THE *Art* OF FAIR ISLE KNITTING

HISTORY, TECHNIQUE, COLOR & PATTERNS

Ann Feitelson

INTERWEAVE.
interweavestore.com

To the memory of Norman Feitelson, who looked and listened and worked carefully.
To Henry Weis, with hopes that he may discover the same pleasures.

Directions for three of the sweaters in this book were originally published in *Knitter's* Magazine, in slightly different form. "Brae" was published in Spring 1993, "Bressay" in Fall 1993, and "Sandwater" in Winter 1993.

Design and production, Marc McCoy Owens
Cover design, Elizabeth R. Mrofka
Photography, unless otherwise noted, Joe Coca
Photography from collections of Shetland Archives, Shetland Museum, Elizabeth Angus, and
    Margaret Stuart; Dennis Coutts
Illustration, Susan Strawn, Lynn Bjork

Interweave Press LLC
201 East Fourth Street
Loveland, Colorado 80537 USA
interweavestore.com

Printed in Singaproe by Tien Wah Press (Pte) Limited.

Library of Congress Cataloging-in-Publication Data:
Feitelson, Ann, 1950–
    The Art of Fair Isle knitting / by Ann Feitelson.
        p. cm.
    Includes bibliographical references and index.
    ISBN 978-1-883010-20-1 (paperback)
    ISBN 978-1-59668-138-5 (hardcover)
    1. Knitting—Scotland—Fair Isle—Patterns. 2. Knitting—
Scotland—Fair Isle—History.
TT819.G72S3624   1996
746.43'20432'0941135—dc20   96-8212
                                              CIP

10 9 8 7 6 5 4 3 2

ACKNOWLEDGEMENTS

I met the kindest people I've ever known in Shetland. Many of them asked me not to publish their names. I wish I could, to thank them thoroughly for sharing their knowledge of knitting so generously. They answered my questions, provided sustaining cups of tea, even the occasional meal, and opened their lives. I came to understand their modesty and their desire for privacy, so I will simply say, to the Shetlanders who helped me so much: I respect and admire you tremendously, I feel extremely fortunate to know you, and I learned a great deal from you. You have my deepest thanks. This book could not have been written without you.

Multitudes of thanks go to the staffs of the Shetland Museum and the Shetland Archives for gracious access to their collections, and for numerous enlightening conversations. I also thank the staffs of the Victoria and Albert Museum, in London, and the Royal Museum of Scotland, in Edinburgh, who were very helpful. I am especially grateful to the Scottish owner of the Fair Isle socks from the 1920s for kind permission to knit a copy of them. I thank Louise Armstrong of Shetland Knitwear Associates for allowing me to knit a swatch copying her 1920s garment. Margaret Stuart of Shetlands from Shetland, and Elizabeth Angus generously shared their private collections and gently educated me; I am grateful to them. Many thanks to the Shetland firm Jamieson & Smith for supplying yarn and assisting with my research.

Several people read and commented on portions of my manuscript-in-progress. Sharing my writing with them enriched both the time I spent working and the content of the book. For their wise advice, my gratitude goes to Ian Tait of the Shetland Museum, Brian Smith of the Shetland Archives, Bill Oedel of the Art History Department at the University of Massachusetts, my aunt Rose Feitelson, and my dear friends Liz Hemley, Sue Peabody, and Steve Ruhl.

I am grateful for many valuable gifts of understanding, enthusiasm, and inspiration from my friends Bruce Burgess, Linda Daniels (who contributed her fine knitting skills to one of the sweaters I designed), Laurel Dickey, Carlton Fletcher, Christy Gallagher, David Kaynor, Mary Alice Rath, and Sue Siegel.

Thanks go to my editors at Interweave Press, Judith Durant and Ann Budd, and technical editor Dot Ratigan, for bringing this project into focus and to fruition.

I thank my mother, Janet Feitelson, for teaching me to knit when I was a child, and for her unflagging support of my endeavors since. Lastly, a big thank-you to my husband, Peter Weis, for paying close, patient attention to my states of mind, my knitting, and my writing.

CONTENTS

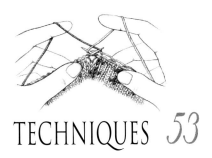
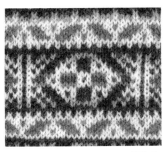
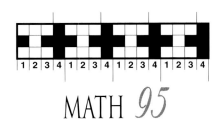

INTRODUCTION

I think of Fair Isle knitting as art, because it is inventive and beautiful, a rich accumulation of the ideas and experience of countless knitters. But as far as almost all Shetlanders are concerned, Fair Isle knitting has been a livelihood and a traditional craft—not an art. A woman whose household needed the income from her knitting had no leisure time. Even if she found a spare moment, it was considered a sin to be idle. There simply was no time for making revisions in her knitting or experimenting with refinements; she didn't think of breaking new ground or of scaling aesthetic heights. One knitter I met, who combines multiple elaborate patterns in resonantly orchestrated shadings, said to me, "I take no pride in my work." I was surprised. I found her work impressive, and I thought she had a right to be proud of it. Rather, the superior, versatile skills of the typical knitter are taken for granted, shrugged off. The fact that most of the Shetland women I came to know did not want their names used in this book speaks of the absence of a concept of art: an individual's stamp is just not important.

But there was pride in the voice of a ninety-four-year-old knitter when she told me forthrightly, "I was always ambitious about my knitting." As a young woman, she had spun twenty subtly different shades of undyed wool for a lace shawl that was selected for presentation to Princess Mary on her marriage to Lord Lascelles in 1922. She also said, "My first sight of Fair Isle knitting [in the 1920s], I thought I had never seen anything so lovely in my life." For her, I am sure, there *was* art in knitting—there was an inner challenge to see patterns and colors anew, to excel. She was once requested to knit a 45-inch sweater in three days, dared to do it, and succeeded. Others, too, must have felt a spark of artistic excitement when they saw Fair Isle patterns and tried them for the very first time.

Despite the conservatism that for most Shetland knitters today dictates staying within the bounds of tradition, there is a tacit understanding that originality is inherent in a good Fair Isle sweater. Some knitters are known for their ways of blending colors and for their preferred patterns. The garments that were presented to royalty in the nineteenth century, discussed further on page 26, and the winning Fair Isle entries in nationwide competitions in the 1920s, such as the one at right and those in illustrations 1-28 and 1-29, must be distinguished as art, as supremely accomplished masterpieces. They were not the only ones. Many another sweater, sold cheaply and forgotten, has heard the whisper of inspiration. While some of the knitting churned out day after day, week after week, year after year, was certainly routine, what is truly remarkable about Shetland is that this small community of isolated, modest people dressed royalty and fashion-conscious people for decades, and that its style of knitting, honed in privation, became common all over the world. The beauty of Fair Isle knitting is continuing inspiration for hand knitters and fashion designers.

Today's Shetland knitter runs a small business producing highly perfected garments that draw from any and all aspects of the past; or knits for that business, either sweaters by machine, or small items—hats, gloves—by hand; or is an ex-

A jumper knitted for a competition. Courtesy Elizabeth Angus.

pert with wide knowledge who experiments with great artistry in the territory already staked out, and has a steady supply of private orders, or intends, one way or another, to sell her work. For the Shetland knitter, the connection between knitting and money has never been lost. For the American or British knitter, who devotes her leisure time to making a gift or a special garment for herself, this is the most dissonant aspect of Fair Isle knitting's history, the hardest part to comprehend. Shetland women knitted because they had to. Today, most of us knit because we love to.

This book is my attempt to pay homage to the hard-working Shetland knitter of the past and the present. I have listened to the recollections of knitters in their forties, fifties, sixties, seventies, eighties, and nineties, and looked at their work. I have read old Shetland newspapers and knitwear catalogs, and examined the collections of knitwear, photographs, and ephemera in museums in Shetland, Edinburgh, and Lon-

don. I have used reproductions from these sources to help tell the story of Fair Isle knitting, its evolution from the first small items sold to fishermen and tourists in the nineteenth century, to the highly fashionable androgynous sweaters of the 1920s, to the large starry Norwegian patterns popular after World War II, to the hand- and machine-made yoked sweaters of the 1960s and 1970s. I am pleased to include many previously unpublished pieces of this story: the earliest depiction of Fair Isle knitting in an 1857 lithograph; the earliest photograph of Fair Isle knitting, c. 1880; pages from a 1920s pattern book which give readers access to past patterns as originally published; a pattern for a pair of socks made in Shetland in the 1920s which also provides direct access to the past; and many historic garments. My aim is to relate the history of Fair Isle knitting in Shetland in a new way, one that considers the relationship of aesthetics to women's lives, fashion, market forces, and the natural environment.

My love of art is the foundation of my interest in Fair Isle knitting and this book. I was trained as an artist in college and in graduate school, and spent ten years struggling to establish a career, painting landscapes and still lifes, and teaching painting and drawing at two colleges. Later, as a journalist, I wrote about the arts, interviewing poets, photographers, painters, weavers, and museum curators. Art school had led me to believe that true art is narrowly defined and practiced by only a very few exceptional people, but my work at the local newspaper where I met and wrote about people deeply involved in a variety of artistic realms broadened my concept of art and the artistic impulse. This more inclusive vision of art is still of utmost importance to me: whatever one finds fascinating and meaningful, undertakes with integrity, steers with the imagination, and practices with skill and courage, is art. While writing for the newspaper, I completed a second graduate degree, in art history.

Throughout all this time I knitted, but entirely as a leisure activity. Knitting seemed outside the realm of the serious or the inventive. I bought patterns and usually followed them to the letter, although I had a grounding in knitwear design. My mother, who taught me to knit when I was about eight years old, was not afraid of venturing into unknown territory with her knitting, and she let my interests lead me. She owned most of the books on knitting and knitwear design then available, and I became thoroughly familiar with them. A close friend of my mother's was a great knitter, too. She designed all of her own clothing and lavished enormous amounts of time on knitting and sewing; her work was ultimately praised by top designers. The friendship of these women and their intense involvement with clothing and fine craftsmanship reverberated throughout my life. Under their guidance when I was a teenager, I knitted the classics of the day—an Aran sweater and a sweater with a patterned yoke, and some of my own designs, none terribly successful. I abandoned many projects. I'd eagerly master a new stitch or pattern, envision how a garment would look, and then move on to a new challenge. As I grew up, I finished what I started and sought more and more challenging projects.

The Fair Isle yoked sweater that I wore in high school (see page 9), ignored in the attic for the past twenty-five years, was important in the genesis of this book as my first acquaintance with Fair Isle knitting. I was, like many teenagers, alienated and unhappy, but felt that I belonged when I wore that sweater. Not only because so many girls wore them, but because wearing them expressed a mutual appreciation of beauty and fine things. I loved the softness of that sweater, its muted, opalescent nuances, and the intricate network of the yoke patterns. That sweater, along with a few other Shetland sweaters I have owned, gave me an identity. It showed the world that I was not the coward I felt I was, but that, like the sweater, I was soft, forgiving, warm, and protective. Some clothing, worn enough, becomes so essential that you are not really yourself without it. I have worn my Shetland sweaters devotedly, relied on them. Clothes are vital indicators of our feelings about ourselves, about what we consider important. Fair Isle and Shetland knitting, worn proudly, indicate, I think, tenderness, a love of beauty, a fascination with intricacy and color, and a respect for the work of women. In a way, I *was* that sweater in high school. I got to know it well, and something about those patterns stayed with me. It gives me a thrill to think that it may actually have been knitted by one of the Shetlanders I have come to know now, twenty-five years later.

My interest in Fair Isle knitting grew by working on and scrutinizing Fair Isle patterns by Patricia Roberts, Sasha Kagan, and Alice Starmore. They did what I too hope to do: express an artistic vision through Fair Isle patterns—but without uprooting them. Knitting became a serious matter for me when I first designed a Fair Isle sweater, about five years ago. It was such a challenge! Every arrangement of colors seemed to generate another. Countless possibilities burgeoned; how could there be so many? Why did colors and patterns, once knitted, look other than what I had envisioned? How could such chromatic wealth come from only two colors in any row, and from so few colors? (A traditional sweater usually contains no more than a dozen colors, often no more than six or eight.)

The Fair Isle yoked sweater that I wore in high school was important in the genesis of this book.

My experience as an art historian made me curious about the history of Fair Isle knitting. What could be learned about the past? My experience as a painter made me curious about the aesthetic principles behind the beauty of Fair Isle knitting. Traditional Fair Isle patterns are relatively simple geometrically—dots, squares, crosses, and diamonds—but, I have discovered, the shading of colors in both the pattern and the background, the shifting relationships of these groups of colors, and the sheer repetition of stitches and patterns give the work its characteristic dazzling complexity. As I have attempted to apply what I know about color and shape, I think I have penetrated the inner logic of Fair Isle patterns. But each new sweater I make, each new group of colors and patterns I select, remains a challenge.

My designs use traditional techniques and patterns which I studied in Shetland formally in a knitting class and informally by talking with many wonderful knitters there. However, I take a personal approach to color. My choice of colors and patterns is usually determined by thinking about the person for whom I'm designing a sweater. I work with their preferences in mind and from my sense of their personality and what would express or complement it. Of course, my own preferences also come into play. I am guided by color theory as well as by the traditional

principles I perceive in Fair Isle knitting. Shetland knitters make color choices differently, relying on what is traditional. White, yellow, or other light colors are often used for the pattern, red or another bright color for the accent in the center row. One Shetlander told me, "If you don't know what color to use in the center row, use strawberry." (What she called strawberry is a dull red flecked with white, Jamieson & Smith #72.) Shetland knitters also base color choices on what will make the pattern show up, the yarns they have left over from previous sweaters, what's fashionable, and their intuitions about what will look good.

I know that some American knitters feel intimidated by the intricacy of this kind of work, by the seemingly infinite number of stitches. They say, "That fine yarn? Those tiny needles? All those stitches? I don't have the patience!" But if you love knitting, and love color, you will find that you have the patience. Fair Isle knitting is really not mind-boggling, nor does it take forever. It looks far more complicated than it is. Each row can be simplified into a rhythm of pattern and background stitches. Three/one three/one goes a row, and, like dancing to music, it's over before you know it. What impels me when I knit is the rhythm of the work. Having a rhythm is essential for speed. I find that working with fine yarn and small needles is actually

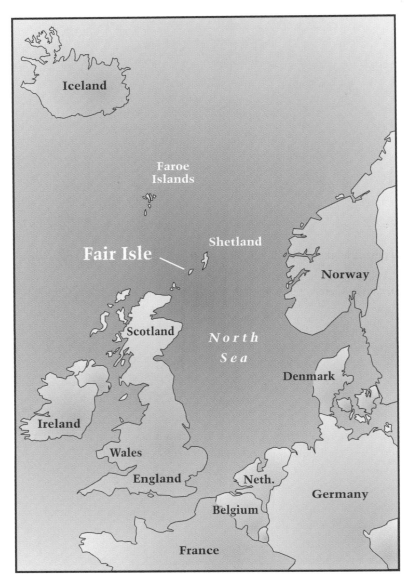

With a current population of about twenty-two thousand, Shetland is isolated in the North Sea.

quicker than working with bulky yarn and fat needles because my motions are more efficient, more concise. Even with my own method of holding yarn, which is in some ways rather primitive—a Shetlander watching me knit said, "That's how children here knit when they first learn"—I can complete a man's pullover in three weeks. I am also impelled by wanting to see how the pattern comes out. It's impossible to tell how the stitches on the needle really look; I have to knit the next round to see them as part of the pattern below. And so I knit another round, and another. It can become obsessive. Just one more! Just one more!

I hope this book beckons you to explore the most colorful, artistic knitting tradition there is, one that, because it is so full of possibilities, can be renewed by all who set their hand to it.

1

HISTORY
OF FAIR ISLE KNITTING

"We are having heavy rain and gales just now. Dark and miserable, but I suppose since it is winter, we can't complain. I have been knitting two jumpers."

"I have been so busy. We have just finished the harvest, with a good crop of vegetables. I was glad to get out of the fields before a persistent gale came from the southeast with lashings of rain. Now the ground is sodden, but it's certainly not cold."

"You will have heard about the calamity of the oil tanker aground at Sumburgh. It's surely a dreadful mess."

"We are well here. It is very wintery today, gales, and cold rain. I have a peat fire on and it is warm, sitting writing. I am knitting one or two small presents for Christmas as it is getting so near, and I have baked my Christmas cake."

"Our weather has been bad all winter and is not much better yet. Rain and gales. I hope summer will be better. We are having the roof repaired just now as the weather has stopped work for so long."

"November so far has been quite wonderful, most days no wind and lots of sunshine. Unfortunately, on the two occasions when the wind gusted gale force, two klondyker vessels went aground. One we can see from our windows, at Bressay lighthouse, the other is on a rock north of Lerwick. There were sixty and seventy-five crew all rescued by helicopter and lifeboat in the darkness of the night. It was a very dangerous mission."

These are excerpts from letters written to me by friends in Shetland. Their letters usually contain a weather report, not to make small talk, but because the weather is such a powerful force in their lives. The memorable 1993 wreck of the *Braer*, a tanker that smashed into pieces near the southern end of Shetland, dispersing its cargo of oil—the calamity referred to above—is a recent example of the harshness of North Sea weather. I've experienced winds in Shetland that make it difficult to walk, and it gets windier than that. The wind can blow you off your feet. Along the shore, the ocean reaches up and splashes you; during a gale it can rise to the top of a three-story building. Because of the constant battering wind, crops must be sheltered in high-walled stone enclosures called plantie crubs, but even with that protection, only those that are close to the ground fare well: oats, barley, cab-bage, potatoes, and turnips.

Fishermen have often drowned in rough weather, leaving households of women to sup-port themselves by crofting (farming) and knit-ting. In 1897, for example, when Fair Isle knit-ting was just becoming popular, and the island's population was about 200, sudden bad weather claimed the lives of eight of its fishermen. News-papers recounted the "sad tale of the sea's mas-tery over human skill and endurance" which left "four widows, twenty-four children, and two aged grandmothers . . . destitute sufferers . . . helpless in the struggle for existence, and stricken with an overwhelming grief." [1]

The wild Shetland weather helps to explain, I think, the intricate, minute precision of its knitting. Cozy woolen garments are the best de-fense against a vast North Sea, the persistent wind and rain. But on a deeper level, focusing on the knitting in one's lap keeps death and uncontrollable forces at bay, it keeps one grounded. Shetlanders would not speculate along these lines, though: for them, knitting was a necessity during most of the nineteenth century and until World War II, not only to keep warm, but to keep the household going, to buy boots and shoes, tea, soap, eggs, butter, sugar, soda, drapery, and dishes, for which knitting was exchanged. Even in the 1950s and 1960s, many households could not have survived without the income (by that time, cash) from knitting.

Bad weather is closely connected with the tale said to explain the origin of Fair Isle knitting. In 1588, a Spanish Armada ship was caught in a storm and blown onto the rocks of Fair Isle. Legend has it that the sailors taught islanders to knit colored patterns. Whether or not this story has any validity for the history of Fair Isle knitting, it sets the two together from the start, weather and knitting, storms and the making of stitches.

With a current population of about twenty-two thousand, Shetland is isolated in the North Sea, about two hundred miles from both Aberdeen and Bergen. Like Orkney and Faroe, its neighbor archipelagoes, Shetland's economy has traditionally relied on sheep and fish. The climate of these islands is wet and windy, the landscape barren with steep rocky cliffs. Faroe is the most isolated and insular of the three, the hardest to get to; Orkney, culturally more like Shetland than Faroe, is closest to Scotland, to which it maintains a strong allegiance. Although also part of Scotland, Shetland has just as strong, if not stronger, cultural and historical ties to Norway.

The terminology concerning Shetland and Fair Isle knitting can be confusing, with multiple meanings for the most commonly used words. The largest and most densely populated of all the Shetland islands—there are more than one hundred, fourteen of them now inhabited—is called either Mainland or Shetland. However, Shetland also refers to the islands in general, so when it is necessary to distinguish the largest island from Shetland as a whole, it is called Mainland. When I am there, no matter on which island, I say that I am in Shetland. (It is not necessary to say that one is in, or on, the Shetland islands, and it is incorrect to speak of "the Shetlands" or "the isles of Shetland" or the "Shetland Isles.") Some inhabitants identify just as much, if not more, with their own island than with Shetland. Shetland includes Fair Isle, the smallest inhabited and most remote island, often inaccessible in storms, but Fair Islanders often regard themselves as independent of Shetland.

"Fair Isle knitting" has come to refer to almost any knitting that uses more than one color, but the term should really be reserved for stranded knitting with two colors, and no more, in any single row. Even that narrower meaning does not accurately define the color-patterned knitting done in Shetland today. Nor is it always the Shetlanders' term of choice, though many use it. Perhaps the most precise term for the patterned knitting done there today would be "Shetland Fair Isle knitting" since the authentic Shetland style is very different from the ways that Fair Isle knitting has been interpreted and reinterpreted in other countries. True Fair Isle knitting uses Shetland wools and traditional Shetland patterns, design principles, and construction methods.

Some Shetlanders, when speaking strictly, distinguish between Fair Isle and Shetland knitting. "Fair Isle" may mean knitting done on that island and nowhere else, while "Shetland knitting" may refer just to lace. I have heard the two distinguished by color: "Fair Isle" or "colored Fair Isle" can mean patterned knitting with dyed yarns, and "Shetland knitting" or "Shetland Fair Isle" can mean patterned knitting using only undyed yarns, called "natural colors" or "Shetland colors." I have heard definitions for three categories of Fair Isle knitting in Shetland: Fair Isle, which includes only the original patterns and colors from that island; Shetland Fair Isle, which refers to variations on that theme developed in Shetland, not necessarily using undyed yarns; and Norwegian Fair Isle, which refers to the large star and vertical panel patterns used since World War II. An eighty-five-year-old knitter told me that in the 1920s people did not speak of "Fair Isle knitting," but of knitting an "allover," that is, a garment with patterns all over it. A woman in her fifties said she has *always* spoken of "allovers," and *never* of "Fair Isle knitting," a term she felt has been indiscriminately used, especially since Shetlanders from other islands have created many of the patterns.

There is no consensus on nomenclature; isolated groups—a town or a family—have developed their own terminology. I have heard the smallest one-, two-, three-, four- or five-row patterns referred to as "peerie" (little) patterns, "in-betweens," and "wrinkles." Diamond-grid patterns are called "allover," "running-on," "continuous," and "a continuation." Many patterns and techniques have no names at all. Passed on by demonstration from mother to daughter, or friend to friend, there has been little need for terms.

In Shetland today, when knitters speak of multicolored knitting using any pattern current during the past 150 years, there is often no real difference in meaning between "Shetland knitting" and "Fair Isle knitting"; the terms are interchangeable. Although Fair Isle is the island where this intricate, colorful style of knitting first coalesced and what it was first called, "Shetland knitting" often supplants it because the center of production since the 1920s has been Shetland, not Fair Isle, and because more multicolored patterned knitting has been done in the rest of Shetland than was ever done on Fair Isle. In fact, very little is done there now. Because Fair Isle is one of the Shetland islands, "Shetland knitting" does encompass what has been made on Fair Isle.

No matter what it is called, Fair Isle knitting has been far from static. The style has changed completely over the last 150 years, evolving sometimes cyclically, sometimes radically. The vagaries of fashion have often been responsible for its evolution. Economic, technological, and political factors have also shaped it. The economic imperative of expedience has eroded the lively variety of early Fair Isle knitting: in the 1920s there would be ten or even twenty different patterns in a sweater, but by the 1950s there might be only two. Since their introduction in the 1930s, knitting machines have contributed to making hand-knitting more precise, simple, and uniform. Political forces have also made their impact, especially during World War II when large numbers of British soldiers stationed

in Shetland increased demand (and therefore, production), and when Norwegian refugees introduced large star patterns. While Fair Isle knitting of the nineteenth century and the present share the common characteristics of two colors per row, stranded across fairly short intervals, very little else is the same. Today, there is an expanded repertoire of patterns, a wider range of colors employed in new ways, and a change in the shape and style of garments. The nineteenth-century Fair Isle knitter would almost certainly not call today's work "Fair Isle"; nor, for that matter, would a Shetland knitter of the 1920s or 1930s.

In an industry that has produced thousands upon thousands of articles, each one unique, a phenomenal amount of individual variation occurs. Originality is intrinsic to Fair Isle knitting; it is like jazz, improvisatory, mutable. Originality is complemented when a knitter is skilled at shading colors or combining complex patterns. One Fair Isle knitter likes to say, "No two sweaters need ever be the same." The Shetland knitting tradition covers a broad territory with flexible boundaries. But opinions are sometimes strong about where the boundaries lie. I have heard "that's not really Shetland" or "that's not traditional" about patterns and groupings of colors I would have thought were well within the bounds of tradition. Too much experimentation may be frowned upon today. It is acceptable to add a personal touch—for example, an unusual accent color or a minor alteration in a pattern—but most knitters stay with the tried and true.

Why such conservatism? Garments had to be sold—the income from selling them was vital—so it was important not to risk rejection by a merchant or the market. Conservative taste is also an unstated rule in a small, closely interwoven community, where one doesn't call attention to oneself. And, in a worldwide market where "Fair Isle" can mean practically anything, and where daring designers employ hosts of third-world knitters to make cheap, bulky sweaters, it is important to be tenacious about the virtually inimitable skills and aesthetics at the heart of Shetland knitting. Tradition is important to Shetland knitters, more so now than in the past, when knitters freely absorbed eclectic influences.

Detail of 1-35. Diamond-grid patterns are called "allover," "running-on," "continuous," and "a continuation."

A dictate adhered to, its limitations are unimportant. Shetlanders today deeply value their tradition not only out of pride and a sense of identity, but because they have been able to rely on earning a living from these traditional skills. Today, "Fair Isle" or "Shetland knitting" means traditional knitting—honoring the past by sustaining it in the present.

THE ARMADA LEGEND

For almost as long as we have known of Fair Isle knitting, it has been said that the patterns are originally Spanish, having come to the island in 1588 with the Armada's *El Gran Grifon*, shipwrecked on the rocky shore after the failed attempt to invade England. If this legend has any bearing on the evolution of Fair Isle knitting, presumably there would be a detectable Spanish influence in the patterns. Is there?

Most of the Spanish patterns illustrated in James Norbury's *Traditional Knitting Patterns from Scandinavia, the British Isles, France, Italy, and other European Countries* are pictorial and bear no resemblance whatever to Fair Isle patterns. The sole exception is a star, shown in illustration 1-1a,[2] which is similar to stars found in Shetland knitting, although Shetland's are usually smaller. It is a type of star so common as to be practically universal in textiles, and could well have evolved independently of Fair Isle knitting. Two thirteenth-century knitted Spanish cushions from a royal monastery shown in Richard Rutt's authoritative study, *A History of Handknitting,* are patterned with pictorial motifs—eagles, fleurs-de-lys, castles, and birds—that do not resemble Fair Isle motifs, although the star appears in the cushion, as does a rosette, shown in illustration 1-1b. The rosette, too, is an almost universal motif in textiles, and is also found in Shetland knitting.[3] While these correspondences may seem provocative, appearing three full centuries before the Armada, an independent evolution is more likely than a direct connection. Closer to the time of the Armada, two sixteenth-century liturgical gloves believed to be Spanish, also shown in Rutt's *A History of Handknitting,*[4] are patterned with complex shapes that bear no resemblance to Fair Isle knitting, although the rosette in illustration 1-1b appears on one of the gloves. Again, the correspondence proves nothing; the star and rosette were rarely used in Shetland when Fair Isle knitting first surfaced and

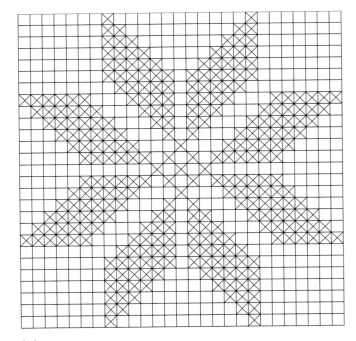

1-1a

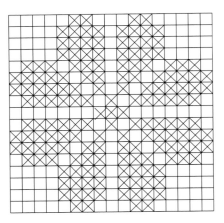

1-1b

1-1a. The "Spanish" star is shown in James Norbury's *Traditional Knitting Patterns from Scandinavia, the British Isles, France, Italy and Other European Countries.*
1-1b. This rosette pattern appears in some sixteenth-century liturgical gloves believed to be Spanish. Like the star in illustration 1-1a, the rosette motif is practically universal in textiles, and is also found in Shetland knitting.

are much more commonly used in the twentieth century. The Europeans who knitted for Spanish royalty and clergy were probably isolated specialists[5] whose skills and knowledge Armada sailors would not have possessed. The Armada sailors were not all Spaniards in any case, but had been recruited from many countries; an Armada sailor who might have knitted or worn knitwear from home could have been Portuguese, French, Dutch, Italian, Scottish, Irish, English, or German.[6]

There is no evidence to support the Armada legend. There is no mention of patterned knitting or a connection between the Armada and knitting done on Fair Isle until 1842, when James Wilson, a scientist/traveler from Great Britain, noted "peculiar patterns of gloves and caps," and attributed their origin to the Armada sailors.[7] Previous writers, such as Janet Schaw of Edinburgh, in a 1774 account of a trip to Fair Isle, spoke of "Island manufactures: such as knit caps, mittens, socks, and the softest cloth I ever saw made of wool," [8] without mentioning either patterns or the Armada.

Fair Isle patterns have so much in common with those in the knitting of its neighbors in Scandinavia, the Baltic states, and the rest of Great Britain that the most likely hypothesis for the origin of Fair Isle knitting is that during the early nineteenth century, knitters in all these countries saw each other's work, and a gradual evolution based on numerous exchanges of patterns and skills occurred. These countries depended on ocean travel for fishing and trade. For example, in the nineteenth century, most wood came to Shetland from Norway, and most of Shetland's herring was exported to the Baltic countries.[9] Cultural exchanges would have accompanied this trade.

On my last trip to Shetland, several Norwegian boats were docked at the Lerwick harbor after a sailing race. Within five minutes, I spotted at least ten unmistakable Norwegian sweaters with complex patterns. In the busy port of Lerwick, the presence of foreigners has been common since the fourteenth century, when merchants of the Hanseatic League bartered with Shetlanders for salted fish. Alert knitters would surely have noticed visitors' knitwear. Shetland

men who sailed to other countries knitted too, and even if they didn't bring knitwear home, they could have observed and copied patterns in foreign ports.

Shetland's longest-standing links are with Norway, which owned it and ruled it until 1469. Shetland's dialect, place names, and people's names are markedly Norse; in fact, the dialect word for knitting, "makkin," is of Norse origin.[10] If any single country has had a major influence on Shetland culture, it is Norway. Fair Isle knitting shares Norwegian knitting's multiplicity of stacked patterns and geometric motifs. Early Fair Isle knitting is undoubtedly eclectic, however.· It also closely resembles Baltic knitting in its use of multiple colors and motifs formed by parallel diagonal shifts (called "OXO" only in the twentieth century when the bouillon cubes by that name first appeared).

Throughout the Baltic Circle, knitting patterns probably evolved through a process rather like a game of "telephone." Borrowing was followed by adaptation and refinement. A pattern traveled, was copied stitch for stitch, if not color for color at first, then perhaps subtly refined, and the refinement was revised by the next knitter. Then it traveled again, was repeated with a slight variation, and altered again. Around the world, the motifs used in other textiles—weaving, oriental rugs, and embroidery, for example—also evolved this way. Many textiles have motifs similar to those in Fair Isle knitting, such as stars, diamonds, and crosses. These geometric shapes derive from diagonal progressions on a square grid: a diamond starts with one stitch, in the next row three stitches are centered above it, five in the next, and so on.

The requisites of the technique of stranded two-color knitting are what really determine pattern possibilities. Fair Isle knitting requires small intervals between stitches, making small shapes. The small intervals make a densely woven, durable fabric, with no long strands susceptible to snagging. The small shapes are easy to remember and speedy to knit, without referring to a chart or having to correct mistakes. Knitting proceeds row by row or round by round, growing vertically; when a plain row intervenes between patterned rows, as it characteristically does

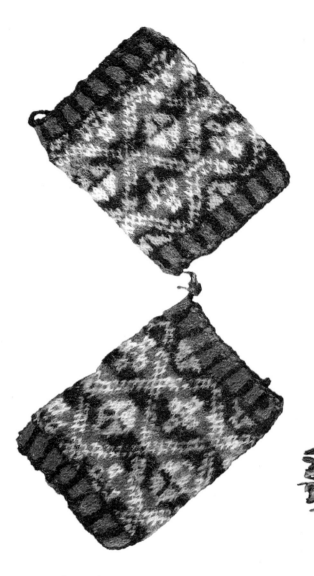

in Fair Isle knitting, the motifs become stacked in bands. Or, when there are no plain rows and pattern stitches shift diagonally, a diamond grid is formed, as seen in the wristlets shown in illustration 1-2. The sheer number of stitches in a garment and the accumulation of pattern upon pattern make Fair Isle knitting look complex. But it does not use highly complex shapes or pictorial elements; in this respect it differs fundamentally from the vast store of elaborate decorative motifs found in printed textiles, embroidery, oriental rugs, and many other textile forms.

The Armada legend has functioned primarily as a marketing device to dramatize Fair Isle knitting and increase its appeal. One knitwear catalog from c. 1900 touts "Fair Isle Goods, Spanish Patterns (Very Rare)."[11] Another cata-

1-2. Wristlets with diamond grid pattern.
©1996, Royal Museum of Scotland.

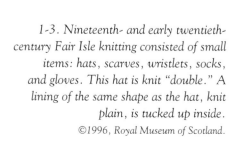

1-3. Nineteenth- and early twentieth-century Fair Isle knitting consisted of small items: hats, scarves, wristlets, socks, and gloves. This hat is knit "double." A lining of the same shape as the hat, knit plain, is tucked up inside.
©1996, Royal Museum of Scotland.

log from the 1920s proclaims, "Originally these patterns were first learned by the girls in Fair Isle from the Spanish sailors who were wrecked there during the days of the Spanish Armada in 1588."[12] Some people in Shetland today insist that Fair Isle patterns absolutely, positively, indisputably come from the Armada—but the strongest advocate of the legend's validity I met was a member of the family that owned one of Shetland's prominent knitwear companies. Others resent the legend's unfair implication that Fair Islanders or Shetlanders could not have developed the patterns on their own and had to have learned them from others—from the continent, where culture might be accorded more respect and legitimacy. Many Shetlanders groan at the very mention of the Armada. To them, the legend has been trite and irreverent for far too long. All the same, travel guides and knitwear merchants are unlikely to give up a story with such romantic appeal, notwithstanding its lack of evidence.

The legend was refuted as far back as 1898, when an article in *The Shetland Times*[13] pointed out inconsistencies: the Spaniards were said to have taught the natives to knit, to knit Spanish patterns, or to dye yarn. Which was it? Dyeing, the article's author asserts, was not part of either Spanish *or* Shetland tradition, but was practiced from "the earliest times" by Norsemen. The lichens used in Shetland for dyeing are known by Norse names, so knowledge of the process probably came to Shetland via Norway. The author also claims: "We have seen nothing in Fair Isle patterns that we have not seen lasses all over Shetland occasionally make 'out of their own heads' as they put it. This shows that the art of knitting the 'brilliantly variegated hosiery' still is and was long, long ago practiced all over Shetland before Armada times." And, the article points out, the shipwrecked men were not welcomed in Fair Isle, where there was barely enough food for residents suddenly outnumbered by the sailors, so "it is somewhat anomalous to imagine the Spaniards teaching the Fair Isle lasses knitting, while their brothers were helping some of them [Spaniards] over the banks!" Not only were Fair Islanders said to have thrown the shipwrecked sailors into the sea, it was also said

1-4. Scarf.
©*1996, Royal Museum of Scotland.*

that they collapsed stone huts onto them and lured them to a feast where they were cut off by the tide and drowned.[14] Another popular topic for speculation often mentioned in connection with the Armada has been whether Spanish blood intermingled with Shetland's. The Armada story has been heavily embroidered; it was a compelling event, after all. Some of these refutations may be groundless, too.

The legend, though it holds just the tiniest germ of plausibility, has little if anything to do with the reality of knitting during the nineteenth and twentieth centuries, and little if any bearing on today's knitters, or their mothers and grandmothers. These knitters' memories, the knitwear that still exists, and archival materials—photographs, catalogs of knitwear companies, and newspaper advertisements—are primary documentation that provide the most credible keys to the past. Romantic as the

1-5. *This 1857 Dutch lithograph contains the earliest known depiction of Fair Isle knitting. The fishermen, who may have traded with Fair Islanders, wear caps with an* **XOX** *pattern on the brim and stripes on the crown, perhaps the same kind of cap Sir Walter Scott described as "striped" in an account of his 1814 visit to Fair Isle.*

Armada legend is, it misses entirely the most important aspect of knitting in Shetland, which is that both patterned and plain, knitting was, and remains, a skill used to earn a living. Economic survival is the true explanation for Fair Isle knitting and for the large numbers of skilled knitters in Shetland.

FAIR ISLE KNITTING IN THE NINETEENTH CENTURY

In 1814, Sir Walter Scott visited Fair Isle and wrote of men wearing "striped worsted caps."[15] In 1822, in *A Description of the Shetland Islands*, Samuel Hibbert described a cap with "the stripes of a signal flag" in "variegated and fantastical colours."[16] The stripes these visitors noted sound like one-color-per-row horizontal stripes, not two-colors-per-row patterning. Could the earliest Fair Isle knitting have been striped rather than patterned?

Patterned Fair Isle double hats known to have been knitted in the middle of the nineteenth century, such as the one shown in illustration 1-3, do appear prominently banded and could have been described as "striped." A hat may have had both stripes and patterns, as in the scarf shown in illustration 1-4. Hats with a striped crown and a patterned brim appear in the 1857 Dutch lithograph shown in illustration 1-5. The hats seem to have Fair Isle patterns, but could certainly be described as "striped." Surrounding the figures in the lithograph, an illustration of contemporary costume and activity, are indications of the fisherman's life: a harpoon, a boat, and a barrel. Voyaging in the Baltic Circle, the men could have traded with Fair Islanders for their hats.[17] So perhaps the earliest Fair Isle knitting, or a variant of it, was made with both stripes and patterns.

The earliest printed notice of Fair Isle knitwear for sale in Shetland, shown in illustration 1-6, appeared in the *Shetland Advertiser* in January 1862. James R. Spence's advertisement for "Fair Isle Hosiery" ran in every weekly issue of this paper during 1862. "Hosiery" refers not just to hose but to *any* kind of knitwear; the term, still widely used in Shetland to refer to knitting

and the knitwear industry, derives from the prominence of socks in earlier trade. In the second half of the eighteenth century, for example, Shetland exported eleven thousand to twenty-three thousand pairs of hand-knitted socks annually[18] when the population was between fifteen and twenty thousand. The socks went to Scotland, Germany, Spain, Portugal, the Caribbean, and America.[19]

The three accompanying advertisements stress practicality: warmth and economy. In contrast, the knitting identified specifically as "Fair Isle" is described as a curiosity, that is, a rare and attention-getting novelty. The Fair Isle product is not aimed at Shetlanders, but at a rising tourist trade interested in collecting souvenirs and exotica. In 1863 Spence changed his ad to appeal to the practical needs of working men. Could he perhaps have stopped promoting Fair Isle knitting because there was not much of a market in Shetland for the "curiously knitted goods?" Around this time, Fair Isle's population dropped by about a third after crop failures and a bad fishing season; islanders on the verge of starvation emigrated en masse to Canada.[20] Without a full complement of knitters, Spence may have temporarily run out of stock.

Most nineteenth-century Fair Isle knitwear consisted of small items such as the aforementioned hats, and wristlets, socks, gloves, and scarves. These are the kinds of things Spence would have sold. Early Fair Isle goods were not intended for the

1-6. Advertisements for knitwear from the Shetland Advertiser, *Monday, January 13, 1862. The advertisement third from the top is the earliest printed notice of Fair Isle knitwear for sale. 'Hosiery' refers to any kind of knitwear; the term, still widely used in Shetland, derives from the prominence of socks in earlier trade, although socks were far from the only Fair Isle patterned goods being made or sold. The three advertisements accompanying the one for Fair Isle goods stress practicality: warmth, and economy. The knitting identified specifically as Fair Isle is described, in contrast, as a curiosity, that is, a rare and attention-getting novelty. Courtesy Shetland Archives.*

SHETLAND HOSIERY.

THICK WARM STOCKINGS for Ladies, Gentlemen, Youths, and Children, to be had at Moderate Prices of
WILLIAM DUNCAN,
GARTH, DELTING.

SHETLAND HOSIERY.— LADIES' STOCKINGS, SHAWLS, VEILS, &c. GENTLEMEN'S HOSE and WORSTED, at the lowest Manufacturing Prices, to be had of
SANDISON BROTHERS,
CULLIVOE, SHETLAND.

FAIR ISLE HOSIERY,

JAMES R. SPENCE, 85 COMMERCIAL STREET, has on hand a var'ed assortment of curiously Knitted Goods from the Fair Isle. Also, an assortment of Plain and Fancy Knitted Goods.

THOMAS LINKLATER begs Respectfully to intimate that he has always on hand the various articles, knitted in the Shetland Isles, consisting of warm Under-clothing, Hosiery, Gloves, &c., for Ladies, Gentlemen and Children. Also, thick warm Shawls and Lace do., Veils, Mitts, Neckties, &c., &c., made from the softest and finest Wool, and specially adapted for cold weather, at the
SHETLAND WOOLLEN WAREHOUSE,
5 CHARLOTTE PLACE, LERWICK,
SHETLAND ISLES.

N.B.—Orders to the value of £3 and upwards sent Carriage free, to any Railway Station in England.

1-7. *Nineteenth-century Fair Isle
socks.* ©1996, *Royal Museum of Scotland.*

1-8. *Beret.*
©1996, *Royal Museum of Scotland.*

Victorian woman who valued and wore Shetland's fine, feminine lace shawls.

Early Fair Isle knitters used both dyed and
undyed yarns. The dyes were imported madder
for red and indigo for blue, both available at
shops, and locally collected organic dyes—
onions, lichens, and other wild plants—for yellows. Undyed yarns existed in a wider range of
colors than is available today. (Sheep are now
bred for white wool, which is easily dyed.) In addition to the brown, brownish black, beige, and
range of grays which have always been available—the "natural" colors we know today—
there was a russet color redder than today's
"moorit," a pinkish beige called "pinky fawn," a
grayish brown called "shaila," and a bluish gray.
Sir Walter Scott described Fair Isle sheep as "mis-
erable-looking hairy creatures, of all colours,
even to sky-blue."[21]

In the earliest knitwear, yellow was usually
paired with brown or blue, and red with white.
Patterns were either continuous diamond-grids
or alternating octagons and X-shapes. Repeats
were not always complete at the end of the
round of knitting, which sometimes left half-
patterns next to whole ones. Patterns were not
always lined up precisely over and under each
other, nor were color divisions always regular or
symmetrical, as in the socks shown in illustration 1-7. Inconsistencies in color divisions and
patterns in work from this time may be partial-
ly attributable to insufficient light. There was
no electricity in a Fair Isle home, and only a few
very small windows; sometimes there were no
windows at all.[22] Long dark winter nights, when
most knitting was done, were illuminated only
by a fire or a paraffin lamp. (In summer and in
daylight, croft work took priority.) The precision of today's knitting may have been impossible, or just not deemed important. Some work,
nevertheless, is quite precise, perhaps a reflection of an individual knitter's skill. See the beret
in illustration 1-8.

By the late nineteenth century, Fair Isle knitting had attained social status. The photograph
in illustration 1-9—the earliest known photograph of Fair Isle knitwear, made in the 1880s—
shows a child wearing Fair Isle socks. Comfort-

1-9. This is the earliest known photograph of Fair Isle knitwear, c. 1880. The child at center front is wearing Fair Isle socks. ©1996, Shetland Museum.

able in their close-fitting clothes, this Shetland family appears well-to-do. They may be landlords or merchants who would not have had to make their own clothing, but could afford to buy it. Their clothing is not utilitarian, but decorative; the women wear brooches, the young girls lacy pinafores. Like the finery of the girls and women, the young child's Fair Isle socks may be a statement of wealth, a sign of worldliness and sophistication. Though the patterns on the child's socks are somewhat difficult to discern, they have a tic-tac-toe grid of Xs and Os and resemble the socks shown in illustration 1-10.

1-10. These socks are similar to those worn by the child in the photograph above. ©1996, Royal Museum of Scotland.

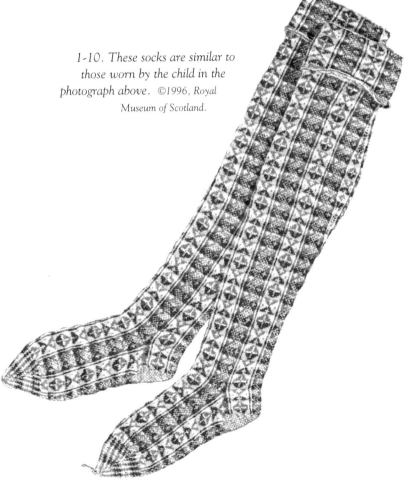

SHETLAND-STYLE PATTERNED KNITTING

Fair Isle knitting was not the only patterned knitting done in Shetland. A different style of patterned knitting was done on mainland Shetland. The mainland style, which I will henceforth call the Shetland style, was simpler, with small patterns in basic geometric units—squares, stripes, or diagonal lines—in only two undyed colors, and with only one pattern in any garment.

The mainland Shetland style of patterned knitting was relatively simple, with small patterns in basic geometric units— squares, stripes or diagonal lines—in only two colors and with only one pattern on a garment. These mittens, a type still worn by working men, are an example of this style. They were made by households for their own use, for wear and for wamth, and not for sale. The person who made these mittens for me, who had resurrected the pattern from the memories of members of her family, told me that they "go back a long way."

The origins of the Shetland style may be found in the knitwear on a man unearthed at Gunnister, in Shetland, in 1951. His clothing and effects included solid-color knitted stockings and gloves, and a purse patterned with small squares in red and white. He possessed coins dated 1690, so he would have died around that time. It is not absolutely certain that the Gunnister man was a Shetlander, nor is it certain that his knitwear was made in Shetland. But the evidence strongly suggests that two-color patterns had been known in Shetland for more than a century when Fair Isle patterns first appeared.

The gloves in illustration 1-11 were made for me by a Shetlander, now in her eighties, as an example of the kind of gloves she remembered her aunt knitting in the 1920s. The aunt was in her seventies then, and had been making this type of patterned gloves for decades. The woman who made my gloves, who, like her aunt, has knitted commercially all her life, told me they were of a type of knitting that preceded Fair Isle knitting in Shetland. "This kind of knitting," she said, referring to the gloves below, "was never called Fair Isle."

1-11. Fair Isle knitting was not the only patterned knitting done in the Shetland islands. These gloves are examples of the mainland Shetland style of patterned knitting. They were made for me by a Shetlander, now in her eighties, as an example of the kind of gloves she remembered her aunt knitting in the 1920s.

1-12. What's the difference between Fair Isle and Shetland knitting? "Fair Isle is lots of different patterns," I was told. This detail from a well-worn jumper from the turn of the century shows a variety of patterns.
©1996, Shetland Museum.

She called the pattern on the gloves a "fern pattern." The same pattern is sometimes called a "fishbone," or "three to the door, three to the fire." This is not only a wonderfully concise description of the shifting, first one way and then the other, of three stitches in relation to the rows below; it also shows the knitter at home, between the door and the fire, the source of light and warmth. But if this pattern was not Fair Isle knitting, I asked, then what *was* Fair Isle knitting? The answer: "Lots of different patterns."

This small gift and short conversation make vividly clear the distinction between the Fair Isle and Shetland styles in the first decades of this century. The Shetland style is the style of these gloves: simple geometric patterns, smaller (nine rows or fewer) than the Fair Isle patterns (usually seventeen or nineteen rows), with only two undyed colors. The Fair Isle style uses more colors, at least four, including dyed yarns. The Shetland style uses a single repeated pattern, but in the Fair Isle style no pattern band mimics another, and each band has two elements, an octagon and an X-shape, or more if the motif inside the octagon varies across the bands, making a seemingly infinite number of patterns as shown above in the detail of a well-

worn jumper from the turn of the century.

Further evidence of distinctions between the two types of patterned knitting is found in knitwear catalogs from early in the century. In one, c. 1910 from Anderson & Co. (a shop still in operation; illustration 1-13), several solid-color gloves are photographed alongside one pair of "Fancy Gloves." The patterned gloves are the same (except for the reversal of dark and light) as the ones that were made for me, shown at left. On the last page of the catalog are "Fair Isle Goods," where gloves also appear. The "Fancy Gloves" on page 14 are separated by several pages from the "Fair Isle Goods" on page 21; they are clearly differentiated. The "Fair Isle Goods" would have come directly from Fair Isle; the "Fancy Gloves" would have been made on mainland Shetland. Shawls for women and underwear for both sexes make up the bulk of the catalog. Edwardian taste in knitwear was still close to the Victorian: women wore delicate lace shawls, not sweaters. And warm underwear, of course, was a practical staple in damp cool climates, and was softer in Shetland wool than in any other wool.

Shetland and Fair Isle gloves are also presented in separate categories in two other cata-

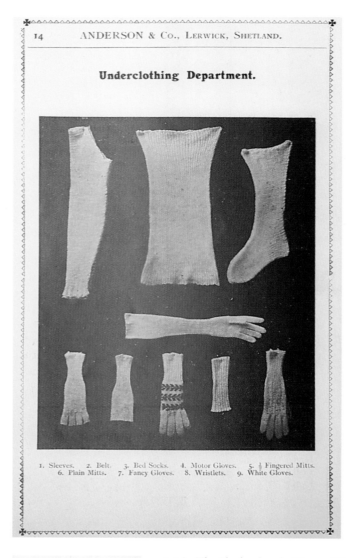

Underclothing Department.

1. Sleeves. 2. Belt. 3. Bed Socks. 4. Motor Gloves. 5. ½ Fingered Mitts.
6. Plain Mitts. 7. Fancy Gloves. 8. Wristlets. 9. White Gloves.

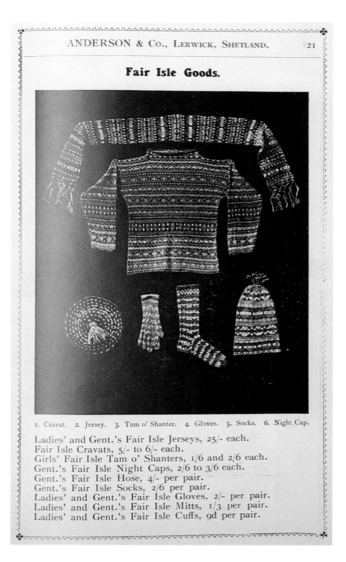

Fair Isle Goods.

1. Cravat. 2. Jersey. 3. Tam o' Shanter. 4. Gloves. 5. Socks. 6. Night Cap.

Ladies' and Gent.'s Fair Isle Jerseys, 25/- each.
Fair Isle Cravats, 5/- to 6/- each.
Girls' Fair Isle Tam o' Shanters, 1/6 and 2/6 each.
Gent.'s Fair Isle Night Caps, 2/6 to 3/6 each.
Gent.'s Fair Isle Hose, 4/- per pair.
Gent.'s Fair Isle Socks, 2/6 per pair.
Ladies' and Gent.'s Fair Isle Gloves, 2/- per pair.
Ladies' and Gent.'s Fair Isle Mitts, 1/3 per pair.
Ladies' and Gent.'s Fair Isle Cuffs, 9d per pair.

1-13. The Shetland-style "Fancy Gloves" shown on page 14 in the catalog are like those in illustration 1-11. They are in a separate category from the Fair Isle Goods on page 21 of the catalog.
Courtesy Shetland Archives.

logs, those of The Shetland Hand-Knit Co., c. 1910,[23] and James A. Smith, Manufacturer, 1926.[24]

These separate listings show that, in the early decades of the twentieth century, there was a clear distinction between Fair Isle and Shetland patterned knitting. Fair Isle knitting is always a separate category, and is always on the last pages.

This consistent placement, behind the steady sellers and practical items, indicates that it was not considered essential or everyday apparel. Along with its higher price, this special designation signifies that it was regarded as valuable and intended for gifts, or souvenirs, or to be worn as stylish accessories.

Patterned knitting was worn proudly by both

1-14. In this turn-of-the-century photograph, the boy on the left wears Shetland-style socks with a pattern similar to that on the gloves in illustration 1-11.
©1996, Shetland Museum.

those who made it and those who bought it. The photograph c. 1920 in illustration 1-14 shows a boy wearing socks with the same Shetland pattern as in the gloves in illustration 1-11. This family group appears to be less well-to-do than the family in the 1880s photograph (illustration 1-9). The turn-of-the-century family wears no jewelry, just their Sunday best, and looks stiff and uncomfortable. The boy on the left wears Shetland-style patterned socks, probably made for him by a family member, not made for sale.

The two early styles, Shetland and Fair Isle, were easily combined, appearing together in some garments. The scarf shown in illustration 1-15, dating from around 1900, shows both styles. The narrow bands include the Shetland fern/fishbone pattern, as well as simple diamonds and squares; the wide bands, knitted with red, yellow, brown, and white, are in the Fair Isle style. Mainland knitters who could knit the Shetland style patterns easily adapted to knitting Fair Isle patterns. The Shetland style gave way to the colorful variety of Fair Isle, but did not vanish completely. (See sidebar on page 22.)

FAIR ISLE KNITTING
IN THE
TWENTIETH CENTURY

Before World War I, Fair Isle knitting was not widely known or seen, although Fair Isle scarves were popular for motoring. Patterns are usually arranged symmetrically in scarves: the first and last patterns are the same, the second and next-to-last are the same, and so on. The pattern at the center of the scarf, which falls at the back of the neck, is unique. This carefully ordered arrangement can be seen in the scarf shown below, and in the scarf shown in illustration 1-4.

The 1920s

The rise in popularity of Fair Isle knitwear in the 1920s is often credited to the Prince of Wales (the future Edward VIII who abdicated his throne to marry the American divorcée Wallis Simpson), who wore a Fair Isle jumper on the golf course in 1922. The boyish, handsome Prince was an arbiter of fashion, so his impri-

1-15. This scarf from around the turn of the century shows both the Shetland and Fair Isle styles. The narrow pattern bands show the Shetland fern pattern and simple diamonds and squares. The wide pattern bands, knitted with red, yellow, brown, and white, are in the Fair Isle style.
©1996, Shetland Museum.

matur was important. The prestige of golf, too, an upper-class sport, shed its light on the sweater, perhaps as much as or more than the sweater lit up the golf course. The head of one of Shetland's major knitwear companies, James A. Smith, had given the sweater to the Prince's equerry, or private secretary, with the request that it be worn for golfing. Smith's motives were obviously promotional; not only did he want the endorsement of royalty, but he visited the buyer at Harrod's department store in London on the same trip.

Royalty had often been given Shetland knitwear. The gifts were offered out of affection and admiration for the crown, and with a sense of national pride as British subjects, and local pride as Shetland's fine knitters—but publicity was always an underlying motive. The subsequent stimulation of sales is one way the Shetland hand knitting industry was established in the nineteenth century. Stockings and gloves were presented to Queen Victoria and the Duchess of Kent in 1837; Princess Alexandra received a shawl on the occasion of her marriage to a previous Prince of Wales in 1863; the Duke of Connaught received Fair Isle knitting when he wed in 1879; Queen Victoria was given a shawl at the International Exhibition in Edinburgh in 1886; Princess May and the Duke of York were presented with a shawl and a Fair Isle cap, cowl and cravat when they married in 1893.[25] The work chosen for these gifts was the best that could be found, "as fine a specimen of our native manufacture as any that have yet been made."[26]

Association with royalty and the upper classes was useful for marketing Shetland knitwear as a luxury product. A catalog of "Shetland Goods Manufactured by Miss Johnston," c. 1914,[27] takes up half its back cover with a list of fifty "distinguished Personages . . . Miss Johnston has had the honour to supply Shetland Hand-Knit Goods to": three Countesses, a Dowager Countess, two Dowager Ladies, an Honorable Dowager Lady, two Viscountesses, two Marchionesses, one Baroness, twenty-eight Ladies, and ten "Honorable Mrs." The complex Fair Isle patterns, which could only be produced by hand at this time, stood out against the increasing presence of machine-made knits; their

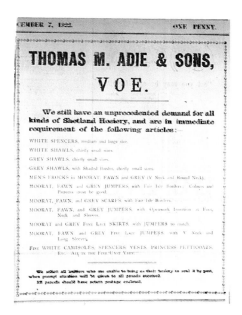

Far left: 1-16. Advertisement from The Shetland News, *Thursday, December 7, 1922. Note the reference to the "unprecedented demand" for knitwear. Until, and even during, the boom years of Fair Isle knitting in the 1920s and 1930s, simple, practical knitwear remained a staple product. For every patterned sweater there were many plain, functional items made.* Courtesy Shetland Archives.

Left: 1-17. Advertisements from The Shetland News, *Thursday, September 21, 1922. These illustrate the proportion of plain to patterned knitting being solicited from knitters in the early 1920s. The style that combines Fair Isle and plain knitting, the Fair Isle bordered sweater, became popular in that decade and remained so into the 1970s.* Courtesy Shetland Archives.

high value as an evident labor-intensive product was no doubt a factor in their increased popularity.

The demand for lace had vanished with the end of the Victorian and Edwardian eras, and competition from machine knitting was beginning to threaten hand knitting; had it not been for Fair Isle knitting, which could not yet be copied by machine, the Shetland hand-knitting industry would not have survived.[28] Those who did not know how to knit Fair Isle patterns learned or combined forces with those who did. I heard of a team of two relatives who worked together; the one who didn't know how to knit with two colors did the plain rows, the other knitted the patterned rows. But until, and even during, the boom years of Fair Isle knitting in the 1920s and 1930s, warm, practical garments remained a staple product. For every patterned sweater, there were many plain, functional items made, such as spencers and undervests (long- and short-sleeved underwear), children's wear, and socks. The proportion of patterned to plain knitting in the early 1920s can be gauged by the advertisements shown in illustrations 1-16 and 1-17. Note the reference to the "unprecedented demand" for knitwear. Later in the 1920s, at the height of the rage for Fair Isle knitting, patterned knitwear made up a greater proportion of overall commercial production, but Shetland knitting was never exclusively Fair Isle.

In the 1920s, virtually every female in Shetland, girl or woman, could knit, and probably did so at every spare moment, and even not-so-spare moments, such as late at night when they would have rather slept. One woman told me, "You never thought about sleep. What was important was just getting on with the work." Another said, "You had to knit into the middle of the night until you felt tears of tiredness." Another talked of knitting "every spare moment, with no respite." Households were dependent on the earnings of their female members. For most, knitting was not the sole means of support, but was a critical supplement to a subsistence living gained from crofting. Knitting was exchanged with the local merchant for the goods a small croft could not produce, such as tea, sugar, dishes, shoes, and fabric; knitters rarely received money. This barter system, known as trucking, dates back at least to 1779, when stockings were accepted as currency for payment of rent and duties.[29] If a knitter did not have wool, she would obtain it from a merchant, incurring the obligation to sell her work back to him at whatever price he set. Paid in goods, she became indebted to the merchant. If, however, she'd been paid with cash, she could have bought her own wool, and sold to any merchant. The very best knitters could sell their knitting directly to Scottish and English shops, and so were less abused by the system, but they were the excep-

"WE HAD TO DO IT."

So many Shetland women have said this to me about knitting. It was absolutely a financial necessity. "The more you could knit, the more you could eat," a ninety-four-year-old woman told me. Despite having no choice about knitting day in and day out (except Sundays), week in and week out, many women were very proud of their work. "You were contributing so much to the family economy that you didn't feel downtrodden. It was a great independent feeling, but you had to work terribly, terribly hard." Some found pleasure in it. "Although we had to do it, we enjoyed it. It's been a godsend to many people who survived on it." I heard about the pride of having mastered knitting skills as small children: "I was selling little Fair Isle mitts when I was about nine or ten years old [in the early 1940s]," one person told me. Another had knitted enough to buy herself a winter coat at the age of six. "I could card, spin, and knit when I went to school before I was seven years old," the same ninety-four-year-old woman said, of the early years of this century.

I sometimes heard a bitter inflection—"we HAD to do it." "Knitters were up half the night, and not for the love of it," a sharp-tongued woman reported. She spoke of the boring, repetitive work forced on her:

"I had to put the fingers in gloves before I went to school [in the morning] so I always vowed I'd never knit for anyone." She still thinks of knitting as "tied in with a lot of hardship." Others told me about the humiliation of being at the mercy of buyers who scrutinized their work and might reject it for capricious reasons or insignificant flaws— that a knot was not tied tightly enough, for example, or that the beginning of the round on a glove belonged on the outside of the hand, not the thumb side. "If you didn't knit it perfectly," one said, "it was thrown back at you."

Some knitters are both proud and bitter. One expert related, "I have always knitted, as a schoolgirl, as a teenager, and especially when my family was young, I had to knit as much as I could manage. For a while in the late 1950s and early 1960s I grafted plain jumpers, putting in the sleeves and necks and cuffs for one of the manufacturers. Then I got my own knitting machine and did plain garments, and later on I did Fair Isle trim (borders at ribs, cuffs and neck) and yokes." This woman's account is factual, and there is real resentment in her voice when she speaks of the past—though she is also very proud of her skills and her heritage, showing it by entering and winning contests.

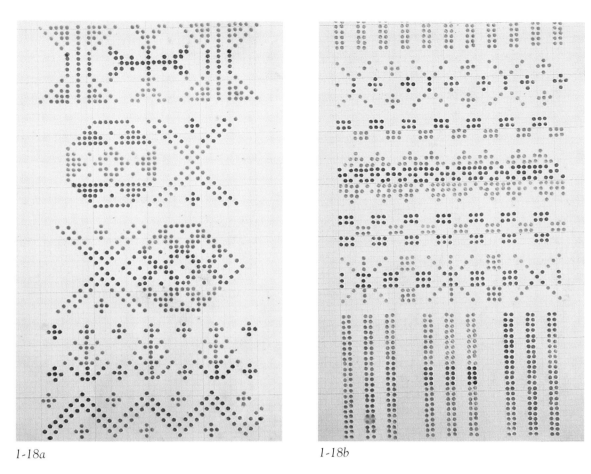

1-18a   1-18b

1-18. A pattern book was published for the first time in the late 1920s, collecting and disseminating new patterns. ©1996, Shetland Museum.

tions. Country women who had their own wool were better off, too, than those living in the main town of Lerwick. Women were very poorly compensated, and many deeply resented it, denouncing the truck system as "oppression and slavery" in letters to the editor in *The Shetland News*.[30] But it is important not to view this barter system solely as exploitation. It afforded women some autonomy and gave them an income. They would have been worse off without it.[31] Many of the knitters I spoke with who had bartered their work for goods during the 1920s thought favorably of the system: they got the household goods they needed for the upcoming week in exchange for their work, and that was sufficient compensation. What they needed, and what they had, was minimal, however; one woman told me that as a girl in the 1930s she would get only two books a year, at Christmas, and that her family had enough food, but never any toys.

As Fair Isle knitting production increased in Shetland, the number of patterns in use expanded dramatically. New patterns evolved from older ones, or were created by inventive knitters who adapted designs from many sources, including linoleum, wallpaper, and magazines. Between 1925 and 1930, a pattern book was published, helping collect and disseminate new patterns. Illustrations 1-18a through 1-18f are pages from this pattern book. Bobby Williamson, a hairdresser, photographer, and painter, stenciled and sold the books at his Commercial Street shop. There were many different editions, some offering twice as many pages of patterns as others. The patterns were indicated in paired colors, red and green, or red and blue, divided symmetrically around the center row, providing the knitter with a guide to where to change colors.

1-18c

1-18d

1-18e

1-18f

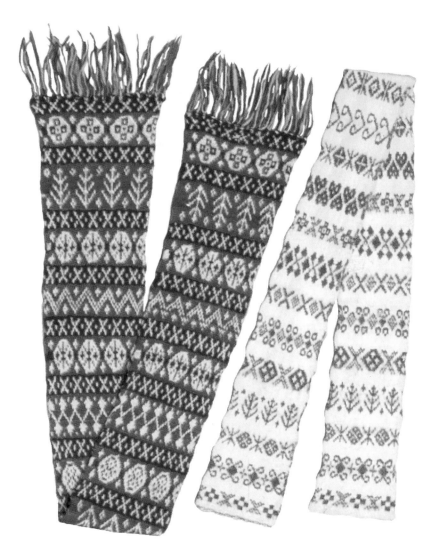

1-19. The colors and color divisions of these scarves from the early 1920s are close to the way they are shown in the pattern book. Red, green, and blue were far from the only colors used at the time, but they were commonly used.
©*1996, Shetland Museum.*

Though red, green, and blue were far from the only colors used at the time, they were commonly used, and the book reflects this. In the scarves from the early 1920s shown in illustration 1-19, the colors and color divisions are remarkably close to the way the pattern book shows them.

Knitters who did not own the Williamson pattern book shared patterns with friends and family by keeping swatches, or copying the last garment made in the household, or memorizing a few patterns and sticking to them. Many knitters charted patterns in graph books of their own. A clever knitter could reproduce a pattern seen on a sweater in passing.

Not only did overall production and the number of patterns increase in the 1920s, so, too, did the number of colors. Spinning mills, founded at the turn of the century, had produced yarn only in undyed colors until the 1920s, when they began to dye it. The dyed yarns were eagerly adopted. Artificial home dyes had been available since before the turn of the century, when they were used to color hand-knitted shawls (both red and black shawls exist) or other woolen, not necessarily knitted, garments. In the twentieth century, artificial home dyes were used to create shades for patterned knitting beyond the limited assortment of colors initially sold by the mills. Even after colored, commercially-spun wool was available, home dyes continued to be used because undyed wool was cheaper than dyed wool. However, some knitters found home-dyeing too much trouble, and stopped doing it once dyed yarn was available, and when they could afford to buy it.

1 9 2 0 s S O C K S

This is a faithful copy of a pair of men's socks that were knitted in Shetland and worn golfing in Scotland in the 1920s. Fair Isle was popular on the links, following the trend set by the Prince of Wales when he teed off in a Fair Isle jumper in 1922. The owner of these socks (the originals), born in 1903, is said to have joked that wearing them would put his opponents at a disadvantage because they would be so distracted by the socks. They are indeed arresting, with varied patterns and bright, sharply contrasting colors.

I wanted to knit a copy of the originals to see what I could discover about the considerations of a 1920s knitter. I also wanted to provide readers with an authentic 1920s colorway, with its strong light-dark contrast and bold colors. I received permission to make a copy of them, and set about analyzing them. First, I examined the patterns and graphed them. Wide and narrow patterns alternate. The narrow ones, with a white pattern on a blue background, are all different: zig-zags, arrows, rosettes, waves, checkers, and so on. The wide pattern bands have octagonal lozenges punctuated by small diamonds. The wide bands are all white on a red background at the three outermost rows, but the central rows alternate two colorways. Seven out of eight of the wide bands have different

motifs inside the lozenge: a rosette, a checkerboard, two kinds of crosses, and three kinds of small, simple stars. The knitter seems to have run out of pattern alternatives when she got to the end of the sock, reusing the third pattern, though with the alternate colorway, so that it really doesn't look at all the same, on the last wide band of the foot.

On the leg, each round begins at the back of the calf. In the wide patterns, the round begins in a way that tends to hide the shift from round to round: not in the middle of the small diamond, which would be where the round would begin if it were strictly centered on the leg, but to the side of the small diamond, so that neither the diamond nor the octagon is disrupted by the shift from one round to another. In the narrow patterns it is not always possible to make the shift smooth, because the repeats of these small patterns are not all divisible into the total number of stitches on the sock. So there is occasionally a kind of stutter where the round ends—a repetition, or a pause. The choice of patterns with such a variety of repeats for the narrow bands suggests that mathematical consistency was a rule that could be bent. The integrity of the wide patterns, however, is maintained, they are never chopped up or interrupted.

I was surprised to find that the rounds begin and end at the *side* of the foot, not the bottom, which is where I would have thought consistency would dictate they begin. Because the ends of yarn are knotted on the inside, I concluded that the reason for shifting the beginning of the round to the side of the foot was to spare the wearer the discomfort of walking on knots. The location in the pattern where the rounds begin, though, is the same: just to the side of the small diamond.

The gauge on the original socks varies between 10 and 11 stitches to the inch. There are 96 stitches at every point of the sock's circumference, except at the Achilles tendon, where a mere 3 stitches are decreased. Hardly enough to compensate for the difference between a muscular calf and a narrow ankle! The socks measure 8 inches around at the foot, and 10 inches at the calf. What accounted for the difference, since the number of stitches was the same in both, I wondered? Had they shrunk from their original dimensions? I did not, I now regret, try on the socks while I was in Scotland, perhaps because I had grown used to the reverence with which one treats textiles in museum collections where

knitting is a highly valuable artifact not to be handled any more than strictly necessary. At these measurements, the original socks would fit the foot, bag at the ankle and tightly hug the calf. I thought perhaps the knitter might have used a larger needle for the leg than the foot. So that's what I did, to try to fit both the narrow boniness of a foot and the breadth of a calf, while keeping to the same number of stitches as the original sock. But I finally concluded that the socks must have been shaped on a curvaceous sock board, and the knitter would not have bothered—or needed—to change needle sizes. When I changed needle sizes from a 1 to a 0, it made only a negligible difference in dimension or in gauge, which was 9¾ stitches to the inch on the larger needle, and 10¼ stitches to the inch on the smaller needle. They still didn't seem like they would fit snugly, so I made a sock board to dress and shape them. (A sock board can be cut out of foam core or plywood.) After being washed and dried on the board, these socks—the copies—measure about 8½ stitches to the inch at the calf, and 11½ inches around; and about 10 stitches to the inch at the foot, where they are 9½ inches around. They fit a small- to medium-sized man, but they remain a little baggy at the ankle.

I did not want to try to improve the fit of the socks by making such radical changes as increasing or decreasing a substantial number of stitches to shape the calf into the ankle, nor did I want to insert a gusset at the heel, or lengthen or shorten the sock by adding or eliminating any patterns at the beginning or end, because those changes

would have fragmented the patterns, and taken away the authenticity I wanted to preserve. While dressing the socks on a sock board does give them a reasonably human shape, a close, hugging fit was evidently not important to the maker or the wearer. This accords with sweater styles of the 1920s, which were loose and boxy.

To improve the fit of these copies I did, however, add some invisible shaping that the originals do not have, hiding it in the plain rows between pattern bands. To give the roominess that a heel gusset provides, I picked up a few additional stitches in the pattern round immediately after the heel, giving that band 105 stitches (9 more than 96—another inch). I decreased back to 96 stitches in the plain row after the following peerie pattern band. I made these decreases opposite the sides of the heel, to achieve some of the effect of a gusset. I also decreased about 10 percent of the total number of stitches before the very last small pattern band at the toe, to draw it in, and again decreased about 10 percent after that band before the final seeded pattern of the toe. This was not done on the original sock; perhaps the original wearer had bigger feet than the person I made these to fit. Both the original toe shaping and my variation are explained in the directions. The foot can easily be lengthened or shortened by working more or less of the seeded pattern at the toe, and the leg can easily be lengthened or shortened by working more or less of the initial ribbing.

The toe decreases of the original socks were done inconsistently, and did not look terribly neat. It's difficult to make decreases neat when they are done every other round at four separate points in a seeded pattern like this one, which is how the socks were shaped. To make the decreases neat in the copies, instead of four single decreases at four points, I worked two double decreases at two points on every round.

Sock Directions

Finished Size: Men's Small to Medium.

Calf circumference: 11½" (29 cm).

Foot circumference: 9½" (24 cm).

Cuff to heel: 16" (40.5 cm).

Heel to toe: 10½" (26.5 cm). *Note:* Instructions include options for a longer foot.

Materials

Yarn: Jamieson & Smith 2-ply jumper weight Shetland yarn (100% wool; 150 yd/oz (137 m/28 g)): #5 very dark brown, #18 bright blue, #21 dark navy, #28 mustard yellow, #32 dull orange, #55 warm red, #66 light yellow, #71 jade green, #202 fawn, 1 oz (28 g) each.

Needles: Leg and Foot—Size 1 (2.25 mm): double-pointed (dpn); Ribbing—Size 0 (2 mm): dpn. Adjust needle sizes if necessary to obtain the correct gauge.

Notions: Marker; tapestry needle.

Gauge: Varies between 8½ and 10 sts to the inch (2.5 cm) with larger needle over St st in color pattern. If you aim for about 9 sts = 1 inch (2.5 cm) as you knit, the finished socks may be shaped on a sock board to make the calf wider and the foot narrower.

Note: Repeats of the narrow pattern bands do not all fit evenly into the total number of sts. On a few rounds, there will be a few sts left over at the end of the rnd; just continue with the pattern. Repeats of the wide pattern bands do fit evenly into the total number of sts except at the Achilles tendon, where one set of diamonds is eliminated by decreasing three sts.

Leg: With dark navy and ribbing dpn, CO 84 sts. Place marker at beg of rnd. Join, being careful not to twist sts.

Ribbing: *k1, p1; rep from * for 2" (5 cm) or desired length. **Increase rnd:** With bright blue and leg dpn, *k7, M1; rep from * 12 times total—96 sts. Follow chart through rnd 93. Rnds 94, 95, and 96: k2tog at beg of each rnd—93 sts rem. Work through Rnd 107. Break yarns.

Heel: Row 108: Slip 21 sts from the right needle to the left needle. With dark navy, k41 sts, turn.

Row 1: (WS) *p1 dark navy, p1 fawn; rep from *, end p1 dark navy, turn.

Row 2: *k1 fawn, k1 dark navy; rep from *, end k1 fawn, turn.

Rep these 2 rows 8 more times, or desired length to heel. End with Row 2 ready to beg a WS row.

Turn heel:

Row 1: Continuing in color pat, p27, p2tog, turn.

Row 2: Continuing in color pat, k14, ssk, turn.

Row 3: Continuing in color pat, p14, p2tog, turn.

Rep rows 2 and 3 until all the sts at the sides of the heel are consumed—15 sts rem.

Foot: Rnd 108 continued: With dark navy, pick up and knit 19 sts along side of heel, k52 instep sts, pick up and knit 19 sts along other side of heel, k15 heel sts—105 sts. Work chart through rnd 114. Rnd 115: With dark navy, *k2, k2tog; rep from * 3 more times, k57, *k2, k2tog; rep from * 3 more times, k6, k2tog, k8—96 sts rem. Sl 8 sts from left needle to right needle to establish the beg of the rnd at the side of the foot, being careful to maintain lineup of patterns along the shin into the top of the foot. Work through rnd 171.

Rnd 172: There are two ways to work this rnd. For a 10½" (26.5 cm) foot (as in the socks pictured), dec about 10% of the sts: with bright blue, *k8, k2tog; rep from *, end k6—87 sts. For a longer foot (as in the original), work the rnd without decs. Work through rnd 178.

Next rnd: **Decrease rnd:** (Dec about 10% of the sts) With dark navy, *k8, k2tog; rep from *, end k7—79 sts. For a longer foot, do not work the decs.

Toe: Divide sts for top and bottom of foot. An odd number of sts is required. Work 2 rnds (or more depending on length of foot desired) alternating k1 dark navy, k1 fawn. **Shape Toe:** Establish dec point at each side of foot. *Sl 1 dark navy st, k2tog with fawn, psso, work to next dec point; rep from *. Work decs every rnd until about 25 sts rem. With dark navy, graft rem sts.

Finishing: Wash in wool-safe detergent. Remove excess water with the spin cycle of a washing machine. Place on a sock board. When dry, remove from the board and reshape the ribbing by wetting and patting it into place, or by steaming it.

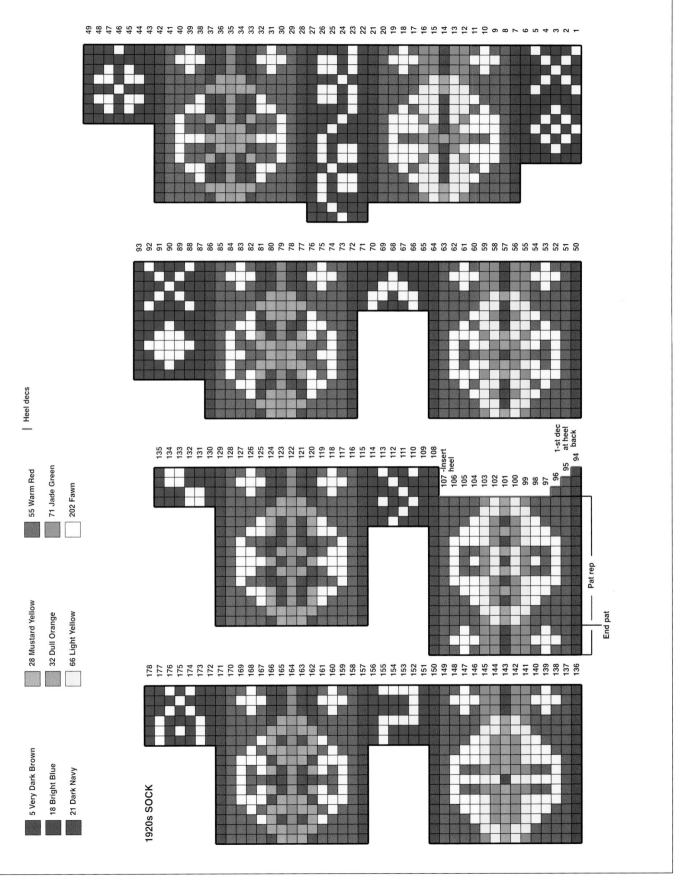

1920s SOCK

Color key:

- 5 Very Dark Brown
- 18 Bright Blue
- 21 Dark Navy
- 28 Mustard Yellow
- 32 Dull Orange
- 66 Light Yellow
- 55 Warm Red
- 71 Jade Green
- 202 Fawn

Heel decs

1-20. A sweater from the 1920s made with wool colored at home with artificial dyes. Courtesy and © Margaret Stuart, Shetlands from Shetland.

1-21. In the expansive climate of the 1920s, the use of color sometimes took new, daring directions. This scarf uses myriad combinations of tropical hot greens, yellows, reds, pinks, and purples. ©1996, Royal Museum of Scotland.

In the expansive climate of the 1920s, the use of color sometimes took new, daring directions. The sweater shown in illustration 1-20 sparkles with brilliant home-dyed pink, tangerine, mint, and light blue on a background of undyed brown and white. The scarf shown in illustration 1-21 uses myriad combinations of tropical hot greens, yellows, reds, pinks, and purples. In these garments, color runs riot—bright, bold, almost discordant, yet somehow satisfyingly right. It demonstrates confident artistic exploration of new territory. The swatch in illustration 1-22, copied from a 1920s garment, is another example of the liberal use of bright color.

1-22. This swatch, copied from a 1920s slipover, shows the liberal use of color during that decade.

1-23. Fair Isle was at the height of fashion in the 1920s, never before and never again so popular. Men's wear on a masculine straight silhouette, the androgynous look, became the rule for women. In this cartoon from Punch, 11 February, 1925, a man in a Fair Isle sweater teases a woman who also wears one about how far she can go towards being a man.

DIEHARD (STROKING HIS BEARD). *"My dear girl, it's our only chance left. As soon as you can imitate this we're done."*

1-24. Quintessential 1920s sweater. The V-neck, originally worn by men to show the tie and adopted by women, is the distinguishing feature of a 1920s Fair Isle sweater.
Courtesy of Margaret Stuart.

How, finally, does one characterize the 1920s style? Fair Isle was at the height of fashion, never before and never again so popular. Tailored wear on a straight silhouette, the androgynous look, became the rule for women. In the cartoon shown in illustration 1-23, a man in a Fair Isle sweater teases a woman who also wears one

about how far she can go towards being a man. The V-neck, a new feature in the 1920s, was first worn by men to show off the tie, and was adopted by women. Sweaters were shapeless, wide and short. The sweater shown in illustration 1-24 is boxy and V-necked, the quintessential 1920s shape. Those in photograph 1-25 are also typi-

1-25. The women in this photograph from the 1920s, playing badminton in their loose-fitting V-necked allovers, with bobbed hair, match the decade's boyish, athletic ideal. The man at lower left is also wearing Fair Isle, a bordered sweater.
©1996, Shetland Museum.

cal of the 1920s. Posing in their allovers, these women are no Victorian matrons cocooned in lace; their hair is bobbed, they play badminton with the boys. Fair Isle was appropriately sporty for the decade's boyish, athletic ideal. The man at lower left in the photograph is also wearing Fair Isle, a bordered sweater.

Competition Jumpers

Almost all the sweaters that were knitted were sold. Only a few were kept for the knitter or her family. A tiny percentage were entered in competitions, such as the one advertised in *The Shetland News*, January 1, 1925, Great Jumper Knitting Competition, sponsored by a Scottish mill (illustration 1-26). Illustration 1-27 is the prize certificate for a competition sponsored by the magazine *Fancy Needlework Illustrated*. Other magazines also sponsored competitions, among them *The Red Letter*. Such contests attest to the spirited, intense nature of knitting at this time, and to the pride women took in their work.

Those who won the substantive prizes offered in these nationwide competitions were at the pinnacle of knitting. Like the gifts given to royalty earlier—"the most excellent to be found"—the winning sweaters were in a different category from those churned out for sale, week after

MUNRO & COMPANY, Ltd
Restalrig Factory, EDINBURGH.

Great
Jumper Knitting Competition

Confined to Residents of Shetland, Orkney, **and** Fair Isle.

FIRST PRIZE - - - - £20.
SECOND PRIZE - - - - £10.
THIRD PRIZE - - - - £5.
15 PRIZES OF £1 EACH.

All Jumpers must be knitted from yarn manufactured by Munro & Co., Ltd., Restalrig, Edinburgh.

Each Competitor can send in as many Jumpers as they desire.

All Jumpers must have a label (which should contain all information) attached with a safety pin. The label can be supplied by any of our Agents.

All entries can be sent direct to Munro & Co., Ltd., Restalrig, Edinburgh, or through any of their Agents, but they must not be despatched before 1st March. However, they should be sent off not later than 10th March.

Entries will close on *28th MARCH*, and judging will take place during the first week in April.

Three gentlemen who have experience of hand-knitted goods will be asked to act as judges, and their names will be published at a later date.

Prize-winners names will be advertised in the Shetland and Orkney papers as soon after the judging as possible.

The following points will be taken into account when judging the Jumper :—
1. Good Knitting. 3. Good Blending of Colours.
2. Originality of Design. 4. Correct Size and Shape.

All Jumpers must bear the price which the Knitter wishes to obtain, and Munro & Co. have the right—if they so desire—to buy the Jumper at this price.

1-26. Advertisement for a knitting competition from The Shetland News, January 1, 1925. Such contests attest to the spirited, intense activity of knitting at this time and the pride women took in their work. Courtesy Shetland Archives.

1-27. Prize certificate for a competition sponsored by a magazine.
Courtesy Elizabeth Angus.

laborious week. Sweaters made for competitions were designed to show off the knitter's skill. The patience and time involved in making complex garments like these reached well beyond what one could ordinarily expect to be paid for. In the sweater made for a competition shown in illustration 1-29, every motif in the round is different; this degree of complexity demands far greater concentration than is required for a repeating pattern. The detail is dazzling. The sweaters in illustrations 1-28a through 1-28c, knitted by two sisters who regularly—regularly!—won prizes in national competitions (and served as judges at local competitions), are exquisite Fair Isle masterpieces. The designs and colors are elaborately varied, harmonious, unusual, and elegantly orchestrated.

The 1930s

In the 1930s, Fair Isle knitting followed fashion—it no longer led it. The stylish silhouette for women, while still slim, was now elongated and more feminine. Traditional patterns were now sometimes applied to non-traditional, feminine shapes, as shown in illustration 1-30. The garments that have survived, in many cases, are those that were made for the knitter's family. As with competition jumpers, more time and imagination was applied to these garments than to those made quickly to sell.

1-28a

1-28b

1-28c

1-28. Competition entries by two sisters who regularly—regularly!—won prizes in national competitions. These are exquisite Fair Isle masterpieces. The designs and colors are elaborately varied, harmonious, unusual, and elegantly orchestrated. Designs ©1996 and courtesy Elizabeth Angus.

1-29. Sweaters made for competitions were designed to show off the knitter's skill. Every motif in the round is different in this sweater; this degree of complexity demands far greater patience, concentration, and time than is required to knit a repeating pattern. ©1996, Royal Museum of Scotland.

The demand for Fair Isle remained strong despite worldwide depression. Knitting was the one bright spot in Shetland's economy, although competition from imitations and knitting machines steadily increased. Taste turned conservative, with somber natural colors harking back to the days when a knitter sheared, carded, and spun her own wool in shades of brown and gray. As a retort to threats from outside manufacturers who falsely labeled goods "Shetland," the undyed wool expressed pride in Shetland and its wool because it was known to be a pure Shetland product, never sent to Scotland to be dyed nor mixed with breeds other than pure Shetland sheep. A garment would be considered truly and unmistakably Shetland when the wool was undyed. An example of the use of natural colors in the 1930s is shown in illustration 1-31.

1-30. In the 1930s, traditional patterns were applied to non-traditional shapes. *Designs ©1996 and courtesy Elizabeth Angus.*

1-31. The natural colors of undyed wool became popular in the 1930s. *©1996, Shetland Museum.*

Browns and blues in combination were also frequently used in the 1930s, as shown in the sweater in illustration 1-32. Color and pattern in this sweater recapitulate earlier themes: white is paired with red, yellow with blue, and the patterns all differ from each other. Despite the wide range of colors now available, the palette in this sweater is limited to the earliest Fair Isle colors. The OXO pattern and the stars are also conservative, in contrast to 1920s innovations. This homage to the past became, from this time on, a tradition in itself. Another example of this neo-traditional style, from the 1940s, is seen in illustration 1-33.

1-32. Browns and blues in combination were frequently used in the 1930s. Color and pattern in this sweater recapitulate previous themes: white is paired with red, yellow with blue, and the patterns all differ from each other. Despite the wide range of colors now available, the palette in the sweater is limited to the earliest Fair Isle colors. ©1996, Shetland Museum.

1-33. Using the colors and/or patterns of the earliest sweaters in an homage to the past became a tradition in itself from this time on. Courtesy and © Margaret Stuart, Shetlands from Shetland.

The 1940s

After the German invasion of Norway in 1940, Norwegian refugees came to Shetland, and their large star patterns were incorporated into the Shetland repertoire as shown in illustration 1-34. The stars were taller and wider than any previously used in Shetland knitting, twenty-five to thirty-one rows and stitches. The new scale and range of shapes marked the biggest stylistic revolution in Fair Isle knitting since its inception. Arranging these patterns vertically, which was also revolutionary, gave them a powerful visual impact. In Norway the stars had been knit-ted with only two colors, usually black and white; Shetlanders applied their ways of using colors to the patterns, shading them and/or putting bright colors in the center rows. The large stars, referred to today as "Norwegian patterns," have been widely used since their introduction.

Norwegian refugees also introduced diagonal grid patterns on a similarly magnified scale as in the sweater shown in illustration 1-35. Smaller diamond-grid designs had long been used, as in the wristlets shown in illustration 1-2 and the swatch in illustration 1-22.

1-34. After the German invasion of Norway in 1940, Norwegian refugees came to Shetland, and their large star patterns—taller and wider than any previously used in Shetland knitting— were incorporated into the repertoire. This bold new scale was the biggest stylistic revolution in Fair Isle knitting since its inception. Arranging patterns vertically was also revolutionary. ©1996, Shetland Museum.

1-35. Norwegian refugees introduced diagonal grid patterns on a similarly magnified scale. ©1996, Shetland Museum.

1-36. The catalog of the Shetland Hand Knitter's Association, c. 1950, shows styles of the time. In the patterned sweaters, there is only one large and one small pattern. The variety seen in earlier work, when every pattern on a sweater was different, has vanished. The Fair Isle bordered sweater had remained popular since its introduction in the 1920s. Its patterned areas were hand knitted, but its plain areas were now speedily done by machine. *Courtesy Shetland Archives.*

As the V-neck was a distinguishing feature of the 1920s, a high neck was common in the 1940s, when styles were snugger.

Shetland knitters were at last emancipated from the truck system during World War II. With soldiers eager to pay cash at realistic prices for hand knitting, the knitter's return doubled and tripled.[32] A cooperative association, The Shetland Hand Knitters' Association, was founded to protect the interests of local knitters by negotiating fair prices, improving marketing, and establishing a trademark. The Association acted as an agent, buying and selling yarn and knitwear.[38]

The 1950s

In the 1950s, hand knitters were better organized and better compensated than they had ever been, but could not withstand the competition from cheaper machine-made knits. The market for hand knitting collapsed. Domestic knitting machines, first introduced into Shetland in the 1930s, had by this time become commonplace; I have heard it said that *every* home had one in the 1950s. This is undoubtedly an exaggeration, but many homes did. The knitwear industry expanded with the widespread use of machines. People who knitted on machines at home would have a regular order from a company for, say, a few dozen plain garments a week. The machines are not remembered fondly by

1-37. An especially easy pattern to knit, shaded diamonds were a new feature in the 1950s. ©1996, Shetland Museum.

1-38. Yoked sweaters were produced in vast numbers in Shetland in the 1960s. This is the sweater that I wore in high school in the 1960s.

those who worked on them daily; the work was noisy and boring, but demanded great concentration and skill. Unlike hand knitting, which requires sitting still and making small movements of the wrists and fingers, machine knitting requires standing or leaning on a stool, and vigorous exertion of the arms, shoulders, and back to push the yarn-holding carriage back and forth across a bed of needles. Knitting became a lonely, mechanized occupation by the 1950s, unlike the communal, sociable carding, spinning, and knitting gatherings often held during the late nineteenth and early twentieth centuries. The advantage of the home knitting machine, like hand knitting up to this time, was that women could care for their children and still contribute to the family income.

The machines had an ineluctable effect on style: there was more and more plain knitting, even in patterned garments. The catalog of the Shetland Hand Knitters Association shown in illustration 1-36 gives a good picture of styles of the time. The Fair Isle border on a plain sweater was still popular. Its patterned areas were hand knitted, but its plain areas were now done by machine. (In the 1920s, the entire sweater would have been hand knitted.) In the catalog's allover patterned hand-knitted sweaters, there is only

one large and one small pattern, repeated without variation, lining up precisely with those above and below. Because it was easier and quicker, the same pattern was done over and over. Hand knitters no longer had the time to learn new patterns, nor the need to remember them. More plain rows fall between patterns, so the work is less patterned altogether, and less complex. The variety of earlier work, when every pattern on a garment differed, has vanished entirely; a kind of monotony has taken hold.

One especially easy pattern to knit became a staple of 1950s styles: shaded diamonds, also known as peaks and waves. Running along the edges of the patterns, shifting step by step from a dark to a light background, they spread the older, more complex patterns far apart, but added visual interest by reversing pattern and background colors. (See illustration 1-37.) The shaded diamonds can also be seen in the catalog in illustration 1-36.

Garments which once would have been entirely hand knitted received a time-saving boost with a machine-knit rib. All the hand-knitted sweaters shown here from the 1940s and the 1950s have solid-color ribbings, made on machines, further evidence of hand knitting's decline.

The 1960s

The yoked sweater shown in illustration 1-38, with a plain machine-made body and a patterned hand-knitted yoke of large Norwegian-style stars, was *de rigueur* in the 1960s. It was remarkably quick to make for a sweater that retained a handmade look. Some Shetlanders spent only five hours, I was told, others, eight, to make a yoked sweater from start to finish—including machine knitting the body, picking up and hand knitting the yoke, grafting the cuffs and neck ribbing to the body, and finishing off ends. For hand knitting the yoke alone, I heard estimates ranging from three to five hours. The woman who told me a yoke could be knitted by hand in three hours, which seems almost incredible, had no doubts about it. "It took three hours if you were good," she said. She knew; she had done it day in and day out. Proficiency with the knitting machine, too, greatly improved performance: it really *is* possible to make the body for a yoked sweater in three hours on a machine.

The sweater in illustration 1-38 is mine, the one I wore and loved in high school. In 1960s America, it seemed as if everyone had one. About 10 percent of the girls photographed in my 1968 Connecticut high school yearbook wore yoked sweaters, and the same percentage wore them in a friend's 1978 Massachusetts high school yearbook. Surely more girls owned them than wore them the day photos were taken; in fact, I was not photographed in mine. Even if the sweaters were, perhaps, more popular in the northeast than elsewhere in America, Shetland, with its population of only about twenty thousand, produced and exported a phenomenal number of sweaters.

A retired designer and owner of one of Shetland's handful of large knitwear companies said that 1966 was her company's biggest year, when forty-one thousand sweaters were produced, with 75 percent of them, or about thirty thousand, yoked. Another retired owner estimated that his company produced about one thousand garments a week in the 1960s, of which about a third, or over seventeen thousand a year, were yoked. By his calculation, among all the knitwear companies in Shetland, a few thousand yoked sweaters—perhaps as many as five thousand, he said—were produced every week from the early 1960s until the mid-1970s; that adds up to about four million during the yoked sweater's heyday. Annual per capita production for adult females would have been approximately fifty yoked sweaters. Of course, some women were otherwise employed or unemployed. Those who did make them produced hundreds of sweaters per year.

Maybe it is the vast numbers they were made in, or just the cycles of fashion, but yoked sweaters have come to seem commonplace, somehow anonymous, and either girlish or dowdy. (The housekeeper in the 1993 movie "Mrs. Doubtfire," a caricature of reliability, safety, and security, wears one.) Nevertheless, the design still merits appreciation, I think. It is flattering the way a necklace is, surrounding the face with a glow. The yoke is visually dramatic, its intricate arc of patterns set off by large plain areas. The design is ingenious in construction: instead of a flat front and a flat back joined in a straight line at the shoulder, as sweaters were constructed up to the 1960s, the shape above the armhole is a funnel.

1-39. Bordered sweaters such as this one, popular since the 1920s, were the predecessors of yoked sweaters. This is another sweater I loved to wear in high school.

Where did the yoked sweater come from? The yoke design evolved from the bordered sweaters of the 1920s, which had remained popular. The sweater in illustration 1-39 shows a bordered sweater, another one I loved to wear in the 1960s. On a sweater like this, with narrow borders, all the shaping is done in the body of the sweater in the plain knitting, where the neck edge is lowered to accommodate the border; the patterned areas are completely unshaped except for decreases between them and the adjacent ribbing.

The first true yoked sweaters were made beginning about 1955 and used larger patterns, as in the sweater shown in illustration 1-38. The shaping in this style is in both the body, which is lowered further and angled along the edge of the yoke; and in the yoke itself, where decreases in the plain rows above and below the large patterns funnel it in. In yoked sweaters made since about 1960, the patterns are larger still, and there is no shaping whatever in the body, which ends with a straight line, the front lower than the back. The yoke is shaped with decreases in the plain rows above and below the large patterns, as well as with decreases that form narrowing branches on pine-tree-like motifs. There is still no machine that can produce a yoke shaped like this. For an example of this style, see the yoked sweaters, my designs, on page 154. Illustration 1-41 shows the shaping of the three styles.

Where did the pine-tree-decrease yoke shaping come from? I found no explanation in Shetland, other than, as some conjectured, one person's invention spread like wildfire. Scandinavian yokes were sometimes mentioned as possible predecessors, but their construction is sufficiently different to rule them out as sources for the Shetland tree design. Trees (without de-

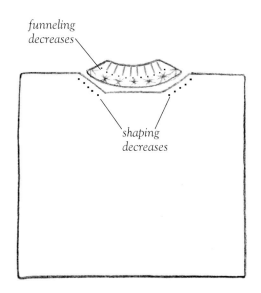

funneling decreases

shaping decreases

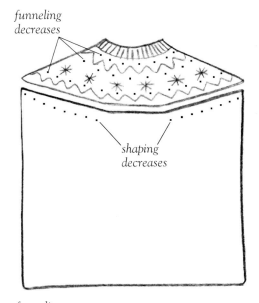

funneling decreases

shaping decreases

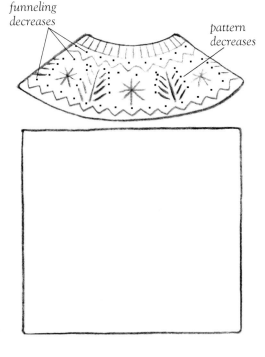

funneling decreases

pattern decreases

1-40. Three stages in the evolution of the yoke. The first drawing shows a bordered sweater like the one in illustration 1-39. The body is shaped with a low, wide front neck. There are no decreases in the borders themselves, but there are decreases between them and the adjacent ribbing. The second drawing shows the first true yoked sweater, like the one in illustration 1-38. The plain knitting ends lower, and the edges of the base of the neck are similarly angled. Decreases spaced evenly all around the yoke draw it in below and above the large patterns. The third drawing shows the yoke design as it is done today. The body ends with a straight edge. The yoke is shaped with decreases that make a triangular tree pattern, as well as with decreases above and below the large patterns as in the second drawing.

creases) have been a common pattern since early in this century; they appear in the 1920s scarves shown in illustration 1-19. The crowns of Shetland hats are shaped with similar decreases that make a narrowing tree-like pattern; perhaps the inventor-knitter was inspired by hats.

In the 1960s, hand knitting styles recapitulated previous styles rather than breaking any new ground. The knitting machine had virtually taken over the knitting industry. In what little hand knitting was done, the large patterns of the 1940s and 1950s were used, in the preferred natural colors. Fewer colors—only four or five or six—were used, in broad bands. Hand knitting was less exclusively commercial than it had been, and less frequently done than before, but people still did it. One of my favorite knitting stories dates to the 1960s. A woman said that when she went to the hospital to have her second baby, she left her first child with her sister-in-law. When she returned a week later to pick up the child, the sister-in-law presented the mother with a new sweater she had made that week, while also taking care of the youngster. The sweater was a vertical panel design, similar

to the one in illustration 1-34, but in browns and greens on a fawn background, with a machine-made rib. Another woman told me she knitted "allovers" only for members of her family because she couldn't charge enough to pay for her time; a yoke, though, she said, paid well enough.

The 1970s to the present

Machines capable of knitting two-color patterns were introduced in Shetland around 1970 and are widely used today. I have been told that "hand knitting is a dying art in Shetland," and I believe it. Although hand knitting is taught to children in schools, young adult women don't do it, and they don't wear it. It is considered passé by most people. Since the construction of an oil terminal in Shetland in the 1970s, employment opportunities have increased and the local economy on the whole has improved; now there are better-paying occupations than knitting by hand *or* by machine. Because knitting is associated with drudgery, more Shetlanders seem happier to be free of it than interested in it. Some women hand knit sweaters for their families because it is traditional, and enter their knitting in agricultural fairs or Women's Rural Institute exhibits, where it appears alongside jams, shortbreads, and home-grown flower arrangements. Many older women, who did most of their knitting before machines became common, still knit by hand as a matter of course, making gloves and mittens for the tourist trade such as the ones shown in illustrations 1-41 and 1-42. The women earn no more than pin money, but as pensioners they can, perhaps, afford to be underpaid; and they would rather work than be idle. Those in their seventies and eighties who do knit have sustained a love of knitting.

A few middle-aged women are passionate about continuing the Shetland art of hand knitting. With a deep and intimate knowledge of its history, they are capable of combining multiple patterns and colors in complex, beautiful, inventive designs. But such women are very rare.

As in the 1960s, hand knitting styles since the 1970s reiterate the past. The end of the road for hand knitting in Shetland, at least in terms of stylistic development, seems to have been

1-41. Mittens, the work of today's older hand knitters.

yarn over the needle. The fingers move just slightly, traveling minimal distances—the equivalent, say, of touch typing. Because the right needle is in a roughly vertical position, and is fixed, the left needle moves up and down over it. As a stitch is placed on the right needle with a downward motion of the left needle, the right finger flicks the yarn over the right needle, and then the left needle is raised to complete the stitch. The left hand, lowering and raising the needle, makes somewhat larger movements than the right hand, but nevertheless motion is minimal. Speed comes from the smallness of the movements of fingers and hands.

HOLDING THE YARN

In Shetland, by far the most common method of holding the yarn is with both strands in the right hand, one going over the index finger and one going over the middle finger, as shown in illustration 2-2. Yarn is sometimes held with one strand on the right index finger and the other on the left index finger (illustration 2-3), though this is less common. I have been told by a Shetlander that some knitters hold both strands on the left index finger, but I've never actually seen anyone do it this way. I've tried it and find it workable but not especially swift. (See illustration 2-4.)

There are a great many other ways knitters around the world hold two strands of yarn, and many individuals have created their own variations. Two particular methods, not part of the Shetland repertoire, offer appealing advantages for Fair Isle knitting. The first involves holding both strands in the left hand, one over the index finger and the other over the middle finger. This works beautifully for those who prefer to hold the yarn in the left hand. A mirror image of the most common Shetland practice, it is Meg Swansen's and is shown in illustration 2-5.

The second method involves holding both strands in the right hand as shown in illustration 2-6. This is my own method, derived I know not when nor where nor how. (My mother, who taught me to knit when I was a child, does not knit this way.) It works well for dominantly right-

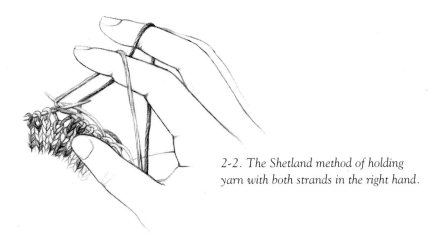

2-2. *The Shetland method of holding yarn with both strands in the right hand.*

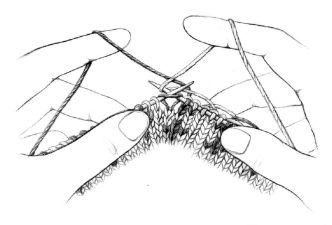

2-3. *Holding one strand of yarn in each hand.*

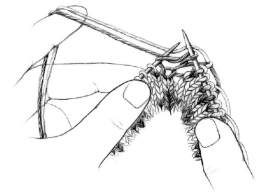

2-4. *One method of holding both strands of yarn in the left hand.*

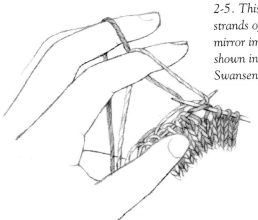

2-5. This method of holding both strands of yarn in the left hand is a mirror image of the Shetland method shown in illustration 2-2, and is Meg Swansen's method.

2-6. My method of holding both strands in the right hand—one pinched lightly between the thumb and index finger, the other between the middle and ring fingers.

handed knitters. It is not unlike the most common Shetland method, differing only in that the strands are held lightly between the fingers, rather than running over the tops of the fingers. This gives the knitter—me, anyway—a surer grip on the yarn. (If I knit like a Shetlander, the strands tend to slide down my fingertips, away from where I need them.) The first strand runs between the thumb and index finger; the second runs between the middle and ring finger. I have a certain, but light, grasp of the yarn. I don't squeeze it tightly; it runs easily through my fingers. The movements I make to knit with either strand are similar, so I can work with a steady rhythm. My motions are not very different than they would be if I were knitting with only one color, which is true of any of the methods that keep both strands in the same hand.

Whatever way *you* find most comfortable to hold two yarns is the best way to do it, and experimenting is worthwhile. There is only one way *not* to do it: dropping one color while knitting with the other. If you do that, you will always be struggling to find the dropped strand and you will lose all rhythm and hope of consistency.

The efficient knitter does not refer frequently, if ever, to a chart. To eliminate the need to keep a chart nearby and stop to look at it—which eats up time—it is necessary to be able to remember the pattern in some way. One aid to memory is to mentally organize the pattern, to find its inner logic. This is not exactly the same as having a mental image of it; rather, it's understanding what the pattern does. For example, if there are two motifs in a row, as there often are—an X and an octagon, say—one usually expands as the knitting progresses while the other contracts, and they both slant in the same direction. The number of stitches between the two motifs always remains the same, so having worked one motif you would always work two stitches (or however many stitches separate them) before working the other motif. If you are working an X of alternating pattern and background stitches, there is either a steadily increasing or a steadily decreasing number of pattern stitches—for example, seven on the first row, six on the next, five on the next, and so on—and then at the top of the pattern there are five and then six and then seven. In a star pattern, the points begin with one stitch on the first row, two stitches on the second row, and three stitches on the third row.

Another way to remember a pattern is to get a fix on its numerical rhythm. I sometimes have a kind of mantra, a counting song, occupying part of my brain, depending on what kind of pattern I'm knitting. It may go: three, three, three, three. Or: three, one-one-one, three, one-one-one, three, one-one-one. Or: three-one-three, one-two-three-four-five, three-one-three, one-two-three-four-five. Or: two-one-two, two-three-two, two-one-two, two-three-two. These mental images and counting songs really do promote faster knitting; you think less and move more automatically, more rhythmically. You can knit easily without looking at the work.

Some patterns, however, *are* too complex to knit without referring to a chart, often or occasionally, or without referring to the patterns already knitted below. But even in these cases, having at least part of the pattern conceptualized—a big curvy X has sides that are always two stitches wide and two rows high, for example—or finding a segment of the pattern that can be simplified and conceptualized numerically, will help the knitting flow smoothly and steadily.

Here is the most important trick for knitting fast, and the most important principle for even knitting. If there is nothing else about technique in this book that you retain, it should be this: You *must* be consistent about which finger holds the background color and which holds the pattern color. There are two reasons for this. First, it is much easier to remember what you're doing, and to work smoothly, because you don't have to stop to think about which strand you should be knitting with. If, for instance, you want to knit two background stitches, you know exactly what to do when you always hold the background strand on the same finger. And the next stitch will, of course, be the pattern color, the one on the other finger. Motions become automatic. You need not stop and deliberate, and you make fewer mistakes.

The second reason to hold the strands consistently is that one strand shows up far more than the other. Which one? Notice that when you hold the colors consistently, one strand goes over the other. (See illustration 2-7.) When knitting with both strands on the right hand, the yarn on the index finger is the one that goes over, and the yarn on the middle finger goes under. The rule in Shetland is that the background strand should go *over* the other strand and the pattern color should go *under* the other strand. It is the pattern strand, the one that comes from underneath, that shows up more than the other. Following the Shetland rule makes the pattern color—and therefore the pattern—show up better. So, the strand on the index finger should be the background color, and the strand on the middle finger should be the pattern color. When knitting with one strand in the left hand and one in the right, the strand in the right hand goes over the strand in the left hand, so the right-hand strand is the background color and the left-hand strand the pattern color. (If you hold your yarn a different way, careful observation of the yarns as they are being knitted will tell you where to hold the background and pattern colors.)

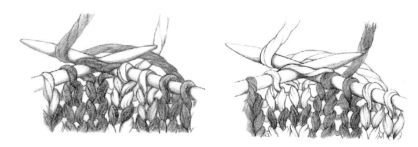

2-7. When yarn is held consistently, one strand goes over the other.

2-8a. Dark colors show up more when the light yarn is held over, the dark under.

2-8b. Light colors are more prominent when the dark yarn is held over, the light under.

2-8c. When yarns are held inconsistently, irregularities are evident.

Illustrations 2-8a through 2-8c show this. In 2-8a, the light yarn went over and the dark yarn went under; the dark shows up more. In 2-8b, the position of the yarns was reversed, so the light colors are more prominent. In 2-8c, the yarns were held inconsistently, sometimes with the dark strand held over, sometimes with the light over. Because there is such a difference in how the two strands show up when held inconsistently, the knitting looks very uneven. This piece of knitting was done before I understood the importance of the rule. It looks hopelessly irregular to me now.

Why does the strand that comes from underneath show up more? Because it travels farther to the needle than the upper strand, which originates closer to the needle. More yarn is used by the farther strand than by the closer strand, so there just is more of it in the finished knitting. Careful observation of the right side of the knitting reveals that, when knitted consistently, with the pattern strand going over and the background strand going under, the pattern stitches actually, and noticeably, originate lower than the background stitches—so much lower that they almost seem to occupy the row below as well as the row they belong to, as shown in illustration 2-9.

The strands carried along the back of the work (what Americans call "floats") must be loose, but they must not be so loose that they form big floppy loops. If they do, the gauge may become distorted, with taller stitches and fewer rows to the inch. Practice is the greatest aid in getting the back strands just loose enough. If the just-knitted work is drawn very gently down along the right needle, that usually guarantees that the floats are just loose enough. If the floats are too short on the wrong side, the knitting will pucker. Some puckering, if it develops, may be eliminated when the garment is washed and stretched on a board (see page 69). Shetlanders' knitting tends to look quite puckered while it is being worked, because the wire is often shorter than the knitting, so the knitting bunches up against the knitting belt. Shetlanders will often gather the knitting below the needles and wrap it with a strand of yarn to keep it from slipping off. This practice also contributes to a tendency to pucker, noticeable in the photograph on page 54

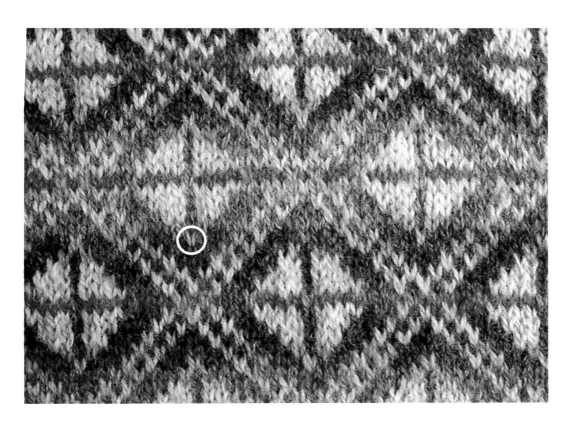

2-9. Pattern strands, the lighter colors, originate noticeably lower than background strands, as in the circled stitch.

CASTING ON

In Shetland, casting on is almost always done with the thumb method, shown in illustration 2-10, because it is quick to do. The path of the yarn, and the results, are identical to the widely known American method, the long-tail cast-on, illustration 2-11, although the motions used in the two methods are completely different. Shetland knitters, I have been told, sometimes use the knitted-on cast-on, illustration 2-12, though I have seen little evidence of it. I like to use a cable cast-on, shown in illustration 2-13, because of its firmness. However, it is time-consuming and the thumb method or long-tail cast-on works just as well.

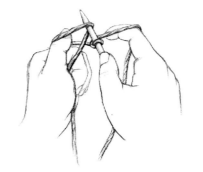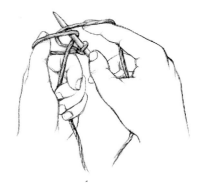

2-10. Thumb Cast-On Method. Make a slip knot and place it on the right needle. Make a loop on your left thumb. Insert the right needle upwards through the loop on your thumb. Wrap the yarn around the needle as if to knit and pull the yarn through the loop on your thumb to complete the stitch.

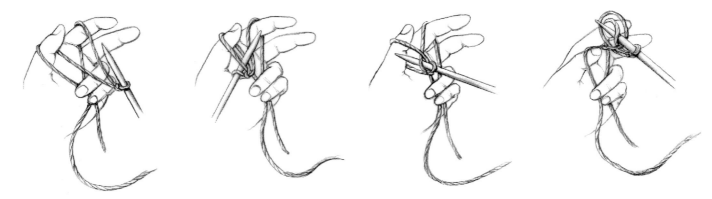

2-11. *Long-Tail Cast-On. Make a slip knot and place it on the right needle, leaving a long tail. Place the thumb and index finger of your left hand between the two threads. Secure the long ends with your other three fingers. Insert the needle into the yarn around your thumb, from front to back. Place the needle over the yarn around your index finger and bring the needle down through the loop around your thumb. Drop the loop off your thumb and tighten the stitch on the needle.*

2-12. *Knitted Cast-On. Make a slip knot and place it on the left needle. Insert the right needle into the loop and wrap the yarn as if to knit. Draw the yarn through to complete the stitch, but do not drop the stitch from the left needle. Slip the new stitch to the left needle as shown.*

2-13. *Cable Cast-On. Cast on two stitches using the knitted cast-on method. Insert the right needle between the two stitches on the left needle. Wrap the yarn as if to knit. Draw the yarn through to complete the stitch, but do not drop the stitch from the left needle. Slip the new stitch to the left needle as shown.*

For a two-color rib, I prefer to cast on with the color that will be used for the rib's purl stitches. (See illustration 2-14a.) It might seem to make more sense to cast on with the color that will be used for the rib's knit stitches, which are more prominent and often the main color of the garment. But if you cast on using the color of the rib's knit stitches, a little bump of the cast-on color will appear in the next purl row, as shown in illustration 2-14b. This, to my eye, jars the lovely flow of colors, though it is hardly a great defect, and not one that would concern most Shetlanders.

If you decide that it is really aesthetically preferable to cast on with the rib's knit color, you can either live with the intrusive tiny bump of color, or work the first row of the rib as follows: *k2 purl color, k2 knit color.* On the following round, begin ribbing: *p2 purl color, k2 knit color*. The bump of the color of the row below will not show with an intermediary row of knit stitches between the cast-on row and the first ribbed row. This method, shown in illustration 2-14c, may make the ribbing curl, at least for the first few rows, before the knitting has any weight, but the curl will disappear when the sweater is washed and stretched on a board. Any two-color ribbing, in fact, may curl, but do not fret if yours does. The curl is easily disciplined into submission after washing and stretching on a jumper board (see page 69).

EXTRA STITCHES

Knitting in the round proceeds very smoothly, but only certain garments are tubular everywhere: scarves, gloves, mittens, hats or berets, and yoked sweaters. None of these are made with flat pieces. But in a sweater, sleeveless or sleeved, the tube of the body must give way to a flat back and a flat front above the armholes.

Some Shetland hand knitters deal with these flat pieces by adding a bridge of extra stitches to connect them, shown in illustration 2-15, so that knitting continues in the round. Later the stitches are cut; stitches for a sleeve or neck ribbing are picked up from them, and the extra stitches become a facing hemmed on the wrong side. I will first explain this method as I learned it in Shetland and then note some variations that I have seen.

At the armhole, body stitches are placed on a holder or threaded on a scrap piece of yarn for the underarm. For a dropped-shoulder sweater, usually one stitch is held in reserve this way; for an indented or a shaped armhole, two to three inches worth of stitches are reserved. Extra stitches that connect the right front with the right back, and the left front with the left back, are cast on. There are twelve extra stitches, worked in vertical stripes. On a pullover, the round begins in the middle of this group of extra stitches. Pattern and background alternate stitch by stitch, to keep the floats short and the knitting as tightly interwoven as possible. Starting at the middle of the armhole, the first six extra stitches of the round are cast on: pattern, background, pattern, background, pattern, background. The last extra stitch, the one next to the body of the sweater, is always in the background color. The pattern on the body continues uninterrupted as the round continues. When the next armhole comes around, twelve extra stitches are cast on as follows: background, pattern, background, pattern, background, *pattern, pattern,* background, pattern, background, pattern, background. At the end of the round, the remaining six extra stitches are cast on, as follows: background, pattern, background, pattern, background, pattern. The two pattern-color stitches next to each other at the center of each bridge make a clear avenue for cutting later.

When the armhole is shaped, decreases are made in the two body stitches adjacent to the extra stitches. When the decrease slants towards the extra stitches, that is, toward the armhole, it is virtually invisible. The method Americans tend to use, with decreases slanting towards the garment and with a one- or two-stitch border of plain knitting at the edge, is obtrusive when used in a Fair Isle pattern (see increasing and decreasing on page 65.)

On a round-neck jumper, stitches at the front neck are put on a holder or threaded on a scrap piece of yarn and another twelve extra stitches are cast on; this group of extra stitches is identical to those at the armhole. Knitting contin-

2-14a. Cast on for ribbing in color of purl stitches.

2-14b. If you cast on for ribbing in color of knit stitches, contrasting bumps will appear in the purl stitches on the first row.

2-14c. Contrasting bumps in the purl stitches can be avoided by knitting one plain row after casting on.

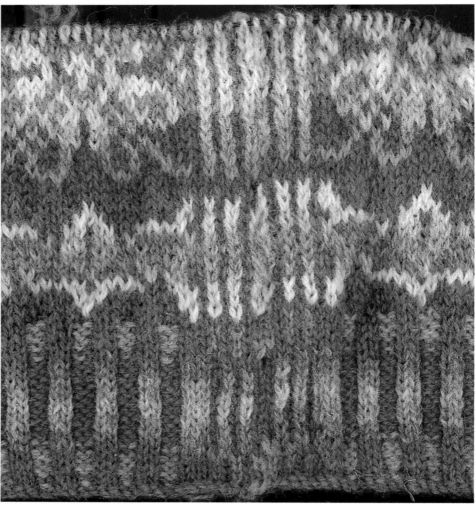

2-15. Two examples of extra stitches forming bridges. On a pullover, twelve extra stitches are worked at the armholes and neck edge. On a sweater that buttons down the front, shown at right, the rounds begin at the center, in the middle of the twelve extra stitches.

ues in the round with three groups of extra stitches. The curve of the neck is shaped with decreases at either side, slanting as they do on a shaped armhole, towards the extra stitches, that is, towards the center of the sweater. In Shetland, the back neck is usually unshaped, being continuous with the shoulder line. But depending on how the patterns meet the back neck, I

avoid truncating a pattern by stopping before it and casting on another group of extra stitches there—making four—decreasing on the final few rounds of the sweater as at the front neck.

On a garment that buttons down the front, the rounds begin at the center front, in the middle of the twelve extra stitches. Above the underarm, the rounds continue to begin at the cen-

For decreases that narrow a sleeve along the underarm, the first decrease, done in the first two stitches of the round, slants right, toward the center underarm line; the second decrease, done in the very last two stitches of the round, slants left, also toward the center. Decreasing this way *does* interrupt the continuity of patterns, causing half-patterns to meet half-patterns, or thirds of patterns to meet other thirds along the line of the sleeve "seam." Despite the importance of maintaining pattern integrity, most Shetland knitters don't mind this fragmentation, because it happens at the part of a sweater that shows least. But some Shetlanders prefer to keep the patterns along the underarm complete by decreasing only in the plain rows between patterns. The decreases in one round must be equal to one repeat, or multiples of one repeat. (This method does not work on a vertical panel garment.) The disadvantage of this method is that the patterns don't line up vertically except along the top of the sleeve—but that is the part of the sleeve that shows the most.

For decreases where the slant of the stitch is irrelevant, such as between sleeve and cuff, or between the pattern bands in a yoke, the easiest decrease—knit two together—suffices nicely.

For decreases that shape a hat or beret crown, three stitches are turned into one. There are three ways to do this: knit three stitches together (illustration 2-21a); slip two together, knit one, pass the 2 sl sts over (illustration 2-21b); or slip one, knit two together, pass slipped stitch over (illustration 2-21c).

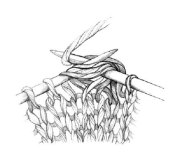

2-21a. K3 tog decrease.

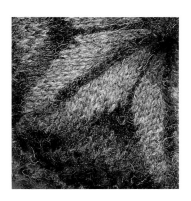

2-21b. Sl 2 tog k1 PSSO decrease. Slip two stitches together, knit one, pass slipped stitches over.

2-21c. Sl 1, k2 tog, PSSO decrease. Slip one, knit two together, pass slipped stitch over.

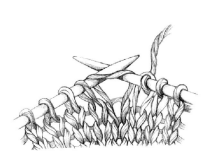
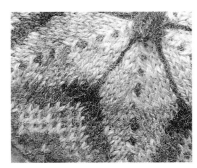

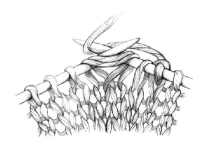

AT THE SHOULDER

Where the front of a sweater meets the back at the shoulder, half a pattern band on one side usually meets half a pattern band on the other, creating a complete pattern. The shoulders can be joined with a three-needle bind-off, which produces a firm edge and matches the stitches of the front and back exactly as shown in illustrations 2-22 and 2-23. Or the front and back can be joined by grafting, using the background color (or whichever color there is more of) in the center row. Then the pattern color (or whichever color there is less of) is duplicate-stitched over the grafted row. A grafted row is always off by half a stitch, though, so I consider this the method of second choice, although it is commonly used in Shetland. Grafting and du-

plicate stitching are more time-consuming and difficult—for me—than binding the shoulders off together. But the elasticity of grafting is more in keeping with the seamless Shetland ideal.

When the patterns do not match half to half at the shoulder, but, instead, a complete pattern on the front meets a complete pattern on the back, then grafting the plain row between patterns makes a completely invisible join.

FINISHING ENDS

When changing colors between the end of one round and the beginning of the next, Shet-landers break off the old color and do no more than knot the new color to the old with a square knot, leaving an end 1/4 inch to one inch long. The strength of a square knot combined with

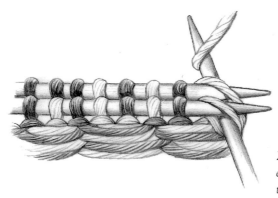

2-22. Shoulders can be joined with a three-needle bind-off. This produces a firm edge and matches the stitches of the front and back exactly. Binding off begins in the middle of the twelve extra stitches. Shown from right are six paired extra stitches and two pattern stitches.

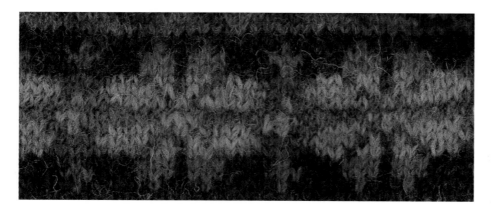

2-23. The shoulder of this sweater was joined with the three-needle cast-off.

the slight felting that occurs when the garment is washed make this a durable finish. It is also speedy, which, as we have seen, has been an important virtue for the Shetland hand knitter who sold her work at the end of every week. In the sweater shown in illustration 2-24, the ends have been treated this way.

There are more time-consuming methods of dealing with color changes and the resulting yarn ends, but they will not necessarily provide a more perfect finish than the preceding method. Knotting the colors as above, but burying them in the floats and/or backs of the stitches with a tapestry needle after the knitting is completed, is one technique. This can take an entire day. One woman told me that she knots the strands as she works her way up the garment, then unknots them when the knitting is completed, adjusts them to the proper tension, and then reknots them. She also said that tying the two ends of the same color together when there is a single row of a color makes the shift where rounds begin and end less visible.

I like to twist the ends in as I knit, as shown in illustration 2-25. This is quick and easy to do, and avoids the inelasticity of a knot. The disadvantage of this method is that it distorts the stitches a little, especially when there are numerous color changes. Here's how it works. Several stitches before the end of the round, lay the new strand over one of the strands you are knitting with and catch it with the next stitch; then begin twisting in the end as you knit. When you do this for several stitches and arrive at the beginning of the round, you're ready to go with the new strand. Twist the old strand or strands in on the first few stitches of the next round.

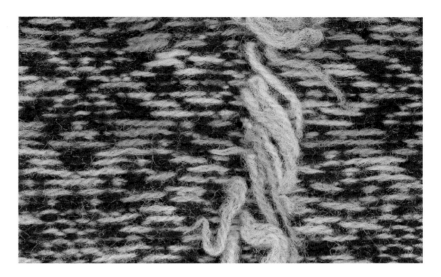

2-24. When changing colors at the end of a round, the ends are knotted and left to felt.

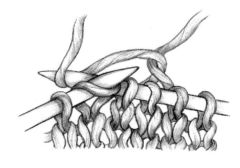

2-25. Twisting. Twist the working and the carried yarns around each other once. Continue knitting with the working yarn.

BOARDS

Shetlanders consider it essential to wash and stretch a garment on a board when the knitting is done. No matter how authentic the yarn, color, and pattern, two-color knitting just won't look like true Shetland Fair Isle knitting unless it is treated this way. There is a remarkable difference in the appearance of the knitting before and after washing and stretching. Textural irregularities in the surface vanish. With the surface evened, the colors become clearer and more assertive, and the pattern becomes fully visible. The wool becomes softer and increases in loft; the fabric seems to relax.

Wash the completed garment in a wool-safe soap. Remove most of the water by spinning it in the final cycle of a washing machine. Place the garment on the board or a framework of proper size immediately. It shouldn't be under a great deal of tension, but slight stretching is necessary to make the knitting even.

Shetland wool is highly malleable when wet. At this final stage, it is easy to make the garment bigger overall, or just a little longer, or to adjust sleeve length or proportions as necessary. (I've—intentionally—enlarged a 40-inch sweater to 44 inches.) This is also the time to round out a shape that is basically square, like a crew neck. When the wet garment is on the board, run a basting thread (cotton or wool) through the neck-band edge and gather it in just slightly. A V-neck may be shaped into a precise angle at this time. With a cardigan, baste the front bands together so that they don't gap. Remove the basting thread when the garment is dry.

The board stretches out the cuff and basque ribbings to the width of the rest of the garment, making them too large. So after the garment is dry and off the board, these ribbings must be shrunk back. In Shetland they are steamed over a boiling kettle, or a steam iron is held on them over a damp cloth, with the ribbing pulled vertically between bouts of steaming. I find it easier to wet the ribbing again by dipping it in water; then I pull and pat it into a narrower shape and allow it to dry again. This does take more time than steaming.

BUTTONHOLES

Shetland button bands are usually worked in one color, in seed stitch or in ribbing. Since the 1940s, body, sleeve, and neckband ribs have usually been machine-made with one color to save time, so to coordinate with the other plain trim, the button band would be worked by hand in one color, too. The button band is often worked in one color even on garments that have two-color ribs at basque and cuffs. Working a two-color rib back and forth is one of the most time-consuming and awkward aspects of two-color knitting, which may be why it is so rarely seen.

This said, however, I like two-color ribs on cardigans but I have had to experiment to find a good way to make a firm, neat buttonhole. The floats on the back of the band tend to cover the buttonhole; the solution to this problem is to twist the two strands together between every stitch as you make the buttonhole.

Here's the method I use for a one-row horizontal buttonhole in a two-color rib. Knit the first stitch of the buttonhole with the appropriate strand. Leaving the yarn at the back of the work, slip the next stitch from the left needle to the right needle. Pull the second stitch on the right needle over the slipped stitch. Slip another stitch from the left needle to the right, and again pass the adjacent stitch on the right needle over the slipped stitch. Repeat this binding-off-without-knitting for as many stitches as desired. A three-stitch buttonhole is usually adequate for most medium-sized buttons. When you have bound off as many stitches as necessary, return the last slipped-and-passed-over stitch to the left needle. Turn the work. Wrap the two strands around each other once. Then, with the appropriate color, cast on a stitch with the knitted-on method, that is, knit into the stitch on the left hand needle, draw the yarn through and place the resulting loop in the left hand needle. Twist the strands together again. Continue casting on, alternating stitches to follow the k2 p2 pattern below, and twisting between every cast-on stitch until you have cast on one more stitch than the number of stitches bound off. Turn the work. Move the extra stitch from what is now the right-hand needle to the left needle and knit it together (or purl it together) with the first stitch on the left needle. Done!

Tiny buttonholes for tiny buttons are very easily made with a yarnover, knit two together. This is the method a Shetlander would use on a one-color button band. For a two-color rib, knit two together with the color of the stitches below; use both strands for the yarnover.

3
COLOR
IN FAIR ISLE KNITTING

There's something so richly luminous about Fair Isle knitting. Why does it glow the way it does? Aside from the choice of colors (discussed in detail below), its radiant effect comes from the qualities of its surface and from the way one color meets another. Any visual medium, in fact, has specific properties based on these features. To take an example completely unrelated to knitting, in oil painting the junctures of colors may be either soft or sharp, so effects are both subtle and bold. An oil-painted surface is glossy, appearing to give off light, yet is also translucent, like stained glass. With the complex detail that can be drawn, magnificent illusions of depth and light can be created. To take another example, practically the opposite effect is found in silkscreen and quilting, where the surface is matte and texturally unvaried, and divisions between colors are uniformly sharp. In silk-screen and quilting, the overall effect is flat, and colors are discrete and well-defined.

Unlike oil painting, or silkscreen, or quilting, Fair Isle knitting made with Shetland wool looks neither deep nor flat, but nebulous. The knitted fabric itself is so soft you can't quite tell exactly where a color begins and ends. A haze of wool fibers is suspended over the surface, making the junctures of colors beneath it blurry. The loft of the yarn means that there is air—therefore light and tiny, practically microscopic shadows, too—in the fabric, which give it a kind of atmospheric mystery. Surface continuity is interrupted where the yarn tucks from front to back, and tiny shadows are also cast in these pockets. Still more indistinctness comes from the jagged shape of a

knitted stitch; where one color meets another, they interpenetrate. Some yarns are spun from a number of different colors—they are called marled, or heathered—and add to the cloudy richness of color.

Because of all of these factors, the salient feature of Shetland wool is the ease with which one color blends into another. Low contrast juxtapositions are indistinguishable (unlike quilting and silkscreen). Relatively high contrast colors like, say, green and purple, may coexist without standing out from each other, making a lively polychromatic surface. For one color to show up against another, which is necessary for a pattern to be distinguishable from the background, a relatively high degree of contrast must be used. Compare Fair Isle knitting with Norwegian knitting, which has a totally different effect. Norway's worsted-spun wool is denser and shinier than Shetland's woolen-spun wool, so the surface is crisper, with more contrast. In Norwegian knitting, similar colors show up more clearly against each other. But the typical colors used in Norwegian knitting are those of utmost contrast—black and white, or red and white— so the effect is bold rather than mysterious.

CHOOSING COLORS

Now to the important matter of choosing colors. Fair Isle patterns are intriguing because of the relationship between groups of closely related, progressively shading colors. Two groupings are far more luminous than one. To my painterly way of thinking, the boost in visual interest from two groupings of color is akin to

3-1

3-2

3-3

the magic of twilight when lights are on indoors but there's still enough light to see well outdoors, or to looking at a shoreline and its reflection in water. Seeing two different worlds of color or light simultaneously is fascinating. The eye follows the logic of one group of related colors, expects a neighboring group to belong to the same realm, and is baffled and entertained when it doesn't. Three groupings are even more luminous than two. To continue these analogies, three groupings is like twilight when there is both fluorescent and incandescent light indoors, as well as a sunset; or like a reflection in water that shimmers in undulating waves. To make an entirely different analogy, three color groupings can resemble music. Melody alone can be dull, but when the bass harmonizes with the treble, it is more interesting, and it is still more interesting when a piece shifts from a major to a minor key, and a number of different instruments are playing.

The most interesting Fair Isle sweaters play one group of colors against another and then another, and colors switch from group to group. For example, a family of colors—say reds and violets—may be used for the pattern in one band, where it is flanked by an opposing family in the background—say royal blue and navy. In the next band, some of those pattern colors— say the violets, this time joined by some grays— will instead be the background colors, and for *this* pattern a third group of colors related to the second group will be used—perhaps deep turquoise and royal blue. To give a more traditional example, a group of light grays and beiges might be the pattern against a background of dark grays and browns in one band; in the next band, the pattern and background would be reversed, with a light gray and beige background and a dark brown and gray pattern; in one flanking peerie band the pattern might be gray and the background black; in another flanking peerie band the pattern might be brown and the background gray. By shifting groups against each other and shifting the colors within groups, a complex effect is achieved.

Despite a lack of any real rules as to what will work with color in a Fair Isle pattern and what won't, it is possible to set out some principles and guidelines for choosing and grouping Shetland colors in patterns. What follows are Shetland principles which I have either heard expressed verbally or deduced from closely examining authentic Fair Isle work. I have phrased these principles in the language of color theory. But color theory is not the touchstone for a Shetland knitter that it is for me. A Shetland knitter chooses colors based on tradition and the yarn she has on hand, or the requirements of an order; a designer may, in addition, use seasonal color forecasts. A Shetland knitter does not think about complementary colors, or about hue, value and intensity, or tint, tone and shade, or even about sequences, at least not in those terms. She does, though, think of shading colors, and of whether colors chosen for the pattern will show up against those chosen for the background. Before beginning a sweater, she probably lines up skeins in a shaded sequence. Her work succeeds because she has a knack for color and a number of tricks up her sleeve gained from long experience with the way colors interact.

In Fair Isle patterns, colors are arranged symmetrically around the pivot point of the center row; the colors mirror each other at the top and bottom of the pattern. The pattern colors form one sequence, the background colors another. Two sequences are not absolutely always used; sometimes there is only one, when the pattern color shades against an unchanging background. (It is rare for the background to shade against an unchanging pattern.) Color effects are most dazzling, though, when both pattern and background are shaded. The center of the pattern is the most exciting part, usually accented with high value contrast such as navy and white, or high color contrast such as red and turquoise, or a very bright color unrelated to the others.

Let me explain these principles in greater detail. First, what is a sequence? Think of what happens when you mix paint. Blue and yellow make green, forming a sequence of blue/green/ yellow as shown in swatch 3-1. Starting with blue paint, and adding white paint at the same time that you add yellow, creates a sequence of blue/light green/pale yellow as shown in swatch 3-2. Starting with yellow paint, and adding white

3-4

3-5

3-6

3-7

paint at the same time that blue is added, the sequence is yellow/light green/light blue, as shown in swatch 3-3.

For a shaded sequence to be smooth and continuous, the steps from one color to the next should be evenly spaced. If there is a big jump between two steps, the sequence will divide, and the break in continuity will become the focus. For example, pale yellow/light green/dark blue, swatch 3-4, does not read as a sequence, but as two categories: light colors and a dark color. The eye is arrested by the line made at the boundary between the dark color and the two much lighter ones. But pale yellow/light green/medium blue-green/dark blue, as shown in swatch 3-5, *does* read as a sequence because the intervals between colors are even.

Between any two colors there is always an intermediate one, which can be interpolated to make a sequence of three. And, from any two colors you can extrapolate the third in the series they begin. For example, between the light pink at the bottom and the medium pink at the top in swatch 3-6, I placed an intermediary pink to make a sequence; taking the same light pink and medium pink next to each other in swatch 3-7, I added the purple beyond them to make a dif-

ferent sequence of three.

Sequences can be composed of any number of colors, as long as there is an even progression from one to the next. Unfortunately, no matter how many colors of yarn you have, there often comes a moment in the design process when you really want a certain color, slightly darker or slightly lighter, slightly brighter or slightly duller, than one you have. You don't have it, and it may not even exist, so you have to work around such limitations. When buying yarn to design a garment, choose colors in grouped sequences like those illustrated in this chapter.

To design with color, it's useful to know the components of color. Standard color theory identifies colors by hue, value, and intensity. Hue defines the color's position on the color wheel. Intensity is a measure of brightness: neutral colors are dull, of low intensity; pure colors are bright, of high intensity. Value refers to lightness or darkness. Standard color theory also makes the following designations. Colors opposite each other on the color wheel are complements. When a pure color is modified with white, it is known as a tint; when it is modified with gray it is known as a tone, and when it is modified with black it is known as a shade.

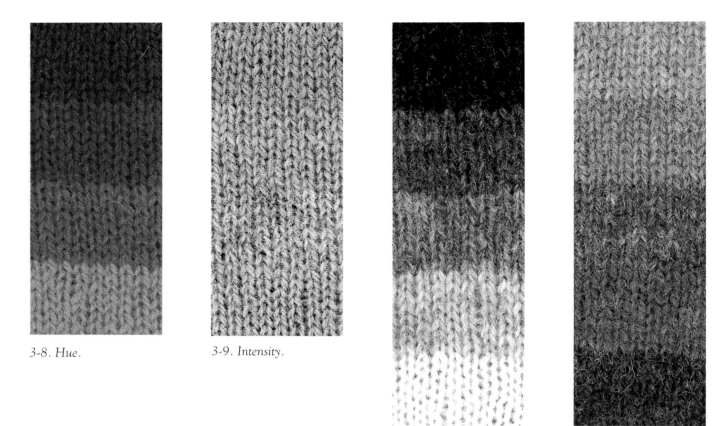

3-8. *Hue*.   3-9. *Intensity*.   3-10. *Value*.   3-11. *Value*

Swatch 3-8 shows a sequence of hues: orange, red-orange, red, red-violet. Swatch 3-9 shows a sequence of diminishing intensity from yellow to tan, and swatch 3-10 a sequence of values graded from white to black. A sequence of values need not be gradations of only one color; many different colors, if arranged in progressing values, will also read as a sequence, as shown in swatch 3-11.

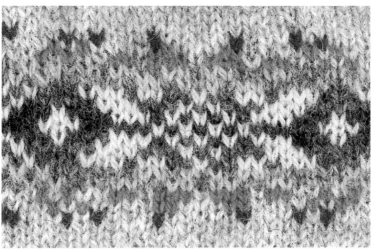

3-13. *This swatch uses the sequences employed in swatches 3-12 and 3-10 in a pattern.*

3-12. *Tint.*

3-14. *Shade.*

3-15. *Tone.*

3-16. *Temperature.*

3-17. *Temperature.*

3-18. *Temperature.*

Swatch 3-12 shows a sequence of tints adding white to red. Swatch 3-14 shows a sequence of shades adding black to green. A sequence of tones is shown in swatch 3-15, adding gray to blue.

Colors may also be characterized by temperature, hot or cold, warm or cool. And although red is generally hot, and blue is generally cool, there may be cool reds, like magenta, and warm blues, like turquoise; a gray is not merely neutral but may be warm, like mouse fur, or cool, like metal. Swatches 3-16 through 3-18 show temperature sequences: 3-16 goes from warm white to cool white, 3-17 moves from warm red to cool, and 3-18 from warm blue to cool blue.

3-19. *Complementary colors.*

3-20. *Complementary colors.*

3-21. *Complementary colors.*

3-22. *Complementary colors.*

When complementary colors are blended with each other they make beautiful sequences as shown in swatches 3-19 through 3-22.

Complementary colors can also be blended as tints, tones, or shades. Swatch 3-23 travels from a tint of red—that is, pink—to a shade of green; swatch 3-24 travels from a tint of green to a shade of red.

3-23. *Complementary colors*.

3-24. *Complementary colors*.

Two more swatches combine some of the sequences from the previous pages to demonstrate how they may be used. Swatch 3-24a uses the colors in 3-23 and 3-15. Swatch 3-24b uses the colors in 3-22 and 3-9.

3-24a

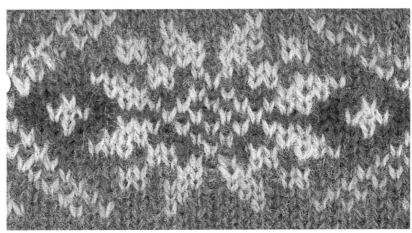

3-24b

USING COLOR PRINCIPLES

The fundamental Shetland rule is that the pattern must be readable and coherent. Patterns are, after all, what this kind of knitting is known for.

For the pattern to show up, there must be sufficient contrast between it and the background. Shetlanders say, "the pattern is either light on dark, or dark on light." In other words, value contrast is the ruling principle. In swatch 3-25, where the pattern colors form a sequence of muted orange/muted red/muted violet, and the background shifts from muted green to muted blue-green, you can barely see the pattern; there is not enough contrast between the pattern and the background, which are both about the same value and intensity. A Shetlander would not use these colors together. Swatch 3-26 uses the identical pattern colors, set against a darker background, and here the pattern is clear. This would be a passable way of using colors for a Shetlander.

Shetlanders also warn, "Don't cut the pattern." Swatch 3-27 shows an example of a "cut pattern": you don't see the pattern, but instead you see the horizontal line where colors change. For the pattern to show up, the contrast between changes of color from row to row must not be greater than the contrast between the pattern and the background. In other words, there has to be more contrast between the pattern and the background than between any two colors in the pattern or in the background.

Complementary colors, color theory goes, enliven each other more than any other combination. But complements close in value will not always show up against each other, as swatch 3-25 shows, where red and green look homogeneous. What's usually required is adding value contrast to complementary contrast by using a tint or a shade of one of the colors, as in swatch 3-26, where light orange appears against dark

3-25

blue and red-violet is against dark green. Colors which are near-complements enliven each other as much as strict complements do; so red-orange looks just as pretty against green as red does. Monochromatic effects—light blue against dark blue, for example—seem dull, and in my opinion should be avoided. As we have seen, for one color to appear distinct from its neighbor, there has to be sufficient contrast between them. But to my eye, this can be a problem, because graphic value contrasts are not rich in color. The challenge is to find rich color effects while not sacrificing clarity.

Another important aspect of color theory is that color is relative. Colors are affected by adjacent colors: the eye naturally polarizes them, maximizing their contrast. We see difference, rather than similarity, when we look at two colors because our eyes overlay a color's after-image—which is its opposite—on adjacent colors. This visual phenomenon is known as simultaneous contrast. Next to a darker color any color looks lighter than it would otherwise; next to a lighter color, it looks darker. Next to a brighter color any color looks duller, and next to a duller color it looks brighter. Two pure colors will push each other apart; for example, when red-violet and blue-violet are paired, they tend to look like red and blue. Next to a bright color, a neutral color tends to look like the bright color's complement. Complements next to each other look brighter than they do in other contexts.

3-26

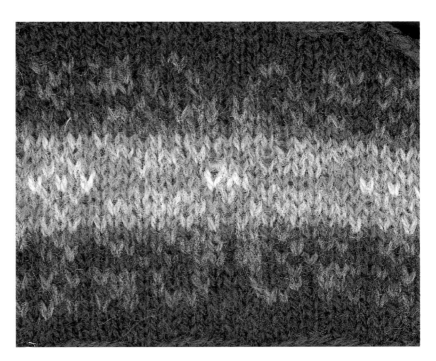

3-27

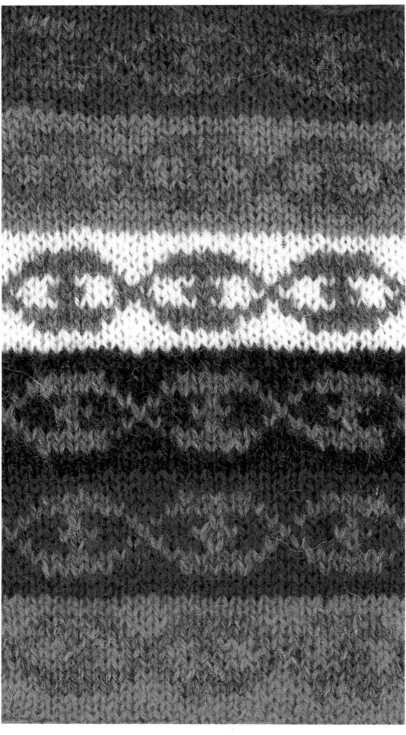

3-28

Swatches 3-28 and 3-29 illustrate the way the eye sees what's *not* there. In swatch 3-28, the same relatively neutral blue-gray is used in all the pattern bands. It tends to look bright next to its complement, orange; dull next to bright blue; light next to dark blue-gray; dark next to white; more like violet next to yellow-orange; more like green next to red-orange. In swatch 3-29, a relatively neutral tan, used in each band, looks bright next to its complement, purple; dull next to bright yellow; light next to dark brown; dark next to white; more like green next to pink; and more like orange next to blue.

Working with Sequences

When I start to design a garment I choose a few colors that I know I want to work with; then I find other colors that make sequences which incorporate them, like those in swatches 3-1 through 3-24. I line up one sequence of balls of yarn next to another sequence and try to imagine how the colors will look when knitted in a pattern. Then I knit a swatch. Once I do, the colors often look completely different from what I imagined. If this happens, I change the color groupings, adding, taking away, or substituting some, and make another swatch.

It often seems to me that nothing is more challenging than taking a group of colors of Shetland yarn and finding a satisfying way to order them in a Fair Isle pattern. No matter how much experience I have making swatches, colors almost always look different knitted together than they do in balls or skeins. It seems one color will show up against another when the skeins are lined up. But instead, in a swatch, the color disappears—or the contrast is too sharp. I want the colors to be varied, to enliven each other, but some colors just look heavy and dull next to each other. And every arrangement suggests another: as I begin a swatch, I find I can think of several variations on the groupings I've chosen that just might improve the swatch, and so I follow those ideas, convinced that they will work, and wind up with more and more swatches.

I usually spend quite a lot of time experimenting with color before I begin a garment, sometimes several weeks, but that doesn't guarantee that I won't rip out portions of semi-completed sweaters, because not only do colors look different than I might predict when I swatch, they look different once several inches of a garment are knitted. So I often make changes after the first few pattern bands of a sweater are knitted, or even later, when the garment is complete, by removing part of the sweater and reknitting it and grafting the new portion to the old. Other times I start over after the first few bands. But a Shetland knitter does not spend much—if any—time swatching, and is not likely to rip out her work. Rather, she enjoys improvising based on past experience, seeming to have a sixth sense about what will work and what won't. On the other hand, designers at small Shetland companies producing hand-framed garments do make numerous swatches and sample garments.

Once I have chosen two sequences of colors, there are, surprisingly, *eight* different ways of juxtaposing them. Either sequence can be used for the background or the pattern, and each is reversible. Usually a sequence travels from light to dark or from dark to light, although some sequences maintain the same value from beginning to end. Depending on how the colors are arranged, a sequence could travel from light at the outer edges of the pattern band to dark at the center, or from dark at the outer edges to light at the center. Swatches 3-30a and 3-30b show all eight permutations. Each uses six colors arranged in two sequences of three. One sequence travels from a shade of blue to a tone of blue, that is, navy to deep dull blue to medium dullish blue, and the other is composed of tints of a warm neutral (the color you would get by mixing blue and orange paint), from orange-brown to beige to oatmeal.

Probably you like some of these arrangements more than others; so do I. But leaving aside preference for a moment, let's analyze the swatches to understand how the ordering and juxtaposition of colors affects the way the patterns look.

Notice first that the background color at the outside of each band is the dominant color in that band. There are two reasons for this. First, there is simply more of it. With two plain rows

3-29

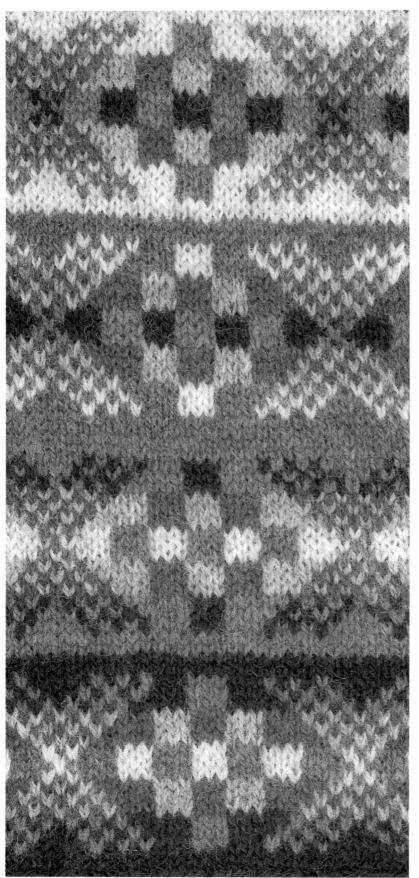

Fourth Band

Background	Pattern
oatmeal	medium dullish blue
beige	deep dull blue
orange-brown	navy
beige	deep dull blue
oatmeal	medium dullish blue

Third Band

Background	Pattern
medium dullish blue	oatmeal
deep dull blue	beige
navy	orange-brown
deep dull blue	beige
medium dullish blue	oatmeal

Second Band

Background	Pattern
orange-brown	navy
beige	deep dull blue
oatmeal	medium dullish blue
beige	deep dull blue
orange-brown	navy

First Band

Background	Pattern
navy	orange-brown
deep dull blue	beige
medium dullish blue	oatmeal
deep dull blue	beige
navy	orange-brown

3-30a

Eighth Band

Background	Pattern
oatmeal	navy
beige	deep dull blue
orange-brown	medium dullish blue
beige	deep dull blue
oatmeal	navy

Seventh Band

Background	Pattern
medium dullish blue	orange-brown
deep dull blue	beige
navy	oatmeal
deep dull blue	beige
medium dullish blue	orange-brown

Sixth Band

Background	Pattern
orange-brown	medium dullish blue
beige	deep dull blue
oatmeal	navy
beige	deep dull blue
orange-brown	medium dullish blue

Fifth Band

Background	Pattern
navy	oatmeal
deep dull blue	beige
medium dullish blue	orange-brown
deep dull blue	beige
navy	oatmeal

3-30b

of it on either side of the pattern, there are, in any one band, ten rows of that color, six rows of the middle color of the sequence, and only three rows of the center background color. Second, the background colors are dominant because in the pattern I used there are more background stitches than pattern stitches on just about every row; there is simply more of that color. Other patterns may have more pattern stitches than background stitches; in those, pattern colors will dominate background colors. But if most of the colors of one sequence are much brighter than the other sequence, the bright colors will dominate, even if there are fewer stitches of them. Because I chose colors of roughly equal brightness, the visual balance of sequences is affected mainly by the proportion of background to pattern stitches.

In the first band of swatch 3-30a (counting from the bottom up), both sequences travel from dark at the outside to light at the center, and the pattern is lighter than the background. In the second band, pattern and background are reversed, with the background lighter than the pattern. In both bands, the lightest colors are at the center. This is the classic way to arrange a pattern, for the eye naturally gravitates to the lightest colors, finding a focal point in the center. I prefer a light pattern on a dark background to the other way around, because a dark pattern on a light ground looks to me like type on a page,

and the light seems to swallow up the pattern; whereas with a light pattern on a dark background, the pattern stands out luminously. Because the eye is drawn to light, a dark pattern against a light background highlights the background rather than the pattern, when, after all, it is the pattern that really matters.

The third and fourth bands turn the sequences of the previous two bands inside out. The darkest colors are at the center and the lightest at the outer edges. Again, because the eye gravitates towards light, these patterns have two focal points, at the outer edges, instead of one, like the first two bands. Depending on taste, two focal points are confusing—or interesting.

In swatch 3-30b (the fifth, sixth, seventh, and eighth bands), I used the background colors in the same order as they appear in the first group of four patterns. In every one of these four bands, one sequence travels from dark at the outside to light at the center, and the other in the opposite direction, from light at the outside to dark at the center. You could call the sequences of the first four bands (swatch 3-30a) "parallel" because both travel the same way, light to dark or dark to light, and the sequences in the second group of four bands (swatch 3-30b) "opposed" because one sequence goes in the opposite direction from the other. With the sequences opposed, the lightest and darkest colors of the six, oatmeal and navy, are adjacent. Colors of minimal contrast, orange-brown and medium dullish blue (which are dull and the same value, so they appear quite similar), are also adjacent to each other. These very high and very muted contrasts appear in all four bands in 3-30b and in none of the bands in 3-30a.

In the fifth and eighth bands, the greatest contrast is at the outer edges, with minimal contrast at the center; in the sixth and seventh bands, the muted contrast is at the outer edges with high contrast at the center. In the sixth and seventh bands, the pattern is difficult to discern at the outer edges, especially compared to the clarity of the center. A Shetlander would not use the sixth or seventh bands because the pattern is not clearly visible; all that can really be seen are the center rows. These two color arrangements are the furthest from classic of the eight bands; opposed sequences are not often used in Shetland. Depending on taste, though, what is difficult to discern may be visually intriguing. Sometimes it's a subtle matter: in the fifth and eighth bands, the same colors are juxtaposed, yet the pattern is visible enough. This may be because the eye can sort out one site of visual confusion, but not two sites at once. Or because the eye prefers having the pattern defined in two places—that is, the outer edges—to having it defined in one place. Or, perhaps, it's because in this particular pattern, all the shapes at the center are squares, easily readable

shapes, whereas at the outer edges of the pattern there is only one nicely readable square, flanked by wide diagonal lines.

Now to my preferences. If I designed a garment based on these swatches, I would probably use the first, third and fifth arrangements. I would use the first because it is so classic and clear, and I would use the third and fifth because they are also readable, and not radically different from the first, but different enough to make an interesting harmony. Or, I might be tempted to design a high-contrast sweater with the first and eighth arrangements, which oppose and set each other off dramatically.

I do not usually make a swatch like this, with all the permutations of the colors I want to use; this one is for illustration only. But isn't it amazing how many possibilities only a few colors allow! And, of course, there are always more possibilities. Suppose you decide to use one of these bands, but on another band, you introduce a different color at the center; or add a fourth step to the shading of three; or darken one sequence (for example, beige/orange-brown/brown, or medium dullish blue/navy/black) or lighten one sequence (for example, beige/oatmeal/white, or deep dull blue/medium dullish blue/light blue); or substitute a completely different sequence for one of these. The possibilities are virtually infinite.

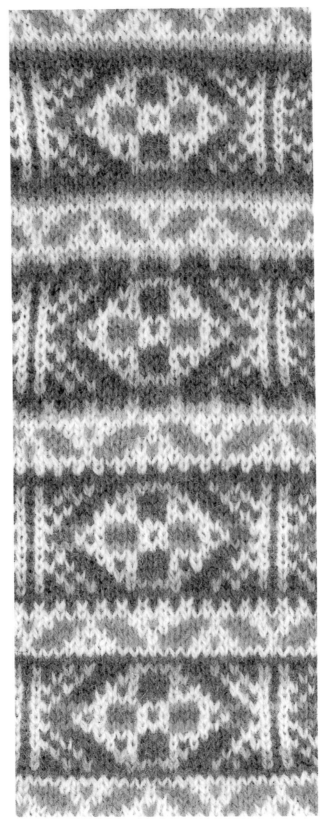

3-31

Transitions Between Bands

Once I've worked out two or three pattern sequences, I'm ready to think about how they might go together to make a sweater. I've chosen groupings of colors and patterns that I like; now, how do the pattern bands look next to each other? The border where one band meets another is a critical area, affecting the overall graphic quality of the sweater. Often, there is a plain row of the background of one band next to a plain row of the background of the next band, making a sharp edge. But there are other ways to treat that juncture that can look blurry or sparkled, contained or open, and make a big difference in the appearance of the garment. Swatches 3-31 and 3-32 illustrate different ways to handle this juncture.

Where the contrast between bands is high, as it is throughout swatch 3-31, the garment will look broadly horizontally striped. Because the eye gravitates to contrast, the outer edges of the pattern bands become focal points, rather than the pattern itself—but those edges ought not to detract from the pattern. The edges of the first band in this swatch (at the bottom of the page) are treated the most simply, and have the greatest degree of contrast: one plain row of white meets one plain row of blue. The variations on the edges in the rest of this swatch and in the next swatch, 3-32, show ways of softening those edges, and diminishing the contrast.

In the second band of swatch 3-31, a row of alternating white and blue stitches, repeated (called cat's teeth, or "een and een" in Shetland dialect, meaning "one and one"), lies at the juncture. This makes the edge appear serrated. It effectively adds another pattern to the two main patterns, increasing visual interest, although the edge is still a focal point. In the third band, pink is added at the edge, making a scallop around the edge of the blue band, softening it. In the fourth band, a plain pink row and a plain red-violet row outline the blue band. This also softens the edge; the progression of values from white to pink to red-violet makes the edge glow because the pink appears to be a suffused halo of the red violet.

Swatch 3-32 uses the same group of colors, the same wide pattern on the same background color, medium blue, and the same narrow pattern, but the contrast between the two bands is greatly diminished by using aqua as the background of the narrow pattern instead of white. The overall effect is less graphic and stark.

In the first band (counting from the bottom up) of swatch 3-32, the outermost row of the blue band is studded with white accent stitches, which have a sparkly effect. The stitches call attention to themselves because they are so much lighter than either the blue or the aqua, so the edge becomes much less noticeable. The stitches are more dispersed at the edge of the band than they are in the pattern (and more so than they are in the second band of swatch 3-31), so the pattern here remains a focal point because of its greater density. In the second band, white diamonds overlap the edge. The effect is similar to, but stronger than it is below; the light diamonds, a more noticeable pattern than the single-stitch sparkles, make the edge seem to recede and diffuse beneath them. In the third band, a four-row zigzag pattern in red-violet overlaps the edge. Now the straight line of the edge has been obscured completely. The red-violet is close in value to both the blue and the aqua, so there is rich color activity at the edge; the strong graphic contrast at the center of the pattern again becomes the focal point. And in the fourth band, the plain row has been replaced by a row of red-violet bordering the pattern. Eliminating the plain blue row makes the background of the band just as prominent as the pattern, so pattern and background seem to join together.

3-32

3-33

Not all this needs to be incorporated into your first design efforts. If you want to do some designing of your own, the simplest approach is to use just one color for the background of the entire garment, as shown in illustration 3-33, a detail of the Lunna jumper, (see page 142). One background color unifies the garment visually, and, because there is only one sequence of color changes to remember from row to row, it's easy to knit. When the background remains the same color, a single sequence of pattern colors would be boring, but two or three different sequences, as there are here, can be quite lively. Keep the background either darker than all the pattern colors, or lighter, so that the patterns will show up. On a heathery middle-value background, patterns do not show up.

The next simplest approach is to use one color for the entire background except the central one, three, or five rows of the patterns, as is shown at right, a detail of the Bressay jumper. (See page 110.)

3-34

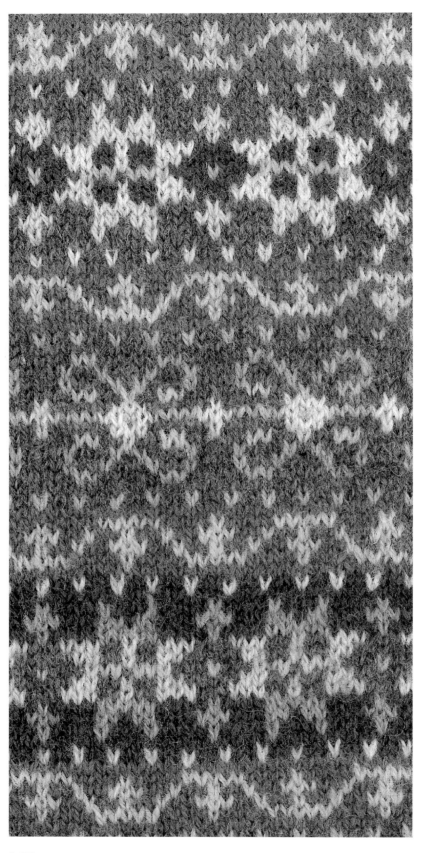

3-35

A slightly more complicated approach is to use closely related colors for the backgrounds: for example, wide bands with backgrounds of bright blue and light blue, flanked by turquoise-background peerie bands. This gives unity *and* variety as seen here in a detail of the Sandwater jumper. (See page 146.)

Switching background and pattern colors—for example, using a wide band with a tan background and purple pattern, flanked by narrow bands with purple background and tan pattern—gives a garment a feeling of complexity and excitement without using very many colors. Alternating light on dark with dark on light, or reversing pattern color and background color, as shown in illustration 3-36, a detail of the Westerwick cardigan (see page 168), is a fundamental construction principle of Fair Isle knitting.

To unify a sweater, it is important to use at least one of the colors from the wide bands in the narrow bands. Wide patterns of red and blue, flanked by narrow ones of gray and white wouldn't look quite right; the narrow pattern would better with gray and white *and* red.

If you've made a swatch and find that one or two rows do not look quite right, you can use duplicate stitch to see how a different color would look. I've duplicate-stitched over the center rows throughout an entire sweater when I realized that it needed a different color than the one I'd first used.

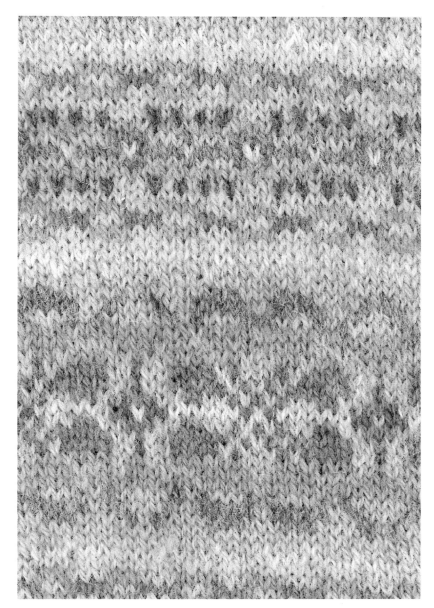

3-36

Designing Ribbing

A simple plan for two-color ribbing is to use just two colors, as I have done in the Sandwater pullover (both colorways) and the Brae cardigan. (See pages 146 and 106.) These ribbings make relatively quiet "frames" for sweaters. Another approach is to repeat sequences from one of the pattern bands in the ribbing. I prefer ribbings with different sequences than are used elsewhere in the sweater, because it makes the overall color effect richer and more complex.

(The ribbing can't be *so* different from the rest of the sweater that it doesn't seem to belong to it.) Shaded k2, p2 ribbing is often quite dynamic; the approximately thirty rows of vertical stripes are effectively the largest pattern in the garment, so they can also be the most graphic.

At right are examples from my search for the most unusual yet most compatible combinations of colors for the ribbing in the Hillswick lumber. (See page 128.)

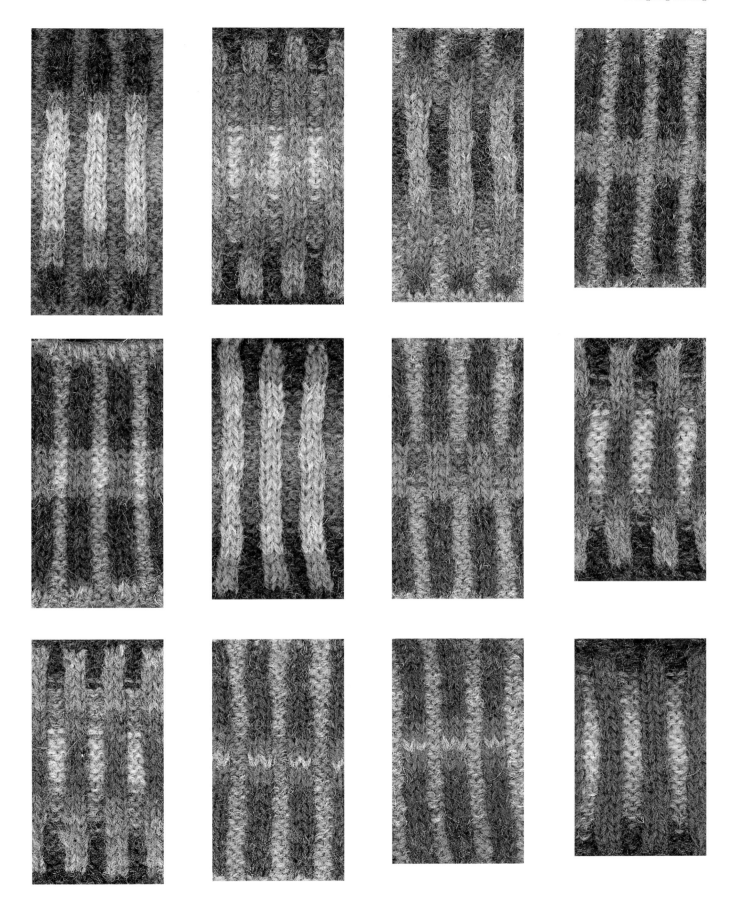

Some patterns have just one element, like the three-row, four-stitch-repeat diamond shown in illustration 4-1. That tiny pattern could be centered in either of two ways: at the center of the diamond, as shown in illustration 4-12, or at the stitch that falls between the diamonds, as shown in illustration 4-13.

Check carefully that you have centered the pattern on the very first round of the sweater and on the first round of subsequent bands. The first round of the sweater and of every new pattern is the hardest, and demands the most concentration and careful counting. After that, there is a reliable guide: the previous row.

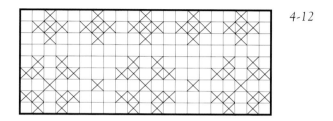

4-12

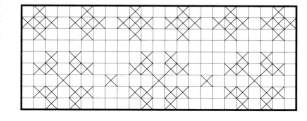

4-13

5
ORIGINAL PATTERNS

If you want to make one of the garments on the following pages, the yarns listed are all readily obtainable. (See Sources of Supply, page 179.) I do not recommend substituting any colors for those specified. Even shifting to an ever-so-slightly darker or ever-so-slightly lighter color may radically change the appearance of the patterns and the garment, creating either a strong horizontally striped appearance and/or obscuring the pattern. I do, however, enthusiastically recommend experimenting with color if you would like to use the patterns but prefer, for example, a different background color, an entirely different palette, or a bolder or subtler effect than the design has. That, in fact, was how I often approached patterns by other designers before I studied in Shetland: I changed the colors radically. Just be sure to make a swatch before you embark!

NOTES ON COLORS

A rose may be a rose may be a rose, but in describing colors, one person's rose may be another person's geranium, or another's dusty pink, or another's medium pink. Poetic names for colors can be wonderful—in poetry, or on lipstick labels—but I'm afraid they may be confusing to the reader, so I don't use them.

The majority of the yarn used in this book comes from the Shetland firm Jamieson & Smith, which doesn't name its colors; they are identified by number. The other yarn that I used, MacAuslan Shetland, is identified by evocative rather than descriptive names. In the directions, colors are listed first by how the company refers to them, followed by a name I have given them using commonly understood terms and taking into account their relationship to each other. So instead of calling three different grays silver gray, pewter gray, and thundercloud gray (which is the lightest? Hm...), I've called them light gray, medium gray and dark gray. They should be readily identifiable, and easily differentiated from, for example, blue gray. As explained in the chapter on color, I usually use colors in ordered sequences, and names given to colors reflect this.

NEEDLES

Most US size #3 needles are 3.25 mm. But some size #3 are 3 mm. I have found that these small differences in dimension make a significant difference in gauge. I tend to get between 7 and 7.5 stitches to the inch on a 3.25 mm needle and 8 stitches to the inch on a 3 mm needle. Be careful not to use one size needle on the body of the sweater and another size on the sleeve, when you switch from a 29" circular needle to a 16" circular needle.

On small parts of the garment—the bottoms of the sleeves and the cuffs especially—I prefer to use circular needles rather than double-pointed needles. I have found that I do not need to switch to double-pointed needles even when the actual dimensions of the narrow end of the sleeve are smaller than the circular needle. Even though it measures as little as 11", the end of the patterned knitting on the sleeve of an adult-size sweater stretches just enough to fit around a 16" circular needle. For the sleeve ribbing, which is too narrow even for that, I use a 29" circular needle, keeping the stitches on only a portion of it, pulling the unused portions of the needle into loops and shifting the location of the loops as the work progresses.

Baltasound Cropped Jumper

BALTASOUND CROPPED JUMPER

This sweater evokes snow, stars, and mid-winter dark. It links two traditional stars usually aligned vertically or horizontally in a continuous diagonal pattern. The stark contrast of black and light gray is tempered by using yarns flecked with motes of gray.

Note: The sleeve pattern is continuous with the body pattern. This is accomplished by picking up stitches in the first round of the sleeve which duplicate the pattern stitches perpendicular and adjacent to them in the body. So, there are two identical rounds: one vertical at the edge of the armhole and one horizontal at the beginning of the sleeve. Because the picked-up round is hidden by the slight ridge formed by the hemmed extra stitches, the duplicate round is not noticeable.

Detail of sleeve-to-body join.

Finished Size: Small/Medium.
Bust/chest circumference: 44" (112 cm).
Body length: 19" (48.5 cm).
Sleeve length: 19" (48.5 cm).
Note: Because of the large pattern repeat and short, boxy shape of this sweater, it is given in one size only. However, it can be made slightly larger or smaller by adjusting the needle size to change the gauge. (See chart above.)

Gauge	Finished Bust/Chest Circumference	Body Length	Sleeve Length
27 sts = 4" (10 cm)	47½" (120.5 cm)	19¾" (50 cm)	19¾" (50 cm)
28 sts = 4" (10 cm)	45¾" (116 cm)	20" (51 cm)	20" (51 cm)
30 sts = 4" (10 cm)	42½" (108 cm)	18½" (47 cm)	18½" (47 cm)
31 sts = 4" (10 cm)	41¼" (105 cm)	18" (45.5 cm)	18" (45.5 cm)

Materials

Yarn: Jamieson & Smith 2-ply jumper weight Shetland yarn (100% wool; 150 yd/oz (137 m/28 g)): #81 black, 8 oz (227 g); #203 light gray, 6 oz (170 g). A few yards of contrast color waste yarn for casting on.

Needles: Body and Sleeves—Size 4 (3.5 mm): 16"/40 cm and 29"/80 cm circular and double-pointed (dpn); Ribbings—Size 2 (2.75 mm): 16"/40 cm and 29"/80 cm circular and dpn; Facings—Size 1 (2.25 mm): 16"/40 cm and 29"/80 cm circular and dpn. Adjust needle sizes if necessary to obtain the correct gauge.

Notions: Marker; four stitch holders; tapestry needle.

Gauge: 29 sts and 29 rnds = 4" (10 cm) with larger needle over St st in color pattern.

Body: With waste yarn, black, and longer facing needle, provisionally CO 288 sts (see page 104). Place marker at beg of rnd. Join, being careful not to twist sts. Beg Body Ribbing chart, k5 rnds facing. Change to longer ribbing needle. Join light gray. **Turning rnd:** *p2 light gray, p2 black; rep from *. **Ribbing:** *k2 light gray, p2 black; rep from * for 5 rnds. **Bottom hem:** Insert longer facing needle into provisional CO rnd. Remove waste yarn. Fold hem at turning rnd so that rib sts are in front. Change to longer body needle and with black, *[(k1 rib st from front needle tog with 1 st from provisional CO rnd) 9 times, M1]; rep from * 31 more times—320 sts total. Beg on rnd 1 of Main Chart, work through rnd 40, and then rnds 1 through 26, for a total of 66 rnds. Break yarns.

Armholes: Rnd 27 of chart: Place 1 st on holder for left underarm, CO 6 extra sts, the first 2 with slip knots and the following 4 with backward loops alternating colors [(light gray, black) 3 times], work 159 front sts in color pattern, place 1 st on holder for right underarm, CO 12 extra sts with backward loops [(black, light gray) 3 times, (light gray, black) 3 times], work 159 back sts in color pattern, and CO 6 more extra sts with backward loops [(black, light gray) 3 times]—318 body sts (and 24 extra sts). Rejoin. Always work the extra sts next to the body of the sweater in black, the 2 center extra sts in light gray, and the rem extra sts in the established striped pattern. Work through rnd 40, then rnds 1 through 40, and then rnds 1 and 2, for a total of 122 rnds.

Shape Front Neck: Rnd 3 of chart: Work 43 left front shoulder sts in color pattern, ssk (the dec slants towards the extra sts), place 69 sts on holder for front neck, CO 12 extra sts as for right underarm, k2tog (the dec slants towards the extra sts), work to end of rnd in color pattern. Work extra sts as for right underarm. Dec 1 st each side of front neck edge in this manner every rnd 6 times total, and *at the same time,*

Shape Back Neck: Rnd 6 of chart: Work in color pattern across front and 43 sts of right back shoulder, ssk, place 69 sts on holder for back neck, CO 12 extra sts as for right underarm, k2tog, work to end of rnd in color pattern. Work extra sts as before. Working decs as for front neck, dec 1 st each side of back neck edge every rnd 6 times total—

39 sts rem on each shoulder. Work through rnd 12, for a total of 132 rnds. Work rnd 13 across front sts only.

Shoulder Seam: Turn work inside out. With black and beg at the center of armhole extra sts, BO all sts together, matching extra sts to each other.

Sleeves: Cut armhole extra sts up the center. With black, RS facing, shorter sleeve needle, and beg at center of underarm, k1 st from holder ("seam" st). With black and light gray, duplicating the pattern of the adjacent sts in the body (the pick up rnd is rnd 34 of the chart), pick up and knit 66 sts (see note above) along one armhole edge, 1 st at shoulder seam, and 66 sts along other armhole edge—134 sts. Place marker. Join. Always work the underarm "seam" st in black. Beg on rnd 33, follow Main Chart in reverse direction, working 22 rnds even, then dec 1 st each side of "seam" st on next rnd and every 3rd rnd 28 times, then every 4th rnd 7 times, working 134 rnds total, ending on rnd

21, and changing to sleeve dpn when necessary. End of sleeve pattern matches beg of body pattern—64 sts rem. **Decrease rnd:** With black and ribbing dpn, dec 8 sts evenly spaced—56 sts rem. **Ribbing:** *k2 light gray, p2 black; rep from * for 6 rnds. **Turning rnd:** *p2 light gray, p2 black; rep from *. **Facing:** With black and facing dpn, k5 rnds. BO loosely. Fold hem at turning rnd and sew loosely in place with yarn.

Neckband: Cut neck extra sts up the center. With black, RS facing, shorter ribbing needle, and beg at right side of back neck, k69 sts from back neck holder, pick up and knit 13 sts along left back and front neck edges, k69 sts from front neck holder, pick up and knit 13 sts along right front and back neck edges—164 sts. Place marker. Join. **Decrease rnd:** *k2 light gray, p2 black; rep from * and *at the same time*, dec 4 sts evenly spaced along each of the 69 sts of front and back neck—156 sts rem. **Ribbing:** Following Neckband Ribbing chart, *p2

light gray, p2 black; rep from * for 5 rnds. **Decrease rnd:** (Dec about 10% of the sts.) With black and shorter facing needle, *k8, k2tog; rep from *—141 sts rem. **Facing:** With black and shorter facing needle, k5 rnds. BO loosely in knit. Fold hem at turning rnd and sew loosely in place with yarn, spacing sts to allow for 10% fewer sts on inner band.

Finishing: Trim the 6 extra sts at neck and armhole edges to 3 or 4 and hem them with a tapestry needle threaded with yarn, turning 1 st under as you go. Wash in wool-safe detergent. Remove excess water with the spin cycle of a washing machine. Place on a jumper board. Using regular sewing thread, a tapestry needle, and long sts, baste the neck edge to shape it and draw it in. When dry, remove the sweater from the board and pull out basting. Reshape the body and sleeve ribbings by wetting and patting them into place, or by steaming them.

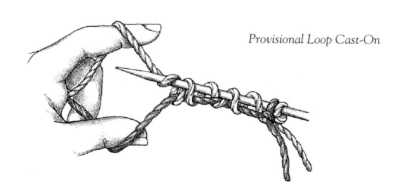

Provisional Loop Cast-On

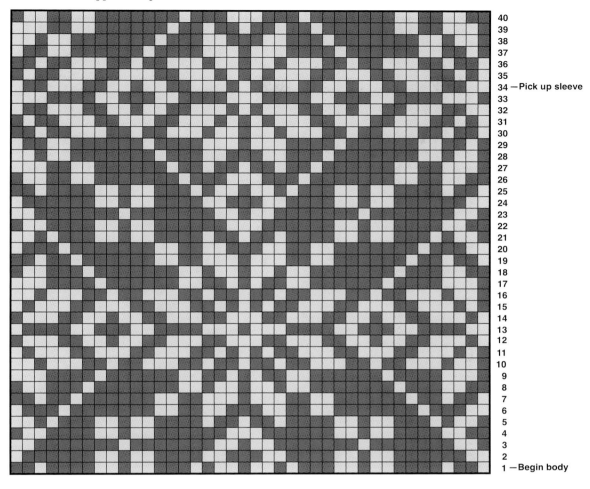

40
39
38
37
36
35
34 —Pick up sleeve
33
32
31
30
29
28
27
26
25
24
23
22
21
20
19
18
17
16
15
14
13
12
11
10
9
8
7
6
5
4
3
2
1 —Begin body

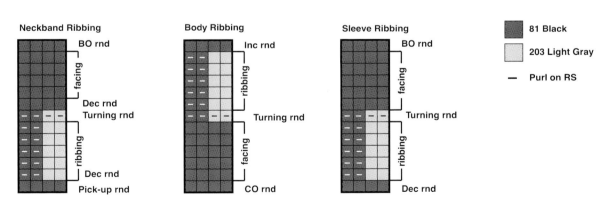

Neckband Ribbing

BO rnd
facing
Dec rnd
Turning rnd
ribbing
Dec rnd
Pick-up rnd

Body Ribbing

Inc rnd
ribbing
Turning rnd
facing
CO rnd

Sleeve Ribbing

BO rnd
facing
Turning rnd
ribbing
Dec rnd

81 Black

203 Light Gray

— Purl on RS

Brae Cardigan

BRAE CARDIGAN

Although this sweater is primarily red and white, it doesn't look monochromatic because of the opposition of warm and cool reds: in the small patterns, warm salmon is paired with cold red; in the large patterns, cool pink is paired with warm red. These colors seem to push each other apart, so the reds tend to look purple or orange. The white is not actually white, but undyed natural wool, which is a pale beige, with a softer effect than pure white. All the patterns are different, though the larger ones are variations on two alternating themes: radiating star/rosettes and curve-bordered diamonds.

Finished Size: Small (Medium, Large). Shown in size Small.

Bust/chest circumference, buttoned: 41 (45, 49)" (104 (114.5, 124.5) cm).

Body length: 20¾ (22¼, 23½)" (52.5 (56.5, 59.5) cm).

Sleeve length: 18½ (19¾, 20¾)" (47 (50, 52.5) cm).

Materials

Yarn: Jamieson & Smith 2-ply jumper weight Shetland yarn (100% wool; 150 yd/oz (137 m/28 g)): #55 warm red, 3 (4, 4) oz (85 (113, 113) g); #202 fawn, 2 (2, 3) oz (57 (57, 85) g); #43 magenta-red, 2 (3, 3) oz (57 (85, 85) g); #FC6 light pink heather, 1 (2, 2) oz (28 (57, 57) g); #123 light red-violet heather, #131 blue-violet, #FC22 deep pink heather, 1 oz (28 g) each.

MacAuslan Shetland yarn (100% wool; 150 yd/oz (137 m/28 g)): Winespark (burgundy heather), 4 (5, 5) oz (113 (142, 142) g); Katrine (salmon), 1 (2, 2) oz (28 (57, 57) g).

Needles: Body and Sleeves—Size 3 (3 mm): 16"/40 cm and 29"/80 cm circular and double-pointed (dpn); Ribbings—Size 1 (2.25 mm): 16"/40 cm and 29"/80 cm circular and dpn. Adjust needle sizes

if necessary to obtain the correct gauge.

Crochet hook: Size C (2.5 mm).

Notions: Markers; three stitch holders; tapestry needle; six 5/8" (1.5 cm) buttons.

Gauge: 32 sts and 32 rnds = 4" (10 cm) with larger needle over St st in color pattern.

Note: At times, each size begins at a different stitch in the pattern repeat.

Body: With burgundy heather and longer ribbing needle, CO 330 (362, 394) sts—318 (350, 382) body sts (and 12 extra sts to be cut later for the center front opening). Place marker at beg of rnd (center front). Join, being careful not to twist sts. **Ribbing:** Work 6 extra sts alternating colors [k1 burgundy heather, k1 warm red] 3 times, *k2 warm red, p2 burgundy heather; rep from * to last 8 sts, end k2 warm red and work rem 6 extra sts [k1 warm red, k1 burgundy heather] 3 times. Work Body Ribbing chart for 2 (2½, 3)" (5 (6.5, 7.5) cm), always working the extra sts next to the body of the sweater in the knit color, the 2 center extra sts in the purl color, and the rem extra sts in the established striped pattern. Change to longer body needle and cold red. **Increase rnd:** Work 6 extra sts, inc 3 sts spaced evenly in the body sts, then work rem 6 extra sts—321 (353, 385) body sts (and 12 extra sts). Except when only one color is used in the rnd, always work the extra sts next to the body of the sweater in the background color, the two center extra sts in the pattern color, and the rem extra sts in the established striped pattern. Beg on rnd 1 of Main Chart, work through rnd 78 (80, 84).

Shape Armholes: Rnd 79 (81, 85) of chart: Work 6 extra sts, work 69 (76, 83) right front sts in color pattern, place 23 (25, 27) sts on holder for right underarm, CO 12 extra sts with backward loops alternating colors [(background, pattern)

3 times, (pattern, background) 3 times], work 137 (151, 165) back sts in color pattern, place 23 (25, 27) sts on holder for left underarm, CO 12 extra sts as for right underarm, work 69 (76, 83) left front sts in color pattern, then work rem 6 extra sts—275 (303, 331) body sts (and 36 extra sts). Work extra sts as for the center front. Work decs at armhole edge as follows: Beg at center front, work extra sts, *work body sts to 2 sts before extra sts, ssk (the dec slants towards the extra sts), work extra sts, k2tog (the dec slants towards the extra sts); rep from *, and work to center front to complete the round. Being careful to keep the pattern motifs in established vertical alignment, dec 1 st each side of armhole edge every other rnd in this manner twice—267 (295, 323) sts, *and at the same time,*

Shape V-Neck: Rnd 84 (86, 88): Work decs at front neck edge as follows: Beg at center front, work extra sts, k2tog, work to 8 sts from center front, ssk, work rem extra sts. Dec 1 st each side of center front extra sts in this manner every 3rd rnd 22 (24, 26) more times—44 (49, 54) sts rem on each shoulder, *and at the same time,*

Shape Back Neck: For size M, work even through rnd 158. For sizes S (L), begin back neck shaping on rnd 144 (158): Work across right front sts and 48 (58) sts of right back shoulder, ssk, place 33 (41) sts on holder for back neck, CO 12 extra sts, k2tog, work to end of rnd. Work extra sts as before. Dec 1 st each side of back neck edge in this manner every rnd 6 times total, ending with rnd 150 (164)—44 (54) sts rem on each shoulder. Work rnd 151 (165) of chart across front sts only (slip sts of left front and 6 left armhole extra sts back to the left end of the circular needle and beg knitting there)—151 (158, 164) rnds total.

Shoulder Seam: Turn work inside out. For sizes S and L: With blue-violet and beg at center of armhole extra sts,

BO all sts together, matching extra sts to each other. For size M: With burgundy heather, *BO 6 extra sts and 49 sts of front shoulder together with 6 extra sts and 49 sts of back shoulder. Begin again at other side and rep from *. BO 12 front extra sts singly. Place rem 49 sts on holder for back neck.

Sleeves: Cut armhole extra sts up the center. With magenta-red (magenta-red, burgundy heather), RS facing, shorter sleeve needle, and beg at center of underarm, k12 (13, 14) underarm sts from holder, pick up and knit 60 (65, 70) sts along one armhole edge, 1 st at shoulder seam, and 61 (66, 71) sts along other armhole edge, and k11 (12, 13) rem underarm sts from holder—145 (157, 169) sts. Place marker. Join. Be careful to center patterns at top of sleeve as they are at the center back of body. Beg on rnd 133 (139, 143), follow Main Chart in reverse direction, dec 1 st each side of underarm marker every 3rd rnd 0 (0, 1) times, every 4th rnd 7 (21, 35) times, and then every 5th rnd 21 (11, 0) times, working 133 (139, 143) rnds total, ending on rnd 1, and changing to sleeve dpn when necessary. End of sleeve pattern matches beg of body pattern—89 (93, 97) sts rem. **Decrease rnd:** With magenta-red and ribbing dpn, dec 21 sts evenly spaced—68 (72, 76) sts rem. **Cuff:** Rnd 1: *k2 warm red, k2 burgundy heather; rep from *. Rnd 2: *k2 warm red, p2 burgundy heather; rep from * until ribbing measures 2 (2½, 3)" (5 (6.5, 7.5) cm). With burgundy heather, BO in knit.

Front Band: Cut center front extra sts up the center. With RS facing, longer ribbing needle, and beg at right front bottom edge alternating k2 burgundy heather, k2 warm red, pick up and knit about 1 st for every rnd, ending k2 burgundy heather—about 169 (181, 191) sts along right front edge, 6 (0, 6) sts along right back neck edge, work 33 (49, 41) sts from back neck holder, 6 (0, 6) sts along left back neck edge, 168 (180, 190) sts along left front edge—about 382 (410, 434) sts total. (Somewhat fewer is acceptable, as long as the number of sts is a multiple of 4 plus 2, but more is not.) Work Front Band Ribbing chart back and forth for 3 rows, keeping floats to the wrong side. **Buttonhole row:** RS facing, rib 2 (3, 4) sts, *work 3-stitch buttonhole (see page 70), rib 16 (17, 18) sts; rep from * 4 more times, work 3-stitch buttonhole—6 buttonholes. Work to end of chart. With burgundy heather, BO in knit. With burgundy heather, crochet about 10 slip sts on the top and bottom edges of the front bands to make them appear continuous with the adjacent cast-on and bind-off edges of the body and neck.

Finishing: Trim the 6 extra sts at neck and armhole edges to 3 or 4 and hem them with a tapestry needle threaded with yarn, turning under 1 st as you go. Overlap the front edges. Using regular sewing thread, a tapestry needle, and long sts, baste the overlapped front edges together so that they will remain flat during blocking. Wash in wool-safe detergent. Remove excess water with the spin cycle of a washing machine. Place on a jumper board. Baste the V of the neck to draw it in and shape it. When dry, remove the sweater from the board and pull out basting. Reshape the body and sleeve ribbings by wetting and patting them into place, or by steaming them. Sew on buttons.

Notes on colors: In the large patterns on rounds 5 to 17, 33 to 45, and so on, the outermost pattern round is deep pink heather, followed by two rounds of light pink heather and three rounds of fawn (undyed natural wool). The background changes from burgundy heather to warm red on the same round that the fawn is introduced. The smaller patterns on rounds 23 to 27, 51 to 55, and so on, use the colder, more purplish magenta-red for the background.

Little three-round diamonds on rounds 1 to 3, 19 to 21, and so on, overlap the background edges. The diamonds are composed of an outer round, rounds 1 and 21, and corresponding repeating rounds, of deep pink heather on the magenta-red background; a center round, round 2, 20, and corresponding repeating rounds, of light red-violet heather on the magenta-red background; and an inner round, rounds 3 and 19, and corresponding repeating rounds, of light red-violet heather on the burgundy heather background.

Brae Cardigan

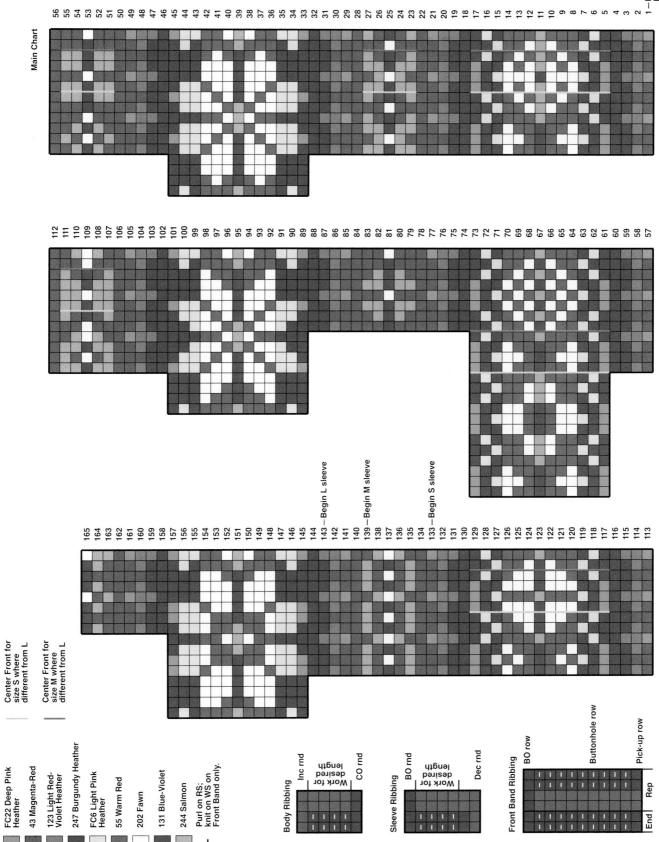

Main Chart

Center Front for size S where different from L

Center Front for size M where different from L

FC22 Deep Pink Heather

43 Magenta-Red

123 Light Red-Violet Heather

247 Burgundy Heather

FC6 Light Pink Heather

55 Warm Red

202 Fawn

131 Blue-Violet

244 Salmon

Purl on RS; knit on WS on Front Band only.

I

Body Ribbing

Inc rnd
Work for desired length
CO rnd

Sleeve Ribbing

BO rnd
Work for desired length
Dec rnd

Front Band Ribbing

BO row
Buttonhole row
Pick-up row

End | Rep

Bressay Jumper

Bressay Jumper

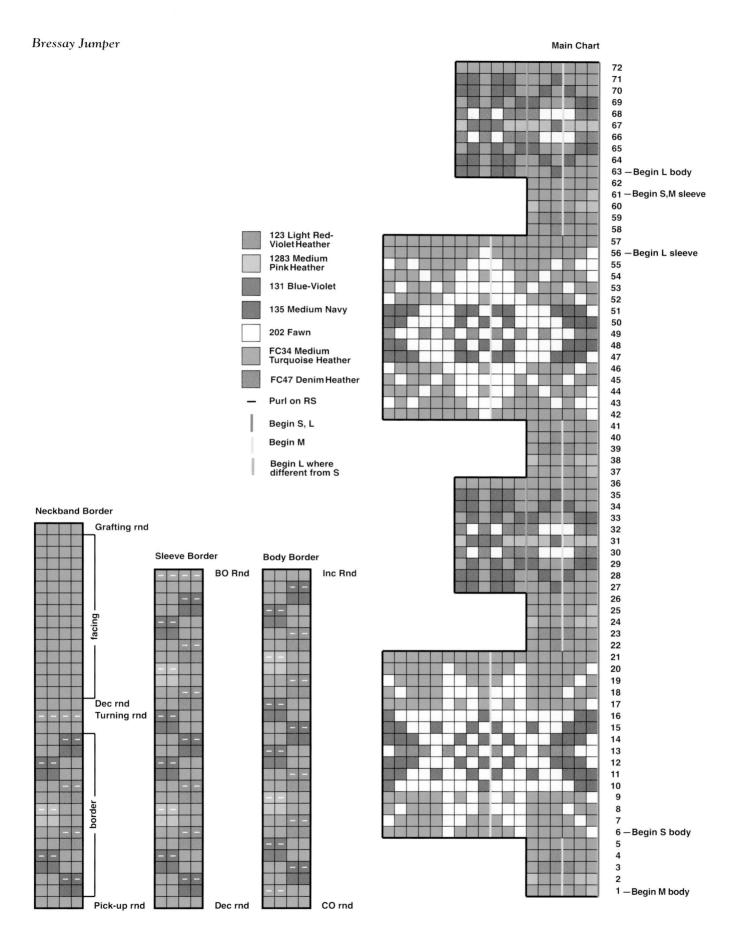

Main Chart

123 Light Red-Violet Heather

1283 Medium Pink Heather

131 Blue-Violet

135 Medium Navy

202 Fawn

FC34 Medium Turquoise Heather

FC47 Denim Heather

Purl on RS

Begin S, L

Begin M

Begin L where different from S

Neckband Border

Grafting rnd

facing

Dec rnd
Turning rnd

border

Pick-up rnd

Sleeve Border

BO Rnd

Dec rnd

Body Border

Inc Rnd

CO rnd

72
71
70
69
68
67
66
65
64
63 — Begin L body
62
61 — Begin S,M sleeve
60
59
58
57
56 — Begin L sleeve
55
54
53
52
51
50
49
48
47
46
45
44
43
42
41
40
39
38
37
36
35
34
33
32
31
30
29
28
27
26
25
24
23
22
21
20
19
18
17
16
15
14
13
12
11
10
9
8
7
6 — Begin S body
5
4
3
2
1 — Begin M body

Burrastow Jumper

BURRASTOW JUMPER

The subject of this sweater is purple. Blue-violets and red-violets, and blues and reds combine in the eye to make purple, like pointillist painting. The colors are muted, with little contrast. The color in the center of the large patterns is actually a dull red, but it takes on a smoldering orange glow because it is next to turquoise, which forces it towards turquoise's complement, red-orange, and because of the otherwise cool context of the rest of the sweater. The patterns are united by repeating motifs of squares, and squares stacked in crosses, and squares interspersed with or superimposed by diamonds.

Finished Size: Small (Medium, Large). Shown in size Medium.

Bust/chest circumference: 40½ (45, 49½)" (103 (114.5, 125.5) cm).

Body length: 23¾ (25¼, 26½)" (60 (65.4, 67.5) cm).

Sleeve length: 20 (20¾, 21½)" (51 (52.5, 54.5) cm).

Materials

Yarn: Jamieson & Smith 2-ply jumper weight Shetland yarn (100% wool; 150 yd/oz (137 m/28 g)): #21 dark navy, #133 medium red-violet heather, #FC48 medium denim heather, 3 (4, 4) oz (85 (113, 113) g) each; #135 medium navy, 3 (3, 4) oz (85 (85, 113) g) each; #123 light red-violet heather, #FC37 blue-violet heather, #19 dull red-violet heather, #142 medium turquoise, #72 light red heather, 1 (1, 2) oz (28 (28, 57) g); #131 blue-violet, #132 very bright turquoise, 1 oz (28 g) each.

Needles: Body and Sleeves—Size 3 (3 mm): 16"/40 cm and 29"/80 cm circular and double-pointed (dpn); Ribbings—Size 1 (2.25 mm): 16"/40 cm and 29"/80 cm circular and dpn. Adjust needle sizes if necessary to obtain the correct gauge.

Notions: Five markers; five stitch holders; tapestry needle.

Gauge: 32 sts and 32 rnds = 4" (10 cm) with larger needle over St st in color pattern.

Note: Each size begins at a different round and at times at a different stitch in the pattern repeat. For sizes Small and Large, the small 5-round pattern repeat needs a slight adjustment in stitch count below the armhole on rounds 13, 18, 37, 42, 55, 60, 79, and 84 to come out even at the end of the round.

Body: With blue-violet and longer ribbing needle, CO 288 (312, 348) sts. Place marker at beg of rnd. Join, being careful not to twist sts. **Ribbing:** *k2 medium navy, p2 blue-violet; rep from *. Work to end of Body Ribbing chart. Change to longer body needle and dark navy (dark navy, medium red-violet heather). **Increase rnd:** For size S: *k8, M1; rep from * 36 times; for size M: *k6, M1, k7, M1; rep from * 24 times; for size L: k3, *k7, M1; rep from * 48 times, end k9—324 (360, 396) sts. After this rnd, adjust the number of sts on designated rnds of the chart, working the incs or decs for size S after the 5th, 158th, 167th, and 320th st; for size L after the 7th, 190th, 207th, and 388th st. (To avoid counting sts every inc and dec rnd, place markers after these sts.) Beg on rnd 1 (1, 19) of Main Chart, work through rnd 84, and then rnds 1 through 6 (18, 37) (do not work st adjustment for size L on the last rnd 37), for a total of 90 (102, 103) rnds (and a total of 324 (360, 396) sts). Break yarns. Discontinue stitch adjustments marked on chart from here on.

Armholes: Rnd 7 (19, 38) of chart: Place 6 (8, 10) sts on holder for half of left underarm, CO 6 extra sts, the first 2 with slip knots and the following 4 with backward loops alternating colors [(pattern, background) 3 times], work 151 (165, 179) front sts in color pattern, place 11 (15, 19) sts on holder for right underarm, CO 12 extra sts with back-

ward loops [(background, pattern) 3 times, (pattern, background) 3 times], work 151 (165, 179) back sts in color pattern, place 5 (7, 9) sts on holder for rem of left underarm, and CO 6 extra sts with backward loops [(background, pattern) 3 times]—302 (330, 358) body sts (and 24 extra sts). Rejoin. Except when only one color is used in the rnd, always work the extra sts next to the body of the sweater in the background color, the 2 center extra sts in the pattern color, and the rem extra sts in the established striped pattern. Work through rnd 59 (78, 17), for a total of 143 (162, 167) rnds.

Shape Front Neck: Rnd 60 (79, 18) of chart: Work 55 (60, 65) left front shoulder sts in color pattern, place 41 (45, 49) sts on holder for front neck, CO 12 extra sts as for right underarm, work to end of rnd in color pattern. Work extra sts as before. Work decs at front neck edge as follows: work to 2 sts before extra sts, ssk (the dec slants towards the extra sts), work extra sts, k2tog (the dec slants towards the extra sts). Dec 1 st each side of neck edge in this manner every rnd 5 times total—50 (55, 60) sts rem on each shoulder. Work through rnd 78 (84, 36), and then for size M only, work rnds 1 through 12, for a total of 162 (180, 186) rnds.

Shoulder: Work back and forth on front sts only (including 6 extra sts at each side and 12 extra sts at front neck) for rows 79 to 82 (13 to 16, 13 to 16) on chart. With medium denim heather and beg at center of armhole extra sts, *graft 6 extra sts and 50 (55, 60) sts of right front shoulder to 6 extra sts and 50 (55, 60) sts of right back shoulder. Begin again at other side and rep from *. BO 12 front neck extra sts singly. Place rem 51 (55, 59) sts on holder for back neck.

Sleeves: Cut armhole extra sts up the center. With dark navy (medium denim heather, medium denim heather), RS facing, shorter sleeve needle, and beg at center of underarm, k6 (8, 10) underarm sts from holder, pick up and knit 148 (160, 170) sts around armhole edge, and k5 (7, 9) rem underarm sts from holder—159 (175, 189) sts. Place marker. Join. Be careful to center patterns at top of sleeve as they are at the center front of body. *Note:* Do not work stitch adjustments marked on chart. Beg on rnd 53 (58, 82), follow Main Chart in reverse direction, dec 1 st each side of underarm marker every 2nd rnd 0 (0, 4) times, every 3rd rnd 19 (38, 48) times, and then every 4th rnd 20 (7, 0) times, working 137 (142, 148) rnds total, ending on rnd 1 (1, 19), and changing to sleeve dpn when necessary. End of sleeve pattern matches beg of body pattern—81 (85, 89) sts rem. **Decrease rnd:** With dark navy (dark navy, medium red-violet heather) and ribbing dpn, dec 17 (21, 21) sts evenly spaced—64 (64, 68) sts rem. **Cuff:** Rnd 1: *k2 medium navy, k2 blue-violet; rep from *. Rnd 2: *k2 medium navy, p2 blue-violet; rep from *. Work to end of Sleeve Ribbing chart. With blue-violet, BO in knit.

Neckband: Cut neck extra sts up the center. With RS facing, shorter ribbing needle, and beg at right side of back neck, *k2 very bright turquoise, k2 light red heather; rep from * across 51 (55, 59) sts from back neck holder, and continuing to alternate colors, pick up and knit 22 sts along left back and front neck edges, knit 41 (45, 49) sts from front neck holder, and pick up and knit 22 sts along right front and back neck edges—136 (144, 152) sts. Place marker. Join. **Ribbing:** Following Neckband Ribbing chart rib 8 rnds. **Turning rnd:** *p2 medium navy, p2 blue-violet; rep from *. **Decrease rnd:** (Dec about 10% of the sts.) With blue-violet, *k8, k2tog; rep from *—123 (130, 137) sts rem. **Facing:** K8 rnds. Break yarn, leaving a long end for grafting.

Finishing: Trim the 6 extra sts at neck and armhole edges to 3 or 4 and hem them with a tapestry needle threaded with yarn, turning under 1 st as you go. Using the long end of yarn from the neckband and a tapestry needle, graft neckband sts on needle to purl bumps and innermost neck extra sts, spacing sts to allow for 10% fewer sts on inner band. Wash in wool-safe detergent. Remove excess water with the spin cycle of a washing machine. Place on a jumper board. Using regular sewing thread, a tapestry needle, and long sts, baste the neck edge to shape it and draw it in. When dry, remove the sweater from the board and pull out basting. Reshape the body and sleeve ribbings by wetting and patting them into place, or by steaming them.

Notes on colors: There are five blues, three red-violets, two blue-violets, and one red in this sweater. In the wide bands—rounds 19 to 35 and 61 to 77—the blues make a sequence from dark to light, going from a dark navy, #21, used in the outer round only; to a medium navy, #135, for the next three rounds; to a heathered medium denim blue, #FC48, on the next two rounds; to a fairly bright medium turquoise, #142, on the next two rounds; and finally to a *very* bright turquoise, #132, in the center round. In the background are two dull red-violet heathers. The darker and slightly redder of the two, #133, medium red-violet heather, is used in the outermost rounds, and the slightly lighter dull red-violet, #19, follows it. So the three-round checkers in rounds 20 to 34 form a sequence of values from the deeper dull red-violet heather, to the lighter dull red-violet heather, to the still lighter red heather in the center three rounds.

In the pattern in rounds 61 to 77, the sequence of colors in both pattern and background is the same, but the background colors occupy a different number of rounds. There are five center rounds of light red heather, with two adjacent rounds of dull red-violet heather.

A brighter, lighter red-violet heather than either of the two aforementioned, #123, is used in the smallest patterns, in rounds 14 to 16, 38 to 40, and so on. The background for these small patterns is the third, middle blue of the sequence of five, #FC48. The lightest, brightest red-violet heather, #123, also appears in the patterns with a dark navy background spanning rounds 84 and 1 to 12, and 42 to 54, in the center three rounds, 5 to 7 and 47 to 49. In these bands, the background shifts from dark navy, used in rounds 84 and 1 to 3 and 9 to 12 (and corresponding repeating rounds) to medium navy in rounds 4 , 5, 7 and 8 (and corresponding repeating rounds); the very bright turquoise is in the center round, rounds 6 and 48.

Of the two similar blue-violets, the darker, unheathered one, #131, is used only in the ribbing. The lighter blue-violet heather, #FC37, heathered with red, is used for the pattern in rounds 1 to 4 and 8 to 11 (and corresponding repeating rounds).

Burrastow Jumper

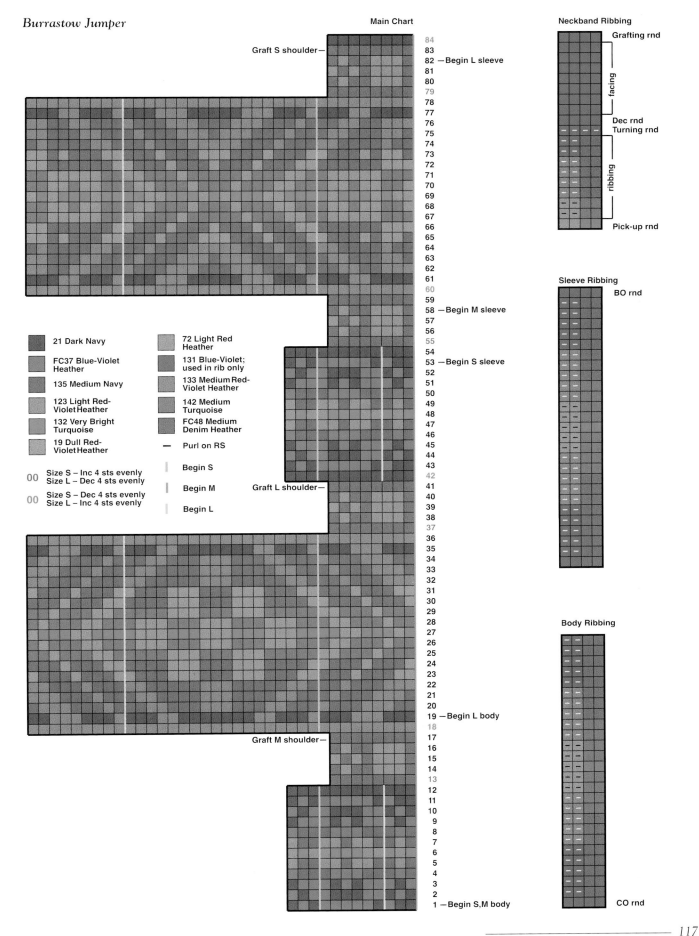

Main Chart

Graft S shoulder—

84
83
82 —Begin L sleeve
81
80
79
78
77
76
75
74
73
72
71
70
69
68
67
66
65
64
63
62
61
60
59
58 —Begin M sleeve
57
56
55
54
53 —Begin S sleeve
52
51
50
49
48
47
46
45
44
43
42
41
40
39
38
37
36
35
34
33
32
31
30
29
28
27
26
25
24
23
22
21
20
19 —Begin L body
18
17
16
15
14
13
12
11
10
9
8
7
6
5
4
3
2
1 —Begin S,M body

Graft L shoulder—

Graft M shoulder—

Neckband Ribbing

Grafting rnd
facing
Dec rnd
Turning rnd
ribbing
Pick-up rnd

Sleeve Ribbing

BO rnd

Body Ribbing

CO rnd

21 Dark Navy

FC37 Blue-Violet Heather

135 Medium Navy

123 Light Red-Violet Heather

132 Very Bright Turquoise

19 Dull Red-Violet Heather

72 Light Red Heather

131 Blue-Violet; used in rib only

133 Medium Red-Violet Heather

142 Medium Turquoise

FC48 Medium Denim Heather

— Purl on RS

| Begin S

| Begin M

| Begin L

00 Size S – Inc 4 sts evenly
Size L – Dec 4 sts evenly

00 Size S – Dec 4 sts evenly
Size L – Inc 4 sts evenly

Cunningsburgh Gloves

CUNNINGSBURGH GLOVES

I started working with these sweet colors after teaching a class of students who favored purples and pinks. I tried using those colors in a yoked sweater, but found them overpowering. I like them much better in small doses. What is interesting about these gloves is the way the triangular border pattern takes a background color from the star—light turquoise heather—and uses it as a pattern color. This kind of shift, where a color moves from background to pattern, enriches the color effect, countering the eye's assumptions, making a color function in more than one way. By giving a color a different context, it takes on a different identity, as if there were two turquoises in the glove. Please refer to page 140 for notes on gloves.

Finished Size: Small.

Palm circumference: 7½" (19 cm).

Note: To make a larger glove, adjust needle size to adjust the gauge. A gauge of 7½ or 7 sts to the inch (2.5 cm) will give a palm circumference of 8" (20 cm) or 8½" (21.5 cm), respectively.

Materials

Yarn: Jamieson & Smith 2-ply jumper weight Shetland yarn (100% wool; 150 yd/oz (137 m/28 g)): #131 blue-violet, 1 oz (28 g); #33 medium blue-gray heather, #1283 medium pink heather, #FC6 light pink heather, #FC22 deep pink heather, #FC34 medium turquoise heather, #FC37 blue-violet heather, #FC43 pale yellow-white heather, 1 oz (28 g) each, or less. A few yards of waste yarn in a contrasting color (CC).

Needles: Size 3 (3 mm) double-pointed (dpn). Adjust needle size if necessary to obtain the correct gauge.

Notions: Marker; two stitch holders; tapestry needle.

Gauge: 8 sts and 8 rnds = 1" (2.5 cm) over St st in color pattern.

Cuff: With blue-violet and dpn, CO 45 sts. Place marker at beg of rnd. Join, being careful not to twist sts. **Ribbing:** *k2, p1; rep from * for 3" (7.5 cm).

Increase rnd: Inc 1 st in every purl st—60 sts. K1 rnd even.

Hand: Beg on rnd 1 of Main Chart, work through rnd 17.

Thumb opening: Rnd 18—center rnd of star: *Left hand:* Work 30 palm sts, sl last 9 sts knit from right needle to left needle, with CC waste yarn, knit these 9 sts again, knit to end of rnd in color pattern. *Right hand:* Work 30 back of hand sts and first 10 palm sts (40 sts total), sl last 9 sts knit from right needle to left needle, with CC waste yarn, knit these 9 sts again, knit to end of rnd in color pattern. Work through rnd 35. With blue-violet, knit 2 rnds. Place palm sts and back of hand sts on holders.

Fingers: *Little finger:* On the side opposite the thumb opening, sl 7 sts from the palm and 8 sts from the back of hand onto dpn, CO 1 st between the fingers—16 sts. Join. Work in St st for 2¼" (5.5 cm) or desired length. *Decrease for tip:* k2tog at four points every rnd 3 times. When 4 or 5 sts rem, k2tog around. Break yarn, thread end through a tapestry needle, draw through rem sts to the inside, and fasten off. *Ring finger:* Sl 8 sts from the palm and 7 sts from the back of hand onto dpn, pick up 2 sts from the inner corner of the little finger—17 sts. Join. Work in St st for 2½" (6.5 cm) or desired length. Dec for tip as for little finger. *Middle finger:* Sl 7 sts from the palm and 8 sts from the back of hand onto dpn, pick up 2 sts from the inner corner of the ring finger—17 sts. Join. Work in St st for 2¾" (7 cm) or desired length. Dec for tip as for little finger. *Index finger:* Sl 8 sts from the palm and 7 sts from the back of hand onto dpn, pick up 1 st from the corner of the middle finger—16 sts. Join. Work for 2½" (6.5 cm) or desired length. Dec for tip as for little finger.

Thumb: Pick up 9 sts from above and 9 sts from below the waste yarn—18 sts. Remove the waste yarn. With medium turquoise heather, work in St st for 2½" (6.5 cm) or desired length. Dec for tip as for little finger.

Finishing: Wash in wool-safe detergent, remove excess water with the spin cycle of a washing machine, and place on a glove board. Or steam carefully.

Notes on colors: The colors in the star make a sequence from dark to light and cool to warm, traveling from a cool, deep pink heather, used on rounds 6 to 9 and 27 to 30; to medium pink heather, used on rounds 10 to 12 and 24 to 26; to a light pink heather, used on rounds 13 to 16 and 20 to 23; and finally to a heathered blend of pale yellow and white in the center three rounds. The background travels from dark to light, too, and from cool to warm, too, from blue-violet to a lighter heathered blue violet—used only on rounds 11 and 25—to a heathered blue-gray on rounds 12, 13, 23 and 24, to medium turquoise heather, which occupies the remaining nine center rounds.

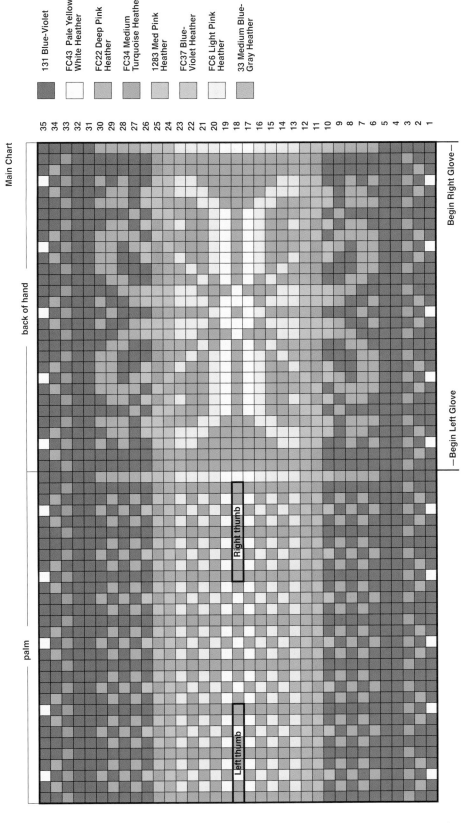

Fridarey Sleeveless Cardigan

FRIDAREY SLEEVELESS CARDIGAN

The ribbing on this sleeveless cardigan forms an opposed sequence, with turquoises shading from dark to light adjacent to red-violets shading from light to dark. I enjoy creating this shimmering effect when I can—the ribbing in the Isleburgh cardigan (page 134) does the same thing. It reminds me of the fascinating refracted quality of a hologram, or glitter, or tinsel, or bubbles—more colors in more places than are logically possible, continuity vying with discontinuity. In the body of the sweater, the patterns are all light on dark. The large patterns shade in parallel sequences, light at the outside and dark at the center, except for a zingy center round in a lighter turquoise. The wide bands and the tiniest bands are pink and red-violet patterns on turquoise backgrounds; they are adjacent to small bands where the red-violet shifts to the background. Reversing pattern and background counters the eye's expectations. The more ways you can use a color, the more interesting the garment.

Finished Size: Small (Medium, Large). Shown in size Small.

Bust/chest circumference, buttoned: 40½ (44¼, 48)" (103 (112.5, 122) cm).

Body length: 21 (23¼, 24¾)" (53.5 (59, 63) cm).

Materials

Yarn: Jamieson & Smith 2-ply jumper weight Shetland yarn (100% wool; 150 yd/oz (137 m/28 g)): #123 light red-violet heather, #142 medium turquoise, #FC41 dark turquoise, 3 (4, 4) oz (85 (113, 113) g) each; #72 light red heather, #75 pale turquoise, #131 blue-violet, #133 medium red-violet heather, #1283 medium pink heather, #FC34 medium turquoise heather, #FC49 light denim heather, 1 oz (28 g) each.

Needles: Body—Size 3 (3 mm): 29"/80 cm circular; Ribbings—Size 1 (2.25 mm): 16"/40 cm and 29"/80 cm circular. Adjust needle sizes if necessary to obtain the correct gauge.

Crochet hook: Size C (2.5 mm).

Notions: Marker; three stitch holders; tapestry needle; six 5/8" (1.5 cm) buttons.

Gauge: 32 sts and 32 rows = 4" (10 cm) with larger needle over St st in color pattern.

Note: Each size begins at a different round and at times at a different stitch in the pattern repeat.

Body: With dark turquoise and longer ribbing needle, CO 302 (330, 362) sts—290 (318, 350) body sts (and 12 extra sts to be cut later for the center front opening). Place marker at beg of rnd (center front). Join, being careful not to twist sts. **Ribbing:** Work 6 extra sts alternating colors [k1 dark turquoise, k1 light red-violet heather] 3 times, *k2 light red-violet heather, p2 dark turquoise; rep from * to last 8 sts, end k2 light red-violet heather and work rem 6 extra sts [k1 light red-violet heather, k1 dark turquoise] 3 times. Work to end of Body Ribbing chart, always working the extra sts next to the body of the sweater in the knit color, the 2 center extra sts in the purl color, and the rem extra sts in the established striped pattern. Change to longer body needle and blue-violet (medium turquoise, dark turquoise). **Increase rnd:** Work 6 extra sts, k2 (4, 6), M1, *k11 (12, 13), M1; rep from * 26 times total, end k2 (4, 6), then work rem 6 extra sts—317 (347, 377) body sts (and 12 extra sts). Except when only one color is used in the rnd, always work the extra sts next to the body of the sweater in the background color, the 2 center extra sts in the pattern color, and the rem extra sts in the established striped pattern. Beg on rnd 1 (20, 8) of

Main Chart, work through rnd 72, then rnds 1 through 6 (35, 35), for a total of 78 (88, 100) rnds.

Shape Armholes and V-Neck: Rnd 7 (36, 36) of chart: Work 6 extra sts, k2tog (the dec slants towards the extra sts), work 58 (65, 71) right front sts in color pattern, ssk (the dec slants towards the extra sts), place 31 (35, 39) sts on holder for right underarm, CO 12 extra sts with backward loops, k2tog, work 127 (135, 145) back sts in color pattern, ssk, place 31 (35, 39) sts on holder for left underarm, CO 12 extra sts as for right underarm, k2tog, work 58 (65, 71) left front sts in color pattern, ssk, then work rem 6 extra sts—249 (271, 293) body sts (and 36 extra sts). Work extra sts as for the center front. Being careful to keep the pattern motifs in established vertical alignment, dec 1 st at each armhole edge in this manner every rnd 10 (11, 12) times total and *at the same time*, dec 1 st at each side of V-neck extra sts every other rnd 0 (5, 9) times, and then every 3rd rnd 25 (22, 22) times total, ending on rnd 5 (41, 41) of the chart, for a total of 149 (166, 178) rnds—27 (29, 32) sts rem on each shoulder. Work rnd 6 (42, 42) of chart across front sts only (slip left front sts and 6 left armhole extra sts back to the left end of the circular needle and beg knitting there). Work rows 7–10 (43–46, 43–46) of the chart back and forth on the front sts only.

Shoulder Seam: With RS facing, dark turquoise, and beg at center of right armhole extra sts, *graft 6 extra sts and 27 (29, 32) front shoulder sts to corresponding 6 extra sts and 27 (29, 32) back shoulder sts. Begin again at the other side and rep from *. BO front neck extra sts singly. Place rem 57 (57, 61) sts on holder for back neck.

Front Band: Cut center front extra sts up the center. With RS facing, longer ribbing needle, and beg at right front bottom edge alternating k2 medium red-violet heather, k2 pale turquoise, pick up and knit about 1 st for every rnd, ending k2 medium red-violet heather—about 177 (196, 207) sts along right front edge, 57 (59, 61) sts from back neck holder, and 176 (195, 206) sts along left front edge—about 410 (450, 474) sts total. (Somewhat fewer is acceptable, as long as the number of sts is a multiple of 4 plus 2, but more is not.) Work Front Band Ribbing chart back and forth for 3 rows, keeping floats to the wrong side. **Buttonhole row:** RS facing, rib 3 (4, 3) sts, *work 3-stitch buttonhole (see page 70), rib 16 (18, 20) sts; rep from * 4 more times, work 3-stitch buttonhole—6 buttonholes. Work to end of chart. With dark turquoise, BO in knit. With dark turquoise, crochet about 10 slip sts on the top and bottom edges of the front bands to make them appear continuous with the adjacent cast-on and bind-off edges of the body and neck.

Armhole Ribbing: Cut armhole extra sts up the center. With RS facing, shorter ribbing needle, and beg at center of underarm, *k2 medium red-violet heather, k2 pale turquoise; rep from * across 16 (18, 20) underarm sts on holder, and continuing to alternate colors, pick up and knit about 7 sts for every 8 rows—about 64 (70, 72) sts along one armhole edge, 1 st at shoulder seam, and 64 (70, 72) sts along other armhole edge, and knit rem 15 (17, 19) underarm sts from holder—160 (176, 184) sts. Place marker. Join. Work to end of Armhole Ribbing chart. With dark turquoise, BO in knit.

Finishing: Trim the 6 extra sts at neck and armhole edges to 3 or 4 and hem them with a tapestry needle threaded with yarn, turning under 1 st as you go. Overlap the front edges. Using regular sewing thread, a tapestry needle, and long sts, baste the overlapped front edges together so that they will remain flat during blocking. Wash in wool-safe detergent. Remove excess water with the spin cycle of a washing machine. Place on a jumper board. Baste the V of the neck to draw it in and shape it. When dry, remove the sweater from the board and pull out basting. Reshape the body and armband ribbings by wetting and patting them into place, or by steaming them. Sew on buttons.

Fridarey Sleeveless Cardigan

Main Chart

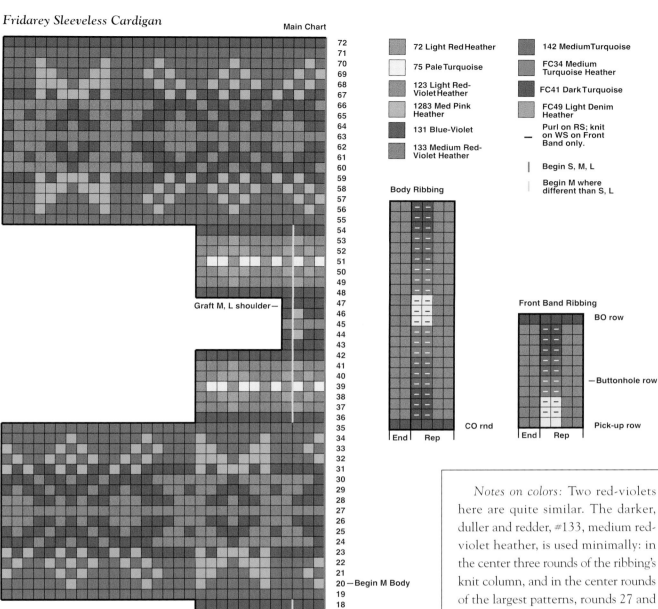

72 Light Red Heather

75 Pale Turquoise

123 Light Red-Violet Heather

1283 Med Pink Heather

131 Blue-Violet

133 Medium Red-Violet Heather

142 Medium Turquoise

FC34 Medium Turquoise Heather

FC41 Dark Turquoise

FC49 Light Denim Heather

— Purl on RS; knit on WS on Front Band only.

| Begin S, M, L

| Begin M where different than S, L

Body Ribbing

BO row

—Buttonhole row

Pick-up row

Front Band Ribbing

CO rnd

| End | Rep

| End | Rep

Armhole Ribbing

BO rnd

Pick-up rnd

Graft M, L shoulder—

Graft S shoulder—

72
71
70
69
68
67
66
65
64
63
62
61
60
59
58
57
56
55
54
53
52
51
50
49
48
47
46
45
44
43
42
41
40
39
38
37
36
35
34
33
32
31
30
29
28
27
26
25
24
23
22
21
20 —Begin M Body
19
18
17
16
15
14
13
12
11
10
9
8 —Begin L Body
7
6
5
4
3
2
1 —Begin S Body

Notes on colors: Two red-violets here are quite similar. The darker, duller and redder, #133, medium red-violet heather, is used minimally: in the center three rounds of the ribbing's knit column, and in the center rounds of the largest patterns, rounds 27 and 63. A lighter, brighter red-violet, #123, is used for the rest of the ribbing's knit stitches; for the pattern in rounds 24, 25, 26, and 28, 29, 30 (and corresponding repeating rounds); for the small diamond pattern's center round, rounds 9 and 45; and for the background in rounds 1, 2, 4 and 5 (and corresponding rounds 13, 14, 16, 17, and so on). The light red heather is also used minimally, only in rounds 3, 15, 39, 51, and so on. The pale turquoise that accompanies the light red heather in those rounds also appears in the ribbing, in the center three rounds of the purl column.

Hillhead Slipover

HILLHEAD SLIPOVER

This pattern is fascinating because of the shifting complexity of positive, negative, and checkered diamonds. The subdued colors—black, dark blues, blue-grays and grays—are given depth and resonance by the small intervals between them. This low-key palette is jolted by a light, bright turquoise. In the ribbing, turquoise is next to the lightest color, gray; in the body of the slipover, the same turquoise is next to black. A light among lights as well as a light among darks, is doubly luminous.

Finished Size: Small (Medium, Large). Shown in size Small.

Bust/chest circumference: 40 (44, 48)" (101.5 (112, 122) cm).

Body length: 24 (25, 26)" (61 (63.5, 66) cm).

Materials

Yarn: Jamieson & Smith 2-ply jumper weight Shetland yarn (100% wool; 150 yd/oz (137 m/28 g): #81 black, 3 (3, 4) oz (85 (85, 113) g); #33 medium blue-gray heather, #FC61 light blue-gray heather, 2 oz (57 g); #203 light gray, 2 oz (57 g); #36 very dark navy, #21 dark navy, #135 medium navy, 1 oz (28 g) each; #1a white, #48 light bright turquoise, #FC47 denim heather, 1 oz (28 g) each.

Needles: Body—Size 3 (3 mm): 29"/80 cm circular; Ribbings—Size 1 (2.25 mm): 16"/40 cm and 29"/80 cm circular. Adjust needle sizes if necessary to obtain the correct gauge.

Notions: Marker; five stitch holders; tapestry needle.

Gauge: 32 sts and 32 rnds = 4" (10 cm) with larger needle over St st in color pattern.

Note: Each size begins at a different round and at a different stitch in the pattern repeat.

Body: With black and longer ribbing needle, CO 300 (328, 360) sts. Place marker at beg of rnd. Join, being careful not to twist sts. **Ribbing:** *k2 medium blue-gray heather, p2 black; rep from *. Work to end of Body Ribbing chart, inc 0 (2, 0) sts on last rnd—300 (330, 360) sts. Change to longer body needle. **Increase rnd:** Beg on rnd 1 (1, 22) of Main Chart, *M1, k15; rep from * 20 (22, 24) times total—320 (352, 384) sts. Work through rnd 28, then rnds 1 through 28 two (two, three) more times, and then rnds 1 through 8, for a total of 92 (92, 99) rnds. Break yarns.

Shape Armholes and V-Neck: Rnd 9 of chart: Place 13 (16, 19) sts on holder for half of left underarm, CO 6 extra sts, the first 2 with slip knots and the following 4 with backward loops alternating colors [(pattern, background) 3 times], k2tog (the dec slants towards the extra sts), work 63 (68, 73) left front sts in color pattern, ssk (the dec slants towards the extra sts), place next st on holder for center front, CO 12 extra sts with backward loops [(background, pattern) 3 times, (pattern, background) 3 times], k2tog, work 63 (68, 73) right front sts in color pattern, ssk, place 25 (31, 37) sts on holder for right underarm, CO 12 extra sts as for center front, k2tog, work 131 (141, 151) back sts in color pattern, ssk, place 12 (15, 18) sts on holder for rem of left underarm, and CO 6 extra sts with backward loops [(background, pattern) 3 times]—263 (283, 303) body sts (1 center st on holder and 36 extra sts). Rejoin. Always work the extra sts next to the body of the sweater in the background color, the 2 center extra sts in the pattern color, and the rem extra sts in the established striped pattern. Being careful to keep the pattern motifs in established vertical alignment, dec 1 st at each armhole edge in this manner every other rnd 11 (13, 14) more times and *at the same time*, dec 1 st at each side of V-neck every 3rd rnd 24 (25, 27) more times, ending on rnd 28 (7, 7)

of the chart—30 (32, 34) sts rem on each shoulder. Work rnd 1 (8, 8) of chart across front sts only—168 (175, 182) rnds total.

Shoulder Seam: Turn work inside out. With RS facing, black (denim heather, denim heather), and beg at center of right armhole extra sts, *BO 6 extra sts and 30 (32, 34) sts of front shoulder together with 6 extra sts and 30 (32, 34) sts of back shoulder. Begin again at the other side and rep from *. BO 12 front neck extra sts singly. Place rem 51 (53, 57) sts on holder for back neck.

Neckband: Cut neck extra sts up the center. With RS facing, shorter ribbing needle, and beg at right side of back neck, *k2 light gray, k2 light bright turquoise; rep from * across 51 (53, 57) sts from back neck holder, and continuing to alternate colors, pick up and knit about 1 st for every row—about 74 (83, 83) sts along left front neck edge, knit the center front st from holder with light gray, and resuming the color alternation, mirroring the colors around the center front st, pick up and knit 75 (84, 84) sts along right front neck edge—201 (221, 225) sts. Place marker. Join. Work to end of Neckband and Armhole Ribbing chart, dec at center front of V-neck every rnd 9 times as follows: slip 2 sts tog (the st just before the center front st and the center front st) as to knit, k1 (the st just after the center front), pass the 2 slipped sts over. With black, BO in knit.

Armhole Ribbing: Cut armhole extra sts up the center. With RS facing, shorter ribbing needle, and beg at center of underarm, *k2 light gray, k2 light bright turquoise; rep from * across 13 (16, 19) underarm sts on holder, and continuing to alternate colors, pick up and knit about 9 sts for every 10 rows—about 65 (70, 71) sts along one armhole edge, 1 st at shoulder seam, and 65 (70, 71) sts along other armhole edge, and knit rem

12 (15, 18) underarm sts from holder—156 (172, 180) sts. Place marker. Join. Work to end of Neckband and Armhole Ribbing chart. With black, BO in knit.

Finishing: Trim the 6 extra sts at neck and armhole edges to 3 or 4 and hem them with a tapestry needle threaded with yarn, turning under 1 st as you go. Wash in wool-safe detergent. Remove excess water with the spin cycle of a washing machine. Place on a jumper board. Using regular sewing thread, a tapestry needle, and long sts, baste the neck edge to shape it and draw it in. When dry, remove the sweater from the board and pull out basting. Reshape the body and armband ribbings by wetting and patting them into place, or by steaming them.

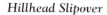

Hillhead Slipover

Main Chart

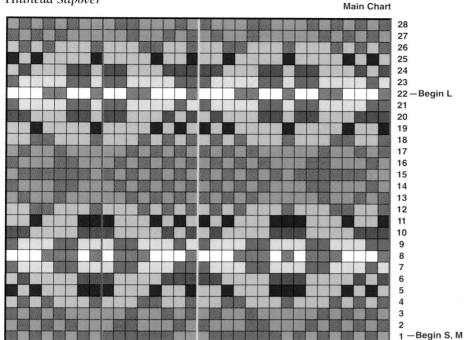

28
27
26
25
24
23
22 — Begin L
21
20
19
18
17
16
15
14
13
12
11
10
9
8
7
6
5
4
3
2
1 — Begin S, M

Body Ribbing

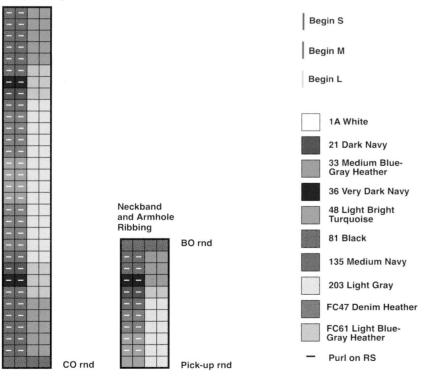

CO rnd

Neckband and Armhole Ribbing

BO rnd

Pick-up rnd

| Begin S

| Begin M

| Begin L

☐ 1A White

■ 21 Dark Navy

▨ 33 Medium Blue-Gray Heather

■ 36 Very Dark Navy

▨ 48 Light Bright Turquoise

▨ 81 Black

▨ 135 Medium Navy

☐ 203 Light Gray

▨ FC47 Denim Heather

☐ FC61 Light Blue-Gray Heather

— Purl on RS

Notes on colors: The colors are arranged in straightforward light-to-dark sequences. The pattern sequence begins with four rounds of black, followed by one round each of very dark navy, dark navy, medium navy and, in the center round, denim blue heather. The background sequence begins with one round of light bright turquoise, followed by two rounds of medium blue-gray heather, three rounds of light blue-gray heather, one round of light gray and one round—the center round—of white.

Hillswick Lumber

HILLSWICK LUMBER

These shady greens are enlivened by three purples: a blue-violet in the center of the rosette pattern, a light red-violet in the center of the diamond pattern, and a deep purple at the edges of the small patterns. The wide patterns are light on a dark background, the narrow patterns dark on a light background. Reversing dark and light and pattern and background creates a complex visual effect akin to the fluctuating nature of reality, to what we see when looking at outdoor space, texture, and light, or any complex environment. For example, a tree in sunlight looks light, but shadows made by the lit leaves on other leaves are dark, and reflected light in the shadows is light. There are darks within the lights and lights within the darks. The tree, no matter how strongly lit, will appear dark against the sky. What looks light in one context may look dark in another. I savor exploring such contradictory, shifting phenomena.

Finished Size: Small (Medium, Large, Extra Large). Shown in size Medium.

Bust/chest circumference, buttoned: 41 (45, 49, 53)" (104 (114.5, 124.5, 134.5) cm).

Body length: 24 (25¾, 26¾, 28¾)" (61 (65.5, 68, 73) cm).

Sleeve Length: 17¼ (18¼, 20, 21)" (44 (46.5, 51, 53.5) cm).

Materials

Yarn: Jamieson & Smith 2-ply jumper weight Shetland yarn (100% wool; 150 yd/oz (137 m/28 g)): #82 dark green, #FC34 medium turquoise heather, 5 (5, 6, 6) oz (142 (142, 170, 170) g) each; #65 emerald green, 4 oz (113 g); #118 olive green, 3 oz (85 g); #20 deep purple, #21 dark navy, #142 medium turquoise, 2 oz (57 g) each; #123 light red-violet heather, #131 blue-violet, #FC24 dull yellow-green, 1 oz (28 g) each.

Needles: Body and Sleeves—Size 3 (3 mm): 16"/40 cm and 29"/80 cm circular and double-pointed (dpn); Ribbings—Size 1 (2.25 mm): 16"/40 cm and 29"/80 cm circular and dpn. Adjust needle sizes if necessary to obtain the correct gauge.

Crochet hook: Size C (2.5 mm).

Notions: Marker; four stitch holders; tapestry needle; nine 5/8" (1.5 cm) buttons.

Gauge: 32 sts and 32 rows = 4" (10 cm) with larger needle over St st in color pattern.

Note: Each size begins at a different round and at times at a different stitch in the pattern repeat.

Body: With emerald green and longer ribbing needle, CO 306 (334, 362, 390) sts—294 (322, 350, 378) body sts (and 12 extra sts to be cut later for the center front opening). Place marker at beg of rnd (center front). Join, being careful not to twist sts. **Ribbing:** Work 6 extra sts alternating colors [k1 emerald, k1 dark] green 3 times, *k2 dark green, p2 emerald green; rep from * to last 8 sts, end k2 dark green and work rem 6 extra sts [k1 dark, k1 emerald] green 3 times. Work to end of Body Ribbing chart, always working the extra sts next to the body of the sweater in the knit color, the 2 center extra sts in the purl color, and the rem extra sts in the established striped pattern. Change to longer body needle and emerald (dark, emerald, dark) green. **Increase rnd:** Work 6 extra sts, k4 (11, 5, 18), M1, *k11 (10, 10, 9), M1; rep from * 26 (30, 34, 38) times total, end k4 (11, 5, 18), then work rem 6 extra sts—321 (353, 385, 417) body sts (and 12 extra sts). Except when only one color is used in the rnd, always work the extra sts next to the body of the sweater in the background color, the 2 center extra sts in the pattern color, and the rem extra sts in the established striped pattern. Beg on rnd 16 (1, 38, 23) of Main Chart, work

through rnd 44, then rnds 1 through 44 once (once, twice, twice) more, and then rnds 1 through 22 (15, 15, 10), for a total of 95 (103, 110, 120) rnds.

Armholes: Rnd 23 (16, 16, 11) of chart: Work 6 extra sts, work 73 (81, 87, 93) right front sts in color pattern, place 15 (15, 19, 23) sts on holder for right underarm, CO 12 extra sts with backward loops alternating colors [(background, pattern) 3 times, (pattern, background) 3 times], work 145 (161, 173, 185) back sts in color pattern, place 15 (15, 19, 23) sts on holder for left underarm, CO 12 extra sts as for right underarm, work 73 (81, 87, 93) left front sts in color pattern, then work rem 6 extra sts—291 (323, 347, 371) body sts (and 36 extra sts). Work extra sts as for the center front. Work through rnd 44, and then rnds 1 through 36, for a total of 153 (168, 175, 190) rnds. Break yarns.

Shape Front Neck: Rnd 37 on chart: Place 12 center front extra sts and 18 (19, 22, 23) sts on either side of them (a total of 48 (50, 56, 58) sts) on holder. With emerald green, CO 6 new extra sts, the first with a slip knot and the following 5 with backward loops, k2tog (the dec slants towards the extra sts) on right front, work around to last 2 sts on left front, ssk (the dec slants towards the extra sts), and CO 6 new extra sts with backward loops. Rejoin. Work extra sts as before. Dec 1 st each side of front neck edge in this manner every rnd 6 more times, and then every other rnd 2 times, and *at the same time,*

Shape Back Neck: Rnd 44 of chart: Continuing to dec at front neck edges, work across right front sts and 52 (59, 62, 67) sts of right back shoulder in color pattern, place 41 (43, 49, 51) sts on holder for back neck, CO 12 extra sts, work to end of rnd. Work extra sts as before. Work decs at back neck edges as follows: Work to 2 sts before back neck extra sts, ssk, work extra sts, k2tog. Dec 1 st each side of back neck edge in this manner every rnd 6 times total, ending with rnd 6 of chart—46 (53, 56, 61) sts rem on each shoulder. Work rnd 7 of chart across front sts only (slip sts of left front and 6 left armhole extra sts back to the left end of the circular needle and beg knitting there)—167 (182, 189, 204) rnds total.

Shoulder Seam: Turn work inside out. With blue-violet and beg at center of armhole extra sts, BO all sts together, matching extra sts to each other.

Sleeves: Cut armhole extra sts up the center. With emerald (dark, emerald, dark) green, RS facing, shorter sleeve needle, and beg at center of underarm, k8 (8, 10, 12) underarm sts from holder, pick up and knit 71 (78, 78, 83) sts along one armhole edge, 1 st at shoulder seam, 72 (79, 79, 84) sts along other armhole edge, and k7 (7, 9, 11) rem underarm sts from holder—159 (173, 177, 191) sts. Place marker. Join. Be careful to center patterns at top of sleeve as they are at the center back of body. Beg on rnd 42 (35, 42, 35), follow Main Chart in reverse direction, dec 1 st each side of underarm marker every 3rd rnd 25 (41, 31, 48) times, and then every 4th rnd 10 (0, 11, 0) times, working 115 (123, 137, 145) rnds total, ending on rnd 16 (1, 38, 23), and changing to sleeve dpn when necessary. End of sleeve pattern matches beg of body pattern—89 (91, 93, 95) sts rem. **Decrease rnd:** With emerald (dark, emerald, dark) green and ribbing dpn, dec 25 (23, 25, 23) sts evenly spaced—64 (68, 68, 72) sts rem. **Cuff:** Rnd 1: *k2 dark green, k2 emerald green;

rep from *. Rnd 2: k2 dark green, p2 emerald green; rep from *. Work to end of Sleeve Ribbing chart. With emerald green, BO in knit.

Neckband: Cut extra sts across neck only (do not cut the center front extra sts yet). With shorter ribbing needle, beg at 6 center front extra sts on holder, [k1 medium turquoise heather, k1 light red-violet heather] 3 times; *k2 light red-violet heather, k2 medium turquoise heather; rep from * across 18 (19, 22, 23) right front sts from neck holder, and continuing to alternate colors, pick up and knit 22 sts along right front and right back neck edges, work 41 (43, 49, 51) sts from back neck holder, pick up and knit 22 along left back and left front neck edges, and work 18 (19, 22, 23) sts of left front from neck holder, then work rem 6 center front extra sts [k1 light red-violet heather, k1 medium turquoise heather] 3 times—122 (126, 138, 142) neckband sts (and 12 extra sts). Place marker. Join. Work to end of Neckband Ribbing chart. With emerald green, BO in knit.

Buttonhole band: Cut center front extra sts up the center. With RS facing, longer ribbing needle, and beg at right front bottom edge alternating k2 medium turquoise heather, k2 light red-violet heather, pick up and knit about 1 st for every rnd, ending k2 medium turquoise heather—about 194 (202, 210, 226) sts total. (Somewhat fewer is acceptable, as long as the number of sts is

a multiple of 4 plus 2, but more is not.) Work Front Band Ribbing chart back and forth for 3 rows, keeping floats to the wrong side. **Buttonhole row:** RS facing, rib 4 sts, work 3-stitch buttonhole (see page 70), *rib 20 (21, 22, 24) sts, work 3-stitch buttonhole; rep from * 7 more times, rib 3 sts—9 buttonholes. Work to end of chart. With emerald green, BO in knit. With emerald green, crochet about 10 slip sts on the top and bottom edges of the band to make it appear continuous with the adjacent cast-on and bind-off edges of the body and neck.

Button band: Work as for Buttonhole Band, omitting buttonholes.

Finishing: Trim the 6 extra sts at front, neck, and armhole edges to 3 or 4 and hem them with a tapestry needle threaded with yarn, turning under 1 st as you go. Overlap the front edges. Using regular sewing thread, a tapestry needle, and long sts, baste the overlapped front edges together so that they will remain flat during blocking. Wash in wool-safe detergent. Remove excess water with the spin cycle of a washing machine. Place on a jumper board. Baste along the outer neck edge to shape it and draw it in. When dry, remove the sweater from the board and pull out basting. Reshape the body and sleeve ribbings by wetting and patting them into place, or by steaming them. Sew on buttons.

Hillswick Lumber

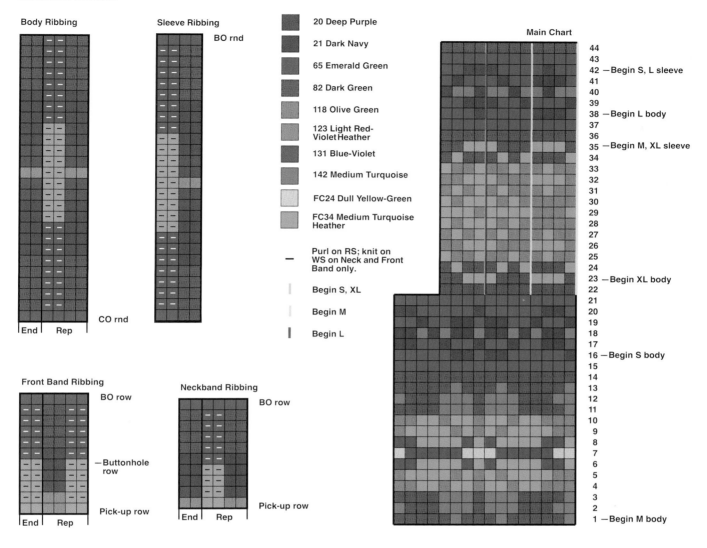

Body Ribbing

Sleeve Ribbing

BO rnd

CO rnd

End | Rep

Front Band Ribbing

BO row

—Buttonhole row

Pick-up row

End | Rep

Neckband Ribbing

BO row

Pick-up row

End | Rep

20 Deep Purple

21 Dark Navy

65 Emerald Green

82 Dark Green

118 Olive Green

123 Light Red-Violet Heather

131 Blue-Violet

142 Medium Turquoise

FC24 Dull Yellow-Green

FC34 Medium Turquoise Heather

— Purl on RS; knit on WS on Neck and Front Band only.

| Begin S, XL

| Begin M

| Begin L

Main Chart

44
43
42 —Begin S, L sleeve
41
40
39
38 —Begin L body
37
36
35 —Begin M, XL sleeve
34
33
32
31
30
29
28
27
26
25
24
23 —Begin XL body
22
21
20
19
18
17
16 —Begin S body
15
14
13
12
11
10
9
8
7
6
5
4
3
2
1 —Begin M body

Notes on colors: The two wide patterns are similar, but have subtle differences. In the rosette pattern on rounds 44 and 1 to 14, the background has four rounds of dark green at the outer edges, followed by two rounds of olive green, with three rounds of blue-violet at the center. The pattern is shaded with three rounds of medium turquoise at the outer edges, followed by three rounds of medium turquoise heather, and a single center round of dull yellow-green. However, in the diamond pattern on rounds 22 to 36, there are only three background rounds of dark green, followed by four of olive green, with a single center round of light red-violet. The pattern color in this band, medium turquoise heather, does not shade at all.

In the small patterns, on rounds 15 to 21 and 37 to 43, the background is emerald green, except for a center round (18 and 40) of medium turquoise, which provides a link to the large patterns. The outer pattern rounds are deep purple, the three inner rounds dark navy.

In the ribbing, the knit column shades from dark green to dark navy to deep purple, with a radiant center round of light red-violet heather. The purl column shades from emerald green to medium turquoise heather.

Isleburgh Cardigan

ISLEBURGH CARDIGAN

This sweater uses colors that are feminine but unusual, oddly deep and discordant for a young girl. Nevertheless, it is festive and lush. In the large pattern, the eye is drawn to the light colors at both the outer edges and the center; like a three-ring circus, there is no place to focus. The small pattern band takes three of the five colors from the large pattern and sets them against a different background color. The ribbing regroups the colors yet again: the knit stitches shade from blue-violet (a background color in the body of the sweater) to light pink heather (a pattern color) via light red-violet heather, while in the column of purl stitches, the medium turquoise from the small pattern bands joins the medium turquoise heather from the large pattern bands. This jumbling of the colors enhances the sweater's flower-garden brilliance.

Finished Size: Child's Small (Medium, Large, Extra Large); approximate ages 2–4 (4–6, 6–8, 8–10). Shown in size Medium.

Bust/chest circumference, buttoned: 28½ (31, 33½, 36)" (72.5 (78.5, 85, 91.5) cm).

Body length: 15¼ (17¼, 18½, 20½)" (38.5 (44, 47, 52) cm).

Sleeve length: 12½ (13½, 14½, 15½)" (32 (34.5, 37, 39.5) cm).

Materials

Yarn: Jamieson & Smith 2-ply jumper weight Shetland yarn (100% wool; 150 yd/oz (137 m/28 g)): #131 blue-violet, 4 (4, 5, 5) oz 113 (113, 146, 146) cm); #142 medium turquoise, #FC22 deep pink heather, 3 (3, 4, 4) oz (85 (85, 113, 113) g) each; #FC34 medium turquoise heather, 2 oz (57 g); #75 pale turquoise, #123 light red-violet heather, #FC6 light pink heather, #FC38 deep orange heather, #FC43 pale yellow-white heather, 1 oz (28 g) each.

MacAuslan 2-ply jumper weight Shetland yarn (100% wool; 150 yd/oz (137 m/28 g)): #244 Katrine (salmon), 2 oz (57 g); #236 Maree (periwinkle), 1 oz (28 g).

Needles: Body and Sleeves—Size 3 (3 mm): 16"/40 cm and 24"/60 cm circular and double-pointed (dpn); Ribbings—Size 1 (2.25 mm): 16"/40 cm and 24"/60 cm circular and dpn. Adjust needle sizes if necessary to obtain the correct gauge.

Crochet hook: Size C (2.5 mm).

Notions: Marker; three stitch holders; tapestry needle; five 5/8" (1.5 cm) buttons.

Gauge: 32 sts and 32 rnds = 4" (10 cm) with larger needle over St st in color pattern.

Note: Each size begins at a different round.

Body: With deep pink heather and longer ribbing needle, CO 214 (234, 254, 274) sts—202 (222, 242, 262) body sts (and 12 extra sts to be cut later for the center front opening). Place marker at beg of rnd (center front). Join, being careful not to twist sts. **Ribbing:** Work 6 extra sts alternating colors [k1 medium turquoise heather, k1 blue-violet] 3 times, *k2 blue-violet, p2 medium turquoise heather; rep from * to last 8 sts, end k2 blue-violet, and work rem 6 extra sts [k1 blue-violet, k1 medium turquoise heather] 3 times. Work to end of Body Ribbing chart, always working the extra sts next to the body of the sweater in the knit color, the 2 center extra sts in the purl color, and the rem extra sts in the established striped pattern. Change to longer body needle and medium turquoise (blue-violet, medium turquoise, blue-violet). **Increase rnd:** Work 6 extra sts, k2 (3, 4, 5), M1, *k11 (12, 13, 14), M1; rep from * 18 times, end k2 (3, 4, 5), then work rem 6 extra sts—221 (241, 261, 281) body sts (and 12 extra sts). Ex-

cept when only one color is used in the rnd, always work the extra sts next to the body of the sweater in the background color, the 2 center extra sts in the pattern color, and the rem extra sts in the established striped pattern. Beg on rnd 18 (1, 18, 1) of Main Chart, work through rnd 26, then rnds 1 through 26 twice more, and then for sizes L and XL only, work rnd 1 through 17, for a total of 61 (78, 78, 95) rnds.

Shape Armholes and V-Neck: Rnd 1 (1, 18, 18) of chart: Work 6 extra sts, k2tog (the dec slants towards the extra sts), work 44 (48, 52, 56) right front sts in color pattern, ssk (the dec slants towards the extra sts), place 15 (17, 19, 21) sts on holder for right underarm, CO 12 extra sts with backward loops alternating colors [(background, pattern) 3 times, (pattern, background) 3 times], k2tog, work 91 (99, 107, 115) back sts in color pattern, ssk, place 15 (17, 19, 21) sts on holder for left underarm, CO 12 extra sts as for right underarm, k2tog, work 44 (48, 52, 56) left front sts in color pattern, ssk, then work rem 6 extra sts—185 (201, 217, 233) body sts (and 36 extra sts). Work extra sts as for the center front. Being careful to keep the pattern motifs in established vertical alignment, dec 1 st each side of armhole edges in this manner every other rnd 3 times total, and *at the same time*, dec 1 st each side of center front extra sts every other rnd 9 (10, 4, 7) times, and then every 3rd rnd 9 (9, 16, 14) times total. After working through rnd 26 once (once, twice, twice) and then rnds 1 through 16 for all sizes, for a total of 103 (120, 129, 146) rnds, *at the same time,*

Shape Back Neck: Rnd 17 of chart: Work across right front sts and 29 (32, 35, 38) sts of right back shoulder, ssk, place 27 (29, 31, 33) sts on holder for back neck, CO 12 extra sts as for right underarm, k2tog, work to end of rnd. Work extra sts as before. Dec 1 st each side of back neck edge in this manner every rnd 4 times total, ending with rnd 20 of chart—27 (30, 33, 36) sts rem on each shoulder. Work rnd 21 of chart across front sts only (slip sts of left front and 6 left armhole extra sts back to the left end of the circular needle and beg knitting there)—107 (124, 133, 150) rnds total.

Shoulder Seam: Turn work inside out. With blue-violet and beg at center of armhole extra sts, BO all sts together, matching extra sts to each other.

Sleeves: Cut armhole extra sts up the center. With medium turquoise (blue-violet, blue-violet, medium turquoise), RS facing, shorter sleeve needle, and beg at center of underarm, k8 (9, 10, 11) underarm sts from holder, pick up and knit 45 (45, 54, 54) sts along one armhole edge, 1 st at shoulder seam, and 46 (46, 55, 55) sts along other armhole edge, and k7 (8, 9, 10) rem underarm sts from holder—107 (109, 129, 131) sts. Place marker. Join. Be careful to center patterns at top of sleeve as they are at the center back of body. Beg on rnd 24 (15, 15, 24), follow Main Chart in reverse direction, dec 1 st each side of underarm marker every 3rd rnd 7 (0, 18, 5) times, every 4th rnd 16 (17, 12, 24) times, and then every 5th rnd 0 (5, 0, 0) times, working

85 (93, 102, 111) rnds total, ending on rnd 18 (1, 18, 18), and changing to sleeve dpn when necessary. End of sleeve pattern matches beg of body pattern, (except for size XL)—61 (65, 69, 73) sts rem. **Decrease rnd:** With medium turquoise (blue-violet, medium turquoise, blue-violet) and ribbing dpn, dec 13 (13, 17, 17) sts evenly spaced—48 (52, 52, 56) sts rem. **Cuff:** Rnd 1: *k2 blue-violet, k2 medium turquoise heather; rep from *. Rnd 2: *k2 blue-violet, p2 medium turquoise heather; rep from *. Work to end of Sleeve Ribbing chart. With blue-violet, BO in knit.

Front Band: Cut center front extra sts up the center. With RS facing, longer ribbing needle, and beg at right front bottom edge alternating k2 light pink heather, k2 medium turquoise, pick up and knit about 1 st for every rnd, ending k2 light pink heather—about 126 (143, 152, 169) sts along right front edge, 4 sts along right back neck edge, 27 (29, 31, 33) sts from back neck holder, 4 sts along left back neck edge, and 125 (142, 151, 168) sts along left front edge—about 286 (322, 342, 378) sts total. (Somewhat fewer is acceptable, as long as the number of sts is a multiple of 4 plus 2, but more is not.) Work Front Band Ribbing

chart back and forth for 3 rows, keeping floats to the wrong side. **Buttonhole row:** RS facing, rib 4 sts, *work 3-stitch buttonhole (see page 70), rib 15 (19, 19, 23) sts; rep from * 3 more times, work 3-stitch buttonhole—5 buttonholes. Work to end of chart. With blue-violet, BO in knit. With blue-violet, crochet about 10 slip sts on the top and bottom edges of the front bands to make them appear continuous with the adjacent cast-on and bind-off edges of the body and neck.

Finishing: Trim the 6 extra sts at neck and armhole edges to 3 or 4 and hem them with a tapestry needle threaded with yarn, turning under 1 st as you go. Overlap the front edges. Using regular sewing thread, a tapestry needle, and long sts, baste the overlapped front edges together so that they will remain flat during blocking. Wash in wool-safe detergent. Remove excess water with the spin cycle of a washing machine. Place on a jumper board. Baste the V of the neck to draw it in and shape it. When dry, remove the sweater from the board and pull out basting. Reshape the body and sleeve ribbings by wetting and patting them into place, or by steaming them. Sew on buttons.

Isleburgh Cardigan

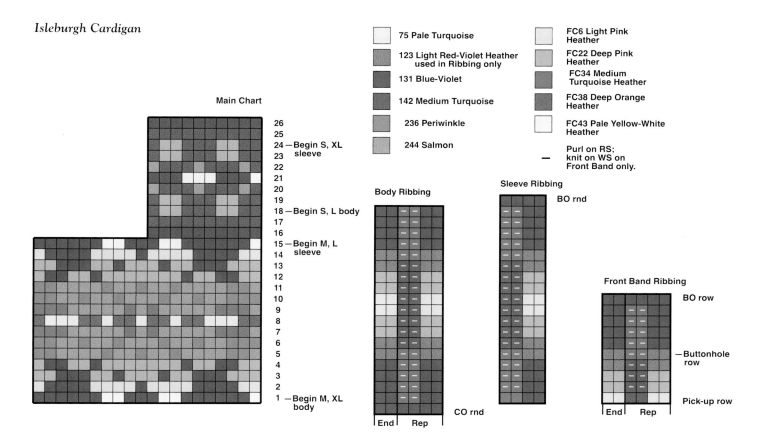

Main Chart

26
25
24 — Begin S, XL sleeve
23
22
21
20
19
18 — Begin S, L body
17
16
15 — Begin M, L sleeve
14
13
12
11
10
9
8
7
6
5
4
3
2
1 — Begin M, XL body

Body Ribbing

End | Rep
CO rnd

Sleeve Ribbing

BO rnd

Front Band Ribbing

BO row
— Buttonhole row
Pick-up row
End | Rep

☐ 75 Pale Turquoise

▨ 123 Light Red-Violet Heather used in Ribbing only

▧ 131 Blue-Violet

▧ 142 Medium Turquoise

▨ 236 Periwinkle

▨ 244 Salmon

☐ FC6 Light Pink Heather

▨ FC22 Deep Pink Heather

▧ FC34 Medium Turquoise Heather

▧ FC38 Deep Orange Heather

☐ FC43 Pale Yellow-White Heather

— Purl on RS; knit on WS on Front Band only.

Notes on colors: In the wide bands, the pattern is edged by one round of pale yellow-white heather, followed by one round of light pink heather, two rounds of deep pink heather, and three rounds of salmon. The center round is deep orange heather. The background changes from a vivid blue-violet to a slightly lighter periwinkle on the same round that the salmon is introduced. This periwinkle occupies two rounds, followed by one round of light turquoise heather, with a center round of pale turquoise.

The light red-violet heather in the ribbing, which makes a transition from blue-violet to deep pink heather, is used nowhere else.

King Harald Street Hats

These hats are based on variations on swatches 30-a and 30-b shown on pages 82 and 83. Each hat starts with the same pattern used throughout that swatch. Hat #1, with a floral group of forest colors, and hat #2, with dusky purples and grays, employ values as they are arranged in the first band of the swatch: a light pattern on a dark background, both traveling from dark at the edges to light at the center. Hat #3, with coffee and cinnamon colors, begins with an arrangement similar to the second band of swatch 3-30: a dark pattern on a light background, both traveling from dark at the edges to light at the center. In each hat, I added a seventh color after the first pattern band and regrouped the colors for the following patterns. None of the hats regroups the colors in the same way. After knitting the first band, some experimenting was required to find the "right" sequences—what looked best—for subsequent bands. Different groups of colors led to different solutions.

Each hat uses a different decrease method on the crown (see page 67). Hat #1 has a centered double decrease, Hat #2 a simple k3tog decrease, and Hat #3 a slip 1, k2tog, psso decrease. If I had to pick a favorite method of these three, it would be k3tog, because it's the easiest to do.

Finished Size: Medium.
Circumference: 21" (53.5 cm).
Depth: 10" (25.5 cm).

Materials

Yarn: Jamieson & Smith 2-ply jumper weight Shetland yarn (100% wool; 150 yd/oz (137 m/28 g)): 1 oz (28 g) (or small amounts) of each color.

Hat #1: #72 light red heather, #82 dark green, #118 olive green, #123 light red-violet heather, #131 blue-violet, #FC12 gold-green heather, #FC41 dark turquoise.

Hat #2: #2 light warm gray, #19 dull red-violet heather, #81 black, #87 dark red-violet heather, #202 fawn, #FC52 blue-beige heather, #FC56 dark blue-violet heather.

Hat #3: #4 medium brown, #5 very dark brown, #61 medium tan, #72 light red heather, #120 caramel, #FC17 light tan, #FC55 dark red heather.

Needles: Base—Size 3 (3 mm): 16"/40 cm circular or double-pointed (dpn); Crown—Size 3 (3 mm): dpn; Ribbing—Size 2 (2.75 mm): 16"/40 cm circular or dpn. Adjust needle sizes if necessary to obtain the correct gauge.

Notions: Marker; tapestry needle.

Gauge: 32 sts and 32 rnds = 4" (10 cm) with larger needle over St st in color pattern.

Base: With ribbing needle, CO 136 sts. Place marker at beg of rnd. Join, being careful not to twist sts. **Ribbing:** Work to end of Ribbing chart. Change to larger needle. **Increase rnd:** K4, *k4, M1; rep from * 32 times, end k4—168 sts. Beg on rnd 1 of Main Chart, work through rnd 47. **Decrease rnd:** *k5, k2tog; rep from * 24 times total—144 sts rem.

Crown: Rnds 1 through 4: With crown dpn, following Crown chart, work even. Each section begins with 24 sts. There are 6 dec points on the crown.

Rnds 5 through 23: Work decs every other rnd as indicated on chart 10 times—24 sts rem. Rnd 24: Work decs again—12 sts rem. Rnd 25: K2tog around—6 sts rem.

Tube: Work a tiny tube on 6 sts with background color for 5 rnds. Break yarn leaving a 6" (15 cm) tail. Thread a tapestry needle with the end, slip sts from dpn onto the tapestry needle, and draw together. Fasten off.

Finishing: Bury the tail end of the yarn in the center of the tube. Wash in wool-safe detergent. Remove excess water with the spin cycle of a washing machine. Place hat over something round of appropriate size to dry.

King Harald Hat #1

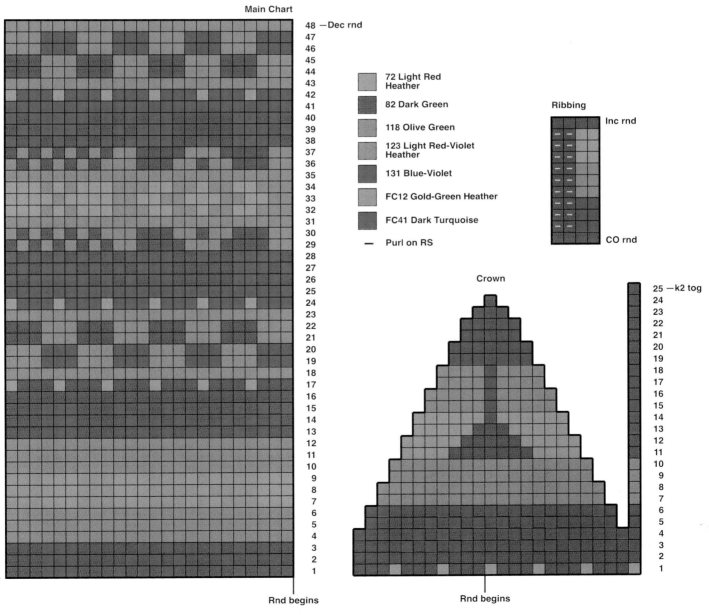

Main Chart

48 —Dec rnd
47
46
45
44
43
42
41
40
39
38
37
36
35
34
33
32
31
30
29
28
27
26
25
24
23
22
21
20
19
18
17
16
15
14
13
12
11
10
9
8
7
6
5
4
3
2
1

Rnd begins

	72 Light Red Heather
	82 Dark Green
	118 Olive Green
	123 Light Red-Violet Heather
	131 Blue-Violet
	FC12 Gold-Green Heather
	FC41 Dark Turquoise
—	Purl on RS

Ribbing

Inc rnd

CO rnd

Crown

25 —k2 tog
24
23
22
21
20
19
18
17
16
15
14
13
12
11
10
9
8
7
6
5
4
3
2
1

Rnd begins

Main Chart

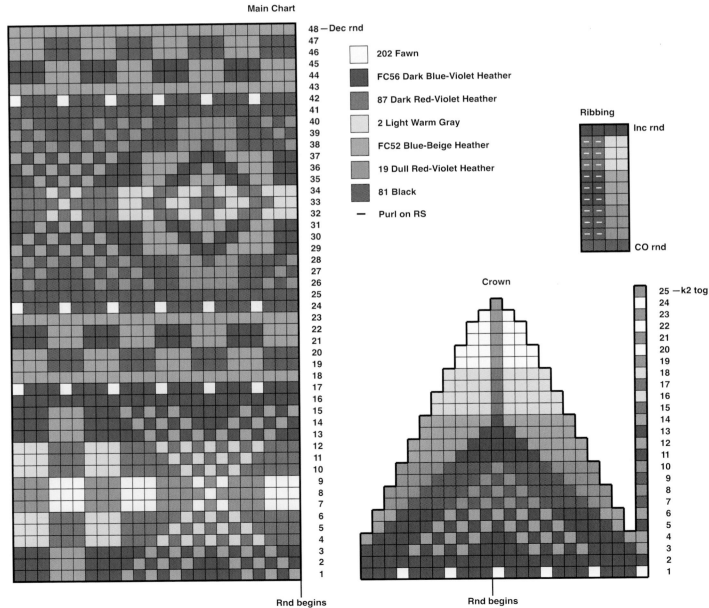

48 — Dec rnd
47
46
45
44
43
42
41
40
39
38
37
36
35
34
33
32
31
30
29
28
27
26
25
24
23
22
21
20
19
18
17
16
15
14
13
12
11
10
9
8
7
6
5
4
3
2
1

☐	202 Fawn
■	FC56 Dark Blue-Violet Heather
■	87 Dark Red-Violet Heather
■	2 Light Warm Gray
■	FC52 Blue-Beige Heather
■	19 Dull Red-Violet Heather
■	81 Black
—	Purl on RS

Ribbing

Inc rnd

CO rnd

Crown

25 — k2 tog
24
23
22
21
20
19
18
17
16
15
14
13
12
11
10
9
8
7
6
5
4
3
2
1

Rnd begins

Rnd begins

King Harald Hat #3

Main Chart

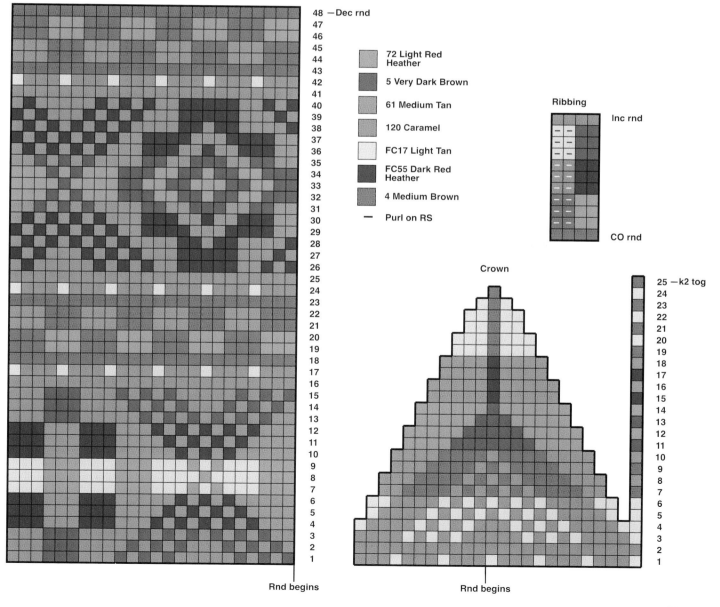

48 — Dec rnd
47
46
45
44
43
42
41
40
39
38
37
36
35
34
33
32
31
30
29
28
27
26
25
24
23
22
21
20
19
18
17
16
15
14
13
12
11
10
9
8
7
6
5
4
3
2
1

	72 Light Red Heather
	5 Very Dark Brown
	61 Medium Tan
	120 Caramel
	FC17 Light Tan
	FC55 Dark Red Heather
	4 Medium Brown
—	Purl on RS

Ribbing

Inc rnd

CO rnd

Crown

25 — k2 tog
24
23
22
21
20
19
18
17
16
15
14
13
12
11
10
9
8
7
6
5
4
3
2
1

Rnd begins

Rnd begins

Knab Fingerless Gloves

I selected this group of misty colors for an artist friend. He asked for earthy greens and browns—landscape colors. These are dull, almost indistinct colors, all but one of the yarns a heathered blend. The insertion of a round of stitches alternating background colors of adjacent bands further mutes contrast by effectively blurring the border between one band and the next.

Notes on Gloves

The hardest thing about making gloves is avoiding making holes at the bases of the fingers. No two knitters in Shetland have the same recipe for overcoming this potential problem. Some recommended picking up more stitches than you need at the joints between the fingers in the first round of the fingers, and then knitting those stitches together on the next round to get the number required. I've been told to tighten the stitches between the fingers by twisting them as they are picked. And I've been told to work into the stitches at the corners twice, once for each finger. Another recommendation is if there are holes when all is said and done, duplicate stitch over them (an adjoining stitches if necessary) to tighten things up. Another way of dealing with loose stitches is to take up the slack yarn by tugging it through several adjacent stitches with a tapestry needle.

Finished Size: Medium.

Palm circumference: 8" (20.5 cm).

Note: To make a larger or smaller glove, adjust needle size to adjust the gauge. A gauge of $8^{1}/_{2}$ or $9^{1}/_{2}$ sts to the inch (2.5 cm) will give a palm circumference of $8^{1}/_{2}$" (21.5 cm) or $7^{1}/_{2}$" (19 cm), respectively.

Materials

Yarn: Jamieson & Smith 2-ply jumper weight Shetland yarn (100% wool; 150 yd/oz (137 m/28 g)): #FC46 olive drab, 1 oz (28 g); #33 medium blue-gray heather, #72 light red heather, #135 medium navy, #141 dull green, #FC34 medium turquoise heather, #FC44 gold-brown heather, #FC48 medium denim heather, 1 oz (28 g) each, or less. A few yards of

Main Chart

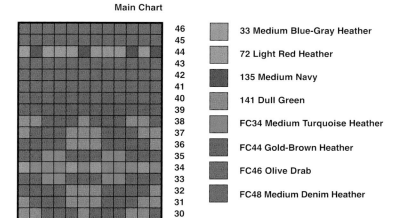

46
45
44
43
42
41
40
39
38
37
36
35
34
33
32
31
30
29
28
27
26
25
24
23
22
21
20
19
18
17
16
15
14
13
12
11
10
9
8
7
6
5
4
3
2
1

33 Medium Blue-Gray Heather

72 Light Red Heather

135 Medium Navy

141 Dull Green

FC34 Medium Turquoise Heather

FC44 Gold-Brown Heather

FC46 Olive Drab

FC48 Medium Denim Heather

Notes on colors: Light red heather runs through the center round of all the patterns. The smallest patterns use a heathered denim blue for the outer rounds and a slightly darker (unheathered) navy in the center, on rounds 4, 24, and 44.

waste yarn in a contrasting color (CC).

Needles: Size 2 (2.75 mm) double-pointed (dpn). Adjust needle size if necessary to obtain the correct gauge.

Notions: Marker; two stitch holders; tapestry needle.

Gauge: 9 sts and 9 rows = 1" (2.5 cm) over St st in color pattern.

Cuff: With olive drab and dpn, CO 50 sts. Place marker at beg of rnd. Join, being careful not to twist sts. **Ribbing:** *k1, p1; rep from * for 3" (7.5 cm). **Increase rnd:** k1, M1, *k2, M1, k3, M1, k2, M1; rep from *—72 sts.

Hand: Beg on rnd 1 of Main Chart, work through rnd 26.

Thumb opening: Rnd 27: *Left hand:* Work 34 palm sts, sl last 9 sts knit from right needle to left needle, with CC

waste yarn, knit these 9 sts again, knit to end of rnd in color pattern. *Right hand:* Work 36 back of hand sts and first 11 palm sts, sl last 9 sts knit from right needle to left needle, with CC waste yarn, knit these 9 sts again, knit to end of rnd in color pattern. Work through rnd 46. With olive drab, knit 2 rnds. Place palm sts and back of hand sts on holders.

Fingers: *Little finger:* On the side opposite the thumb opening, sl 9 sts from the palm and 9 sts from the back of hand onto dpn—18 sts. Join. Work k1, p1 rib for 6 rnds. BO in knit. *Ring finger:* Sl 9 sts from the palm and 9 sts from the back of hand onto dpn, pick up 1 st from the inner corner of the little finger. Work k1, p1 rib across 9 sts from palm, CO 1 st, work k1, p1 rib across 9 sts from the back

of hand, rib rem picked-up st—20 sts. Join. Work k1, p1 rib for 6 rnds. BO in knit. *Middle finger:* Work 20 sts same as ring finger. *Index finger:* Rib 9 sts from palm and 9 sts from back of hand—18 sts. Join. Work k1, p1 rib for 6 rnds. BO in knit. *Thumb:* Pick up 9 sts from above and 9 sts from below the waste yarn, and an extra st at each corner—20 sts. Remove the waste yarn. With olive drab, work k1, p1 rib for six rnds. BO in knit.

Finishing: Wash in wool-safe detergent, remove excess water with the spin cycle of a washing machine, and place on a glove board. Or steam carefully.

Lunna Jumper

LUNNA JUMPER

Two sequences, one of red-violet, pink, and white, and another of blue-violet, blue, and white are set against a navy background. What makes these relatively monochromatic groupings interesting is that in one pattern (the larger, using pink and red-violet) white is at the center, providing one focal point, while in the other, white is at the outer edges, making two focal points. The logic the eye seeks is subverted as visual information oscillates. To further counter expectations, the sequence of blues travels in the opposite direction in the ribbing, with white at the center and blue-violet at the edges. The little checker that courses between the wide bands weaves them together by placing red-violet squares next to the blue band, and blue squares next to the red-violet band.

The background color stays the same throughout this sweater, so it is quicker to knit than garments with more frequent color changes.

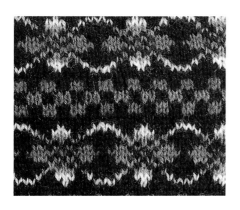

Detail of shoulder join.

Finished Size: Extra Small (Small, Medium, Large, Extra Large). Shown in size Medium.

Bust/chest circumference: 37¼ (41, 44¾, 48½, 52¼)" (94.5 (104, 113.5, 123, 132.5) cm).

Body length: 21¾ (23½, 24¼, 25½, 27)" (55 (59.5, 61.5, 65, 68.5) cm).

Sleeve length: 19½ (19½, 19½, 20, 21¼)" (49.5 (49.5, 49.5, 51, 54) cm).

Materials

Yarn: Jamieson & Smith 2-ply jumper weight Shetland yarn (100% wool; 150 yd/oz (137 m/28 g)): #21 dark navy, 8 (8, 9, 10, 10) oz (227 (227, 255, 284, 284) g); #1a white, 3 (3, 3, 3, 4) oz (85 (85, 85, 85, 113) g); #123 light red-violet heather, #1283 medium pink heather, 1 (1, 1, 2, 2, 3) oz (28 (28, 57, 57, 85) g) each; #FC6 light pink heather, #FC15 light blue, #75 pale turquoise, #FC37 blue-violet heather, 1 (1, 1, 2, 2) oz (28 (28, 28, 57, 57) g) each.

Needles: Body and Sleeves—Size 3 (3.25 mm): 16"/40 cm and 29"/80 cm circular and double-pointed (dpn); Ribbings—Size 1 (2.25 mm): 16"/40 cm and 29"/80 cm circular and dpn. Adjust needle sizes if necessary to obtain the correct gauge.

Notions: Five markers; five stitch holders; tapestry needle.

Gauge: 30 sts and 30 rnds = 4" (10 cm) with larger needle over St st in color pattern.

Note: Each size begins at a different round and at times at a different stitch in the pattern repeat. For sizes Extra Small, Small, Large, and Extra Large, the 12-st, 13-rnd pattern repeat needs a slight adjustment in stitch count below the armhole on rounds 7 and 19 to come out even at the end of the round. The total number of stitches given throughout this pattern refer to the row that the size is on at that time.

Body: With dark navy and longer ribbing needle, CO 272 (300, 324, 352, 376) sts. Place marker at beg of rnd. Join, being careful not to twist sts. **Ribbing:** *k2 dark navy, p2 blue-violet heather; rep from *. Work to end of Body Ribbing chart. Change to longer body needle and dark navy. **Increase rnd:** For sizes XS (S, M, L): *k34 (24, 27, 29), M1; rep from

* 8 (12, 12, 12) times total, end k0 (12, 0, 4); for size XL: *k18, M1, k19, M1; rep from * 10 times, end k6—280 (312, 336, 364, 396) sts. These sts represent the adjusted st numbers for sizes S and XL for the first pattern band. After this rnd, adjust the number of sts on rnds 7 and 19 of the chart, working the incs or decs for size XS after the 2nd, 137th, 142nd, 277th st; for size S after the 4th, 149th, 158th, and 303rd st; for size L after the 7th, 174th, 189th, and 356th st; for size XL after the 8th, 187th, 204th, and 383rd st. (To avoid counting sts every inc and dec rnd, place markers after these sts.) Beg on rnd 20 (7, 1, 20, 7) of Main Chart, work through rnd 46, then rnds 1 through 46, and then rnds 1 through 7 (7, 7, 28, 20) (do not work stitch adjustment for sizes S and XS on the last rnd 7), for a total of 80 (93, 99, 101, 106) rnds (and a total of 280 (308, 336, 364, 392) sts). Break yarns. Discontinue st adjustments marked on the chart from here on.

Shape Armholes: Rnd 8 (8, 8, 29, 21) of chart: Place 4 (6, 7, 9, 10) sts on holder for half of left underarm, CO 6 extra sts, the first 2 with slip knots and the following 4 with backward loops alternating colors [(pattern, background) 3 times], work 133 (143, 155, 165, 177) front sts in color pattern, place 7 (11, 13, 17, 19) sts on holder for right underarm, CO 12 extra sts with backward loops [(background, pattern) 3 times, (pattern, background) 3 times], work 133 (143, 155, 165, 177) back sts in color pattern, place 3 (5, 6, 8, 9) sts on holder for rem of left underarm, and CO 6 extra sts with backward loops [(background, pattern) 3 times]—266 (286, 310, 330, 354) body sts (and 24 extra sts). Rejoin. Except when only one color is used in the rnd, always work the extra sts next to the body of the sweater in the background color, the 2 center extra sts in the pattern color, and the rem extra sts in the established striped pattern. Work decs at armhole edges as follows: Beg at center of left armhole, *work extra sts, k2tog (the dec slants towards the extra sts), work to 2 sts before extra sts, ssk (the dec slants towards the extra sts); rep from *, work rem extra sts. Being careful to keep the pattern motifs in established vertical alignment, dec 1 st each side of armhole in this manner every other rnd 3 (4, 5, 6, 7) times total—254 (270, 290, 306, 326) sts rem. Work through rnd 46, then rnds 1 through 6 (6, 6, 25, 25), for a total of 125 (138, 144, 144, 157) rnds.

Shape Front Neck: Rnd 7 (7, 7, 26, 26) of chart: Work 46 (50, 54, 58, 62) left front shoulder sts, place 35 (35, 37, 37, 39) sts on holder for front neck, CO 12 extra sts with backward loops, work to end of rnd in color pattern. Work extra sts as for right underarm. Work decs at front neck edge as follows: work to 2 sts before extra sts, ssk, work extra sts, k2tog. Dec 1 st each side of neck edge in this manner every rnd 6 times total—40 (44, 48, 52, 56) sts rem on each shoulder. Work through rnd 23 (23, 23, 46, 46), and then for sizes L and XL only, work rnds 1 through 4, for a total of 142 (155, 161, 169, 182) rnds.

Shoulder Seam: Turn work inside out. With dark navy, *BO 6 extra sts and 40 (44, 48, 52, 56) sts of front shoulder together with 6 extra sts and 40 (44, 52, 56) sts of back shoulder. Begin again at other side and rep from *. BO 12 front neck extra sts singly. Place rem 47 (47, 49, 49, 51) sts on holder for back neck. With light blue (light blue, light blue, light red-violet heather, light red-violet heather) and following rnd 24 (24, 24, 5, 5), duplicate stitch over the seam line to make the patterns at the shoulder appear continuous. (See detail on previous page.)

Sleeves: Cut armhole extra sts up the center. With dark navy, RS facing, shorter sleeve needle, and beg at center of underarm, k4 (6, 7, 9, 10) underarm sts from holder, pick up and knit 61 (61, 61, 67, 75) sts along one armhole edge, 1 st at shoulder seam, and 62 (62, 62, 68, 76) sts along other armhole edge, and k3 (5, 6, 8, 9) rem underarm sts from holder—131 (135, 137, 153, 171) sts. Place marker. Join. Be careful to center patterns at top of sleeve as they are at the center front of body. *Note:* Do not work stitch adjustments marked on chart. Beg on rnd 6 (6, 6, 46, 6), follow Main Chart in reverse direction, dec 1 st each side of underarm marker every 3rd rnd 0 (0, 0, 4, 26) times, every 4th rnd 15 (20, 20, 30, 15) times, and then every 5th rnd 13 (9, 9, 0, 0) times, working 125 (125, 125, 132, 138) rnds total, ending on rnd 20 (20, 20, 7, 7), and changing to sleeve dpn when necessary—75 (77, 79, 85, 89) sts rem. **Decrease rnd:** With dark navy and ribbing dpn, dec 15 (13, 15, 17, 17) sts evenly spaced—60 (64, 64, 68, 72) sts rem. **Cuff:** Rnd 1: *k2 dark navy, k2 blue-violet heather; rep from *. Rnd 2: *k2 dark navy, p2 blue-violet heather; rep from *. Work to end of Sleeve Ribbing chart. With dark navy, BO in knit.

Neckband: Cut neck extra sts up the center. With dark navy, RS facing, shorter ribbing needle, and beg at right side of back neck, k47 (47, 49, 49, 51) sts from back neck holder, pick up and knit 19 (19, 19, 27, 27) sts along left front neck edge, k35 (35, 37, 37, 39) sts from front neck holder, and pick up and knit 19 (19, 19, 27, 27) sts along right front neck edge—120 (120, 124, 140, 144) sts. Place marker. Join. Next rnd: *k2 dark navy, k2 white, rep from *. **Ribbing:** *k2 dark navy, p2 white; rep from *. Following Neckband Ribbing chart, rib 8 rnds. **Turning rnd:** *p2 dark navy, p2 blue-violet heather; rep from *. **Decrease rnd:** (Dec about 10% of the sts.) With dark navy, *k8, k2tog; rep from *—108 (108, 112, 126, 130) sts rem. **Facing:** K8 rnds. Break yarn, leaving a long end for grafting.

Finishing: Trim the 6 extra sts at neck and armhole edges to 3 or 4 and hem them with a tapestry needle threaded with yarn, turning under 1 st as you go. Using the long end of yarn from the neckband and a tapestry needle, graft neckband sts on needle to purl bumps and innermost neck extra sts, spacing sts to allow for 10% fewer sts on inner band. Wash in wool-safe detergent. Remove excess water with the spin cycle of a washing machine. Place on a jumper board. Using regular sewing thread, a tapestry needle, and long sts, baste the neck edge to shape it and draw it in. When dry, remove the sweater from the board and pull out basting. Reshape the body and sleeve ribbings by wetting and patting them into place, or by steaming them.

Lunna Jumper

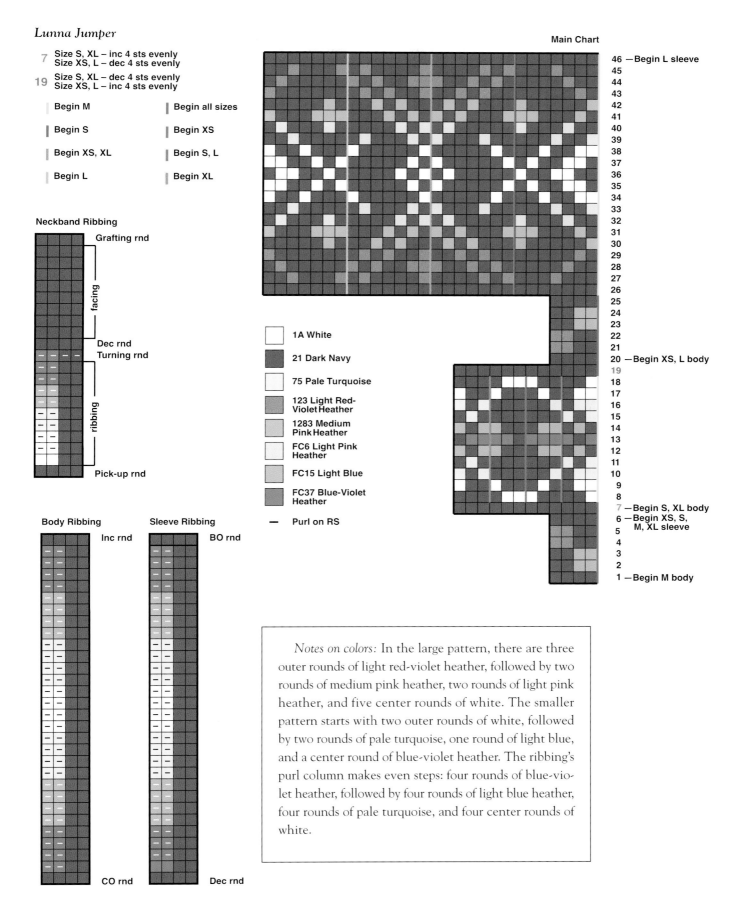

7 Size S, XL – inc 4 sts evenly
   Size XS, L – dec 4 sts evenly

19 Size S, XL – dec 4 sts evenly
    Size XS, L – inc 4 sts evenly

Begin M		Begin all sizes
Begin S		Begin XS
Begin XS, XL		Begin S, L
Begin L		Begin XL

Neckband Ribbing

Grafting rnd

facing

Dec rnd
Turning rnd

ribbing

Pick-up rnd

Body Ribbing   **Sleeve Ribbing**

Inc rnd   BO rnd

CO rnd   Dec rnd

☐ 1A White

■ 21 Dark Navy

☐ 75 Pale Turquoise

▨ 123 Light Red-Violet Heather

▨ 1283 Medium Pink Heather

☐ FC6 Light Pink Heather

▨ FC15 Light Blue

▨ FC37 Blue-Violet Heather

— Purl on RS

46 —Begin L sleeve
45
44
43
42
41
40
39
38
37
36
35
34
33
32
31
30
29
28
27
26
25
24
23
22
21
20 —Begin XS, L body
19
18
17
16
15
14
13
12
11
10
9
8
7 —Begin S, XL body
6 —Begin XS, S, M, XL sleeve
5
4
3
2
1 —Begin M body

Notes on colors: In the large pattern, there are three outer rounds of light red-violet heather, followed by two rounds of medium pink heather, two rounds of light pink heather, and five center rounds of white. The smaller pattern starts with two outer rounds of white, followed by two rounds of pale turquoise, one round of light blue, and a center round of blue-violet heather. The ribbing's purl column makes even steps: four rounds of blue-violet heather, followed by four rounds of light blue heather, four rounds of pale turquoise, and four center rounds of white.

Sandwater Jumper

Main Chart

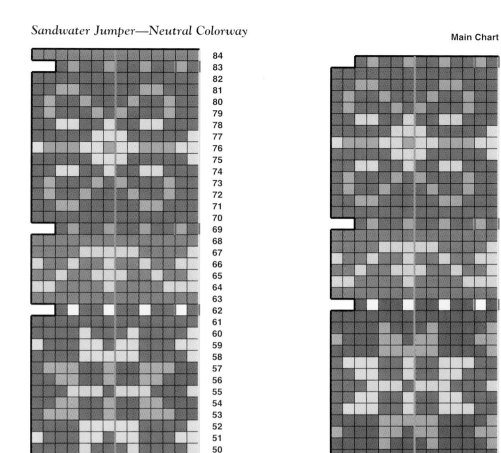

84
83
82
81
80
79
78
77
76
75
74
73
72
71
70
69
68
67
66
65
64
63
62
61
60
59
58
57
56
55
54
53
52
51
50
49
48
47
46 —Begin S, M, L sleeve
45
44
43
42

41
40
39
38
37
36
35
34
33
32
31
30
29
28
27
26
25
24
23
22
21
20
19
18
17
16
15
14
13
12
11
10
9
8
7
6 —Begin S, L body
5
4
3
2
1 —Begin M body

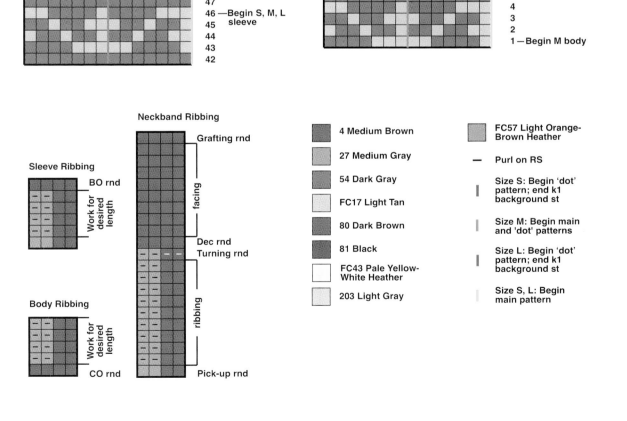

Sleeve Ribbing

BO rnd
Work for desired length

Body Ribbing

Work for desired length
CO rnd

Neckband Ribbing

Grafting rnd
facing
Dec rnd
Turning rnd
ribbing
Pick-up rnd

	4 Medium Brown
	27 Medium Gray
	54 Dark Gray
	FC17 Light Tan
	80 Dark Brown
	81 Black
	FC43 Pale Yellow-White Heather
	203 Light Gray

FC57 Light Orange-Brown Heather

— Purl on RS

| Size S: Begin 'dot' pattern; end k1 background st

| Size M: Begin main and 'dot' patterns

| Size L: Begin 'dot' pattern; end k1 background st

| Size S, L: Begin main pattern

Scalloway Yokes

SCALLOWAY YOKES

In their background colors, these two sweaters are opposites, one dark, one light. In the dark sweater, the main color is a shade of purple. This dark, dull color is sparked by flecks of many other colors, so it looks varied, even vivid, with an inner heat. The colors in the yoke are the components of the shade of purple—purple and black—and gray, which seems quite bright among these deep, dull colors. In the light yoked sweater, where the background is natural undyed fawn, the pattern colors bear no relation to the main color. Against this pale, utterly neutral background, I used a rainbow of deep hues—a green, a purple, a red, two blues.

Notes on Yokes

The yoked sweater has become so classic it's hard to see it as anything other than very conservative, if not outdated. But I wanted to see if it was possible to make the design appealing to contemporary taste.

First, let's talk about the size of the sweater and its relationship to the size of the yoke. In shops in Shetland today, women's small and medium sizes (from 32 to 40 inches) are usually made with six-star yokes; women's large sizes (42 and 44 inches) are usually made with seven-star yokes. A six-star yoke has six stars and six trees, and 276 stitches at the beginning of the star-tree pattern; a seven-star yoke has seven stars and seven trees and 322 stitches at the beginning of the star-tree pattern. The yokes on all sizes from 32 to 40 are identical; between sizes 40 and 42 the base circumference of the star-tree pattern jumps by almost 6 inches. The yoke is the same on sweaters designed for people who vary in measurement by as much as 8 inches. What an enormous amount of latitude in the relationship of the yoke to the body!

Such sweaters are designed to allow only 2 inches of ease in the body. In other words, the sweater measures 2 inches more than the bust; a size 32 measures 34 inches. This is snugger than I find comfortable and than is currently fashionable in America. But if a sweater is designed to fit more loosely, the yoke does not need to expand as much as the body; a well-fitting yoke on no matter how roomy a sweater ought to fit the shoulders relatively closely. So, even if the body of a sweater is to have more ease than the typical Shetland sweater, say 6 to 8 inches, or even 10 inches, a six-star yoke would still be right for a women's small, a seven-star yoke would still be right for a large; and a medium could really go either way. There's no greater science to it than this; the tree decreasing makes a yoke that fits extremely well around the shoulders—anyone's shoulders—because it fans out so gradually, so steadily. As long as the dimensions of the yoke fall between those of the body and the neck, a good fit is guaranteed.

The most commonly made yoke today has 25-row stars, and trees with a base of 17 stitches, with 2 plain stitches between the star and the tree. The number of stitches per star-plus-tree, or per repeat, therefore, is 46. A six-star yoke like this, as noted above, has 276 stitches at the beginning of the star-tree pattern; a seven-star yoke has 322 stitches; an eight-star yoke would have 368 stitches (I've never seen one). I have seen yokes of slightly different dimensions using larger 27- or 31-row stars or smaller 19- or 21-row stars (these could have eight or even ten stars), and with only one plain stitch between the tree and the star, or with as many as three or four stitches between the tree and the star.

The tree decreases are not the only decreases used to shape the yoke. Because the body-plus-sleeves has more stitches than the base of the star-tree pattern in the yoke, decreases are made in the plain rows after the lower border pattern on the yoke. Decreases are made again in the plain rows between the star-tree pattern and the upper border, and yet again in the plain rows after the upper border, before the neck ribbing. The borders around the yoke are indispensable aesthetic elements in the yoke design, framing it and setting it off from the plain knitting. And they fall at convenient places for decreases.

Machine Knitting vs. Hand Knitting

The body of every yoked sweater made in Shetland is machine knitted. A Shetland knitter would not take the time to hand knit the body of a yoked sweater; yoked sweaters are made to sell, and there is an immense time saving in machine knitting vs. hand knitting. In keeping with tradition, the bodies of these yoked sweaters were made on a machine. Also in keeping with tradition, the yokes were hand knitted. American knitters knit for the pleasure of it, to occupy time pleasantly rather than to save time, so I have given directions for hand knitting these sweaters. I did study machine knitting in Shetland, and I learned enough to manage (not without help), to knit these sweaters on a machine. I don't feel experienced enough as a machine knitter to give directions for machine knitting these sweaters, or to detail the machine-knitting techniques used in Shetland. The following information about machine knitting, though, may be of interest to hand knitters.

Machine-knitted solid-color yoke bodies are worked circularly, without side seams, though the ribbings have seams. Two bottom ribbings, a front and a back, are knitted first, and the entire body is knitted directly up from them. The cuff and neck ribbings are also knitted flat, but separately, and grafted on at the end of the process. There are a number of ways Shetlanders sew seams in these ribbings, some more invisible than others; some harder to do than others; the perfectly invisible methods were difficult for me—and for many Shetlanders—to master. The sleeve is knitted from the top down, before knitting the yoke. Stitches are picked up at the armhole edges by a method known as 'the peerie loop:' one new horizontal row is picked up for every two vertical rows; the new sleeve stitch is attached to the body in the piece of yarn that travels from the end of one vertical row to the beginning of the next (this is the 'peerie loop'). This is why the ratio of stitches from horizontal to perpendicular, from sleeve to body, is one to two; the 'peerie loop' occurs every other row. While this makes the sleeve narrower along the body edge than it would be if it were picked up according to the gauge—that is, with 6.5 stitches per 8 rows, instead of the 4 stitches per 8 rows that are actually picked up—the difference is compensated for along the top of the sleeve at the yoke, where as many stitches as necessary are created.

On the machine, it's easier to knit the sleeves from the top down, so that's how the sleeves on these sweaters were done; I have given hand knitting directions for knitting them from the top down or from the bottom up; the two methods are equally good. Your choice would be based on when you wanted to do plain knitting (all before knitting the yoke if you knit the sleeves from the bottom up, or some before and some after if you knit the sleeves from the top down) and whether you are comfortable doing a provisional cast-on to begin the yoke before the sleeves are made.

Centering the Yoke

At the center front of the yoke there is always a star. If there is an even number of stars in the yoke (six or eight, say), there will be a star centered at the center back, too. If there is an odd number of stars (seven, say), there will be a star centered at center front and a tree centered at center back. Centering the border patterns and the star pattern on the yoke is of utmost importance, aesthetically. The center front and center back stitches of the body of the sweater should be marked from the very beginning, or you should be confident of finding them by counting stitches (this is not difficult) when you begin to knit the yoke.

Centering the patterns is more im-portant than where the yoke rounds begin in relation to where previous rounds began. That is to say, it is perfectly permissible to shift the location of the beginning of the round. It is also important to locate the beginning of the round between a tree and a star; you don't want to begin the round in the middle of the tree or the star because that would make the jog where the rounds end and begin horribly obvious. For this reason, too, it may be desirable to shift the location of the beginning of the round. In directions for the large and extra-large size seven-star yoke sweaters (page 156), it happened to work out very nicely that the yoke rounds began at the juncture of right back and right sleeve, but on the small and medium sizes, the beginning of the round was shifted 13 stitches to the left after the border pattern and first non-patterned decrease round were completed. The directions will specify this, but do double-check, before beginning the star patterns, that the star will be centered at center front. Count, from the center front stitch, 12 stitches for half of the star, and then multiples of 46 stitches per star-plus-tree, to the beginning of the round.

Finished Size: Small (Medium, Large, Extra Large). Light colorway shown in size Medium; dark colorway shown in size Large.

Bust/chest circumference: 39¾ (43½, 47, 50¾)" (101 (110.5, 119.5, 129) cm).

Body length: 24¾ (26, 27, 27½)" (63 (66, 68.5, 70) cm).

Sleeve length: 18½ (19, 19½, 20)" (47 (48.5, 49.5, 51) cm). (Includes allowance for turning up cuff.)

Materials

Yarn: Jamieson & Smith 2-ply jumper weight Shetland yarn (100% wool; 150 yd/oz (137 m/28 g)).

Light colorway: #202 fawn (MC), 12 (12, 13, 13) oz (340 (340, 368, 368) g); #19 dull red-violet heather, #21 dark navy, #55 warm red, #65 emerald green, #135 medium navy, 1 oz (28 g) each.

Dark colorway: #FC56 dark blue-violet heather (MC), 12 (12, 13, 13) oz (340 (340, 368, 368) g); #2 light warm gray, #19 dull red-violet heather, #81 black, #87 dark red-violet heather, #FC52 blue-beige heather, #FC53 medium purple-gray heather, 1 oz (28 g) each.

Needles: Body and Sleeves—Size 3 (3.25 mm): 16"/40 cm and 29"/80 cm circular and double-pointed (dpn); Ribbings—Size 1 (2.25 mm): 16"/40 cm and 29"/80 cm circular and dpn. Adjust needle sizes if necessary to obtain the correct gauge.

Notions: Marker; five holders; tapestry needle.

Gauge: Ribbing needle—30 sts = 4" (10 cm). Body needle—26 sts and 32 rnds = 4" (10 cm) over St st. Body needle—30 sts and 30 rnds = 4" (10 cm) over color pattern.

Note: Instructions are written for both colorways: the light colorway/the dark colorway. At times, each size begins at a different stitch in the pattern repeat.

Body: With fawn/dark blue-violet heather and longer ribbing needle, CO 258 (282, 306, 330) sts. Place marker at beg of rnd. Join, being careful not to twist sts. **Ribbing:** *k1, p1; rep from * for 3" (7.5 cm). Change to longer body needle. For light colorway only, k2 rnds plain, and then work Bottom Border chart. For both colorways, work in St st until piece measures 15 (16, 17, 17)" (38 (40.5, 43, 43) cm), or desired length to underarm.

Shape Armholes: K9 (10, 11, 12) sts, place these sts on holder for half of left underarm, k111 (121, 131, 141) front sts, place 18 (20, 22, 24) sts on holder for right underarm, place 111 (121, 131, 141) sts on holder for back, and place 9 (10, 11, 12) sts on holder for rem of left underarm.

Front: Work back and forth on front sts only for 28 (30, 30, 34) rows, and *at the same time*, dec 1 st at each armhole edge every 4th row 1 (3, 4, 4) times—109 (115, 123, 133) sts rem. Place sts on holder.

Back: Work back and forth on back sts only for 38 (40, 40, 44) rows, and *at the same time*, dec 1 st at each armhole edge every 4th row 1 (3, 4, 4) times—109 (115, 123, 133) sts rem. Leave sts on body needle.

Sleeves:

Bottom-up method: With fawn/dark blue-violet heather and ribbing dpn, CO 68 sts. Place marker. Join, being careful not to twist sts. **Ribbing:** *k1, p1; rep from * for 4" (10 cm). Change to sleeve dpn. **Increase rnd:** Inc 10 (10, 16, 16) sts evenly spaced—78 (78, 84, 84) sts. For light colorway only, k1 rnd, and then work Sleeve Border chart. For dark colorway only, work 1" (2.5 cm) even. For both colorways, inc 1 st at end of next rnd. Then inc 1 st each side of marker every 4th rnd 11 (9, 13, 5) times and every 3rd rnd 0 (4, 0, 12) times—101 (105, 111, 119) sts. Change to circular

needle when possible. Work 5" (13 cm) even, for a total of 18½ (19, 19½, 20)" (47 (48.5, 49.5, 51) cm), or desired length to underarm. **Graft sleeve to body:** Beg at center of underarm, *graft 9 (10, 11, 12) underarm sleeve sts on needle to 9 (10, 11, 12) underarm body sts on holder, graft 14 (15, 15, 17) sleeve sts to every other row of body along front armhole edge, place 50 (50, 54, 56) sts on holder to be worked as part of yoke, graft 19 (20, 20, 22) sleeve sts to every other row of body along back armhole edge, and rem 9 (10, 11, 12) underarm sleeve sts on needle to 9 (10, 11, 12) underarm body sts on holder.

Top-down method: *Left Sleeve:* Work body as directed above. With fawn/dark blue-violet heather and longer body needle, provisionally CO 50 (50, 54, 56) sts (see page 104) between front and back for each sleeve and then work yoke to completion. With shorter sleeve needle and beg at center of left underarm, k9 (10, 11, 12) underarm sts from holder, pick up and knit 14 (15, 15, 17) sts along front armhole edge, k50 (50, 54, 56) sts from provisional cast-on, pick up and k19 (20, 20, 22) sts along back armhole edge, then k9 (10, 11, 12) rem underarm sts from holder—101 (105, 111, 119) sts. Place marker. Join. (*Right sleeve:* K9 (10, 11, 12) underarm sts, pick up and knit 19 (20, 20, 22) sts along back armhole edge, k50 (50, 54, 56) provisional cast-on sts, pick up and knit 14 (15, 15, 17) sts along front armhole edge, then k9 (10, 11, 12) rem underarm sts.) Work even for 5" (13 cm). Then dec 1 st each side of marker every 3rd rnd 0 (4, 0, 12) times and then every 4th rnd 11 (9, 13, 5) times, changing to sleeve dpn when necessary—79 (79, 85, 85) sts. On next rnd, dec 1 st at end of rnd—78 (78, 84, 84) sts rem. For light colorway, work Sleeve Border chart in reverse direction, and then k1 rnd with fawn; for dark

colorway, k7 rnds even. Sleeve measures 14½ (15, 15½, 16)" (37, 38, 39.5, 40.5 cm). **Decrease rnd:** Dec 10 (10, 16, 16) sts evenly spaced—68 sts rem. Change to ribbing dpn, *k1, p1; rep from * for 4" (10 cm). BO loosely in ribbing.

Yoke: Beg at left end of longer body needle holding 109 (115, 123, 133) back sts, slip 50 (50, 54, 56) left sleeve sts, 109 (115, 123, 133) front sts, and 50 (50, 54, 56) right sleeve sts from holders onto longer body needle—318 (330, 354, 378) sts. Rejoin at right back shoulder. For light colorway, work rnds 1 through 7 of chart; for dark colorway, work 6 rnds even, then rnds 1 through 4 of chart. **Decrease rnd:** For size S: *k6, k2tog, k5, k2tog; rep from * 21 times total, end k3; for size M: k1, *k2tog, k4; rep from * 54 times total, end k9; for size L: *k2 tog,

k9; rep from * 32 times total, end k2; for size XL: *[k5, k2tog] 3 times, k4, k2tog; rep from * 14 times total—276 (276, 322, 322) sts rem. For sizes S and M (both colorways), k14 sts in background color to establish new beg of rnd. For all sizes, double check that the star/tree pattern will be centered by counting back 104 sts from the center front st (not counting the center front st) to the beg of the rnd. For light colorway, work rnds 9 through 34 of chart (tree decs begin on rnd 18); for dark colorway, work rnds 6 through 31 (tree decs begin on rnd 15)— 180 (180, 210, 210) sts rem. **Decrease rnd:** For sizes S and M (both colorways): *k8, k2tog; rep from * 18 times total; for sizes L and XL (both colorways): *k3, k2tog; rep from * 42 times total—162 (162, 168, 168) sts rem. Change to shorter body needle. For light colorway, work

through rnd 42; for dark colorway, work through rnd 36. **Decrease rnd:** Dec 42 (38, 40, 36) sts evenly spaced—120 (124, 128, 132) sts rem. **Neckband Ribbing:** Change to shorter ribbing needle. *k1, p1; rep from * for 2¾" (7 cm); fold ribbing to inside, and sew loosely in place with yarn.

Finishing: Wash in wool-safe detergent. Remove excess water with the spin cycle of a washing machine. Place on a jumper board. Using regular sewing thread, a tapestry needle, and long sts, baste the neck edge to shape it and draw it in. When dry, remove the sweater from the board and pull out basting. Reshape the body and sleeve ribbings by wetting and patting them into place, or by steaming them.

Scalloway Yoke—Light Colorway

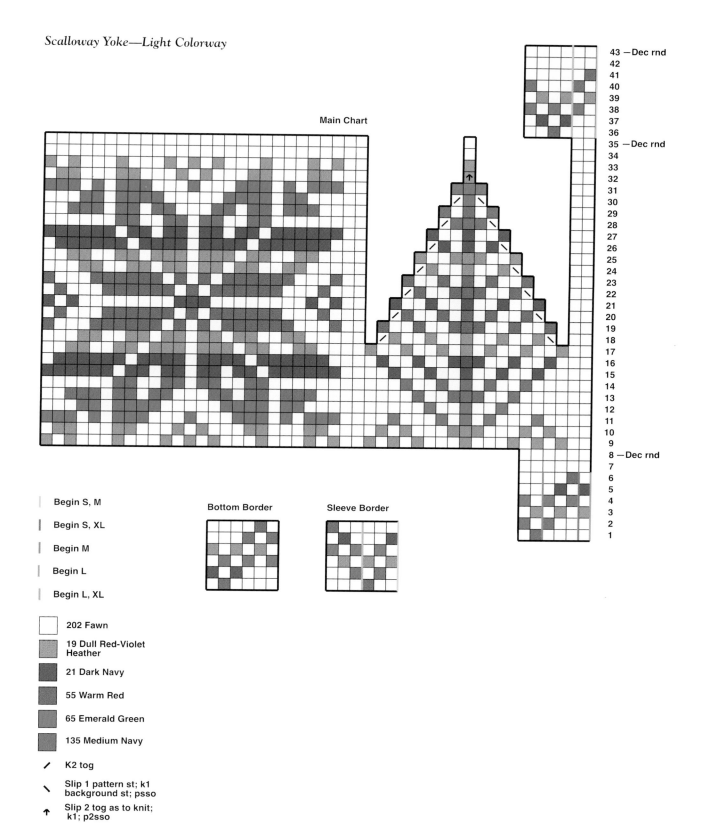

Main Chart

43 — Dec rnd
42
41
40
39
38
37
36
35 — Dec rnd
34
33
32
31
30
29
28
27
26
25
24
23
22
21
20
19
18
17
16
15
14
13
12
11
10
9
8 — Dec rnd
7
6
5
4
3
2
1

Begin S, M

Begin S, XL

Begin M

Begin L

Begin L, XL

Bottom Border   Sleeve Border

202 Fawn

19 Dull Red-Violet
Heather

21 Dark Navy

55 Warm Red

65 Emerald Green

135 Medium Navy

⁄ K2 tog

＼ Slip 1 pattern st; k1
background st; psso

↑ Slip 2 tog as to knit;
k1; p2sso

Scalloway Yoke—Dark Colorway

Main Chart

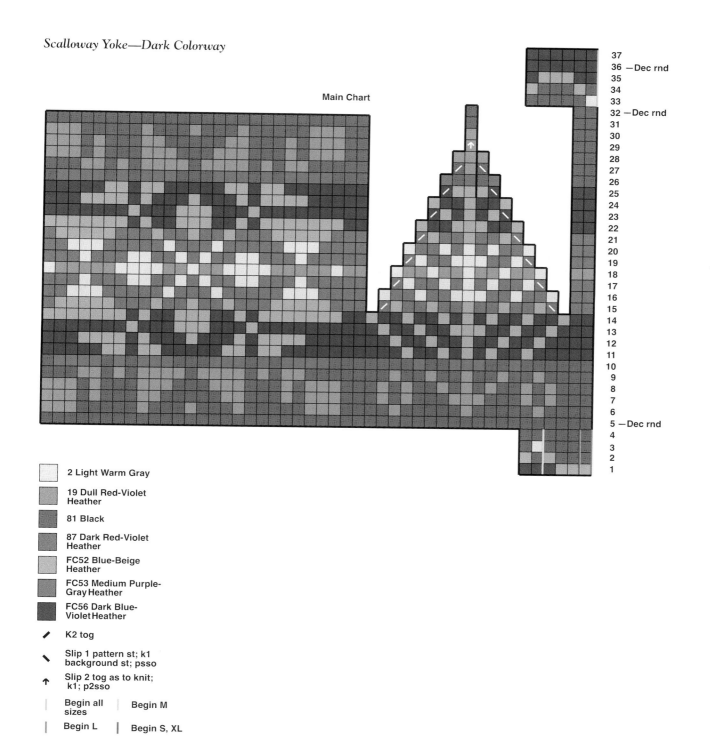

2 Light Warm Gray

19 Dull Red-Violet
Heather

81 Black

87 Dark Red-Violet
Heather

FC52 Blue-Beige
Heather

FC53 Medium Purple-
Gray Heather

FC56 Dark Blue-
Violet Heather

K2 tog

Slip 1 pattern st; k1
background st; psso

Slip 2 tog as to knit;
k1; p2sso

Begin all   Begin M
sizes

Begin L   Begin S, XL

Tingwall Jumper

Tingwall Jumper

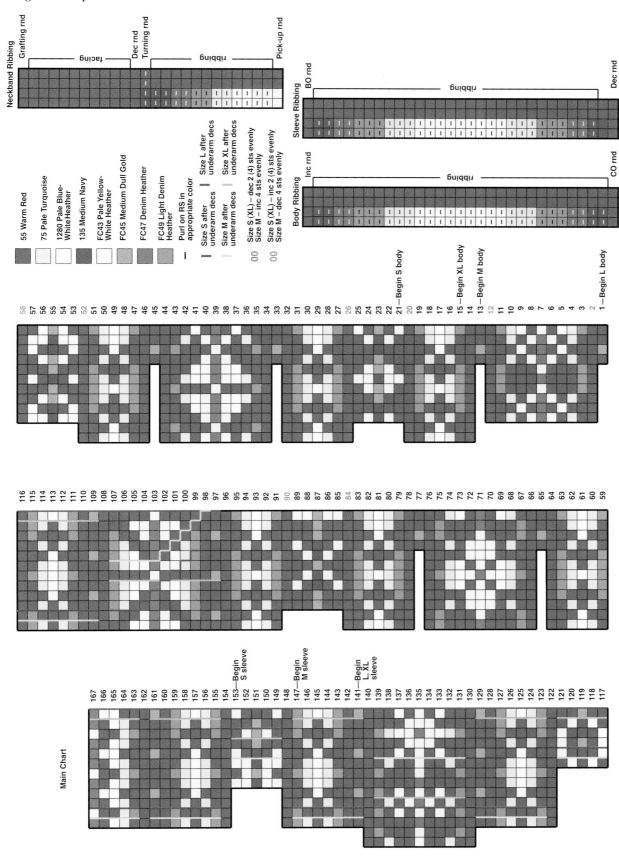

Neckband Ribbing

Grafting rnd · facing · Dec rnd · Turning rnd · ribbing · Pick-up rnd

Sleeve Ribbing

BO rnd · ribbing · Dec rnd

Body Ribbing

Inc rnd · ribbing · CO rnd

55 Warm Red
75 Pale Turquoise
1280 Pale Blue–White Heather
135 Medium Navy
FC43 Pale Yellow–White Heather
FC45 Medium Dull Gold
FC47 Denim Heather
FC49 Light Denim Heather

Purl on RS in appropriate color

Size S after underarm decs
Size L after underarm decs
Size M after underarm decs
Size XL after underarm decs

00 Size S (XL) – dec 2 (4) sts evenly
Size M – inc 4 sts evenly
00 Size S (XL) – inc 2 (4) sts evenly
Size M – dec 4 sts evenly

21—Begin S body
15—Begin XL body
13—Begin M body
1—Begin L body

153—Begin S sleeve
147—Begin M sleeve
141—Begin L, XL sleeve

Main Chart

Vaila Slipover

VAILA SLIPOVER

This pattern is borrowed from a garment made circa 1918 which is in the collection of the Royal Museum of Scotland, Edinburgh. It is reproduced in Sheila MacGregor's *The Complete Book of Traditional Fair Isle Knitting*, opposite page 72. The 1918 garment has only four colors: white and yellow diamonds set on a red and brown background. I retained the light, bright diamonds and the warm background, but used several surprisingly bright accent colors—orange, yellow, pink, light blue—which, scattered in small amounts, do not alter the predominantly neutral feel of the slipover, or the clarity of the light pattern on the darker background.

Detail.

Finished Size: Small (Medium, Large). Shown in size Medium.

Bust/chest circumference: 37¼ (42½, 48)" (94.5 (108, 122) cm).

Body length: 22 (23½, 24¾)" (56 (59.5, 63) cm).

Materials

Yarn: Jamieson & Smith 2-ply jumper weight Shetland yarn (100% wool; 150 yd/oz (137 m/28 g)): #FC43 pale yellow-white heather, 3 (4, 5) oz (85 (113, 142) g); #122 orange-brown heather, 3 (3, 4) oz (85 (85, 113) g); #19 dull red-violet heather, #FC9 medium purple-gray heather, 1 (2, 2) oz (28 (57, 57) g) each;

#14 pale blue, #121 mustard, #203 light gray, #FC7 light orange heather, #FC21 pale purple heather, #FC22 deep pink heather, #FC37 blue-violet heather, #FC63 red-brown heather, 1 oz (28 g) each.

Needles: Body—Size 3 (3.25 mm): 29"/80 cm circular; Ribbings—Size 1 (2.25 mm): 16"/40 cm and 29"/80 cm circular. Adjust needle sizes if necessary to obtain the correct gauge.

Notions: Marker; four stitch holders; tapestry needle.

Gauge: 30 sts and 30 rnds = 4" (10 cm) with larger needle over St st in color pattern.

Note: Size Small begins at a different stitch in the pattern repeat.

Body: With orange-brown heather and longer ribbing needle, CO 268 (304, 340) sts. Place marker at beg of rnd. Join, being careful not to twist sts. **Ribbing:** *k2 orange-brown heather, p2 dull red-violet heather; rep from *. Work to next to last rnd of Body Ribbing chart. **Increase rnd:** Continue k2, p2 ribbing and *at the same time,* inc 12 (16, 20) sts as follows: Size S: *rib 22 sts, M1; rep from *, end rib 4. Size M: *rib 19 sts, M1; rep from *. Size L: *rib 17 sts, M1; rep from *—280 (320, 360) sts. Change to longer body needle. Beg on rnd 1 of Main Chart, work through rnd 20, then rnds 1 through 20 three more times, and then for size L only, work through rnd 10, for a total of 80 (80, 90) rnds. Break yarns.

Shape Armholes and V-Neck: Rnd 1 (1, 11) of chart: Place 11 (13, 18) sts on holder for half of left underarm, CO 6 extra sts, the first 2 with slip knots and the following 4 with backward loops alternating colors [(pattern, background) 3 times], work 59 (67, 72) left front sts in color pattern, place next st on holder for center front, CO 12 extra sts with backward loops [(background, pattern) 3 times, (pattern, background) 3 times],

work 59 (67, 72) right front sts in color pattern, place 21 (25, 35) sts on holder for right underarm, CO 12 extra sts as for center front, work 119 (135, 145) back sts in color pattern, place 10 (12, 17) sts on holder for rem of left underarm, and CO 6 extra sts with backward loops [(background, pattern) 3 times]—237 (269, 289) body sts (1 center st on holder and 36 extra sts). Rejoin. Always work the extra sts next to the body of the sweater in the background color, the 2 center extra sts in the pattern color, and the rem extra sts in the established striped pattern. Work decs at armhole and V-neck edges as follows: Beg at center of left underarm, *work extra sts, k2tog (the dec slants towards the extra sts), work to 2 sts before extra sts, ssk (the dec slants towards the extra sts); rep from *, work rem extra sts. Being careful to keep the pattern motifs in established vertical alignment, dec 1 st at each armhole edge in this manner every other rnd 9 (12, 13) times and *at the same time,* dec 1 st at each side of V-neck every other rnd 6 (0, 6) times and then every 3rd rnd 18 (25, 21) times total. After working a total of 140 (150, 160) rnds, ending on rnd 20 (10, 20) of the chart, *at the same time,*

Shape Back Neck: Rnd 1 (11, 1) of chart: Work across front sts and 29 (33, 35) sts of right back shoulder in color pattern, ssk, place 39 (41, 45) sts on holder for back neck, CO 12 extra sts as for right underarm, k2tog, work to end of rnd in color pattern. Work extra sts as before. Dec 1 st each side of back neck edge in this manner every rnd 4 more times, ending with rnd 5 (15, 5) of chart—26 (30, 32) sts rem on each shoulder. Work rnd 6 (16, 6) of chart across front sts only—146 (156, 166) rnds total.

Shoulder Seam: Turn work inside out. With pale purple heather (orange-brown heather, pale purple heather) and beg at center of right armhole extra sts,

BO all sts tog, matching extra sts to each other.

Neckband: Cut neck extra sts up the center. With RS facing, shorter ribbing needle, and beg at right side of back neck, *k2 orange-brown heather, k2 pale yellow-white heather; rep from * across 39 (41, 45) sts from back neck holder, and continuing to alternate colors, pick up and knit about 1 st for every row—about 68 (77, 77) sts along left back and front neck edges, knit the center front st from holder with orange-brown heather, and resuming the color alternation, mirroring the colors around the center front st, pick up and knit 69 (78, 78) sts along right front and back neck edges—177 (197, 201) sts. Place marker. Join. Work to end of Neckband and Armhole Rib-bing chart, dec at center front of V-neck every rnd 9 times as follows: slip 2 sts tog (the st just before the center front st and the center front st) as to knit, k1 (the st just after the center front), pass the 2 slipped sts over. With orange-brown heather, BO in knit.

Armhole Ribbing: Cut armhole extra sts up the center. With RS facing, shorter ribbing needle, and beg at center of underarm, *k2 pale yellow-white heather, k2 orange-brown heather; rep from * across 11 (13, 18) underarm sts on holder, and continuing to alternate colors, pick up and knit about 7 sts for every 8 rows—about 55 (65, 66) sts along one armhole edge, 1 st at shoulder seam, and 55 (65, 66) sts along other armhole edge, and knit rem 10 (12, 17) underarm sts from holder—132 (156, 168) sts. Place marker. Join. Work to end of Neckband and Armhole Ribbing chart. With orange-brown heather, BO in knit.

Finishing: Trim the 6 extra sts at neck and armhole edges to 3 or 4 and hem them with a tapestry needle threaded with yarn, turning under 1 st as you go. Wash in wool-safe detergent. Remove excess water with the spin cycle of a washing machine. Place on a jumper board. Using regular sewing thread, a tapestry needle, and long sts, baste the neck edge to shape it and draw it in. When dry, remove the sweater from the board and pull out basting. Reshape the body and armhole ribbings by wetting and patting them into place, or by steaming them.

Vaila Slipover

Main Chart

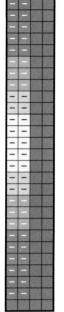

20
19
18
17
16
15
14
13
12
11
10
9
8
7
6
5
4
3
2
1 Inc rnd

Body Ribbing

Neckband and Armhole Ribbing

BO rnd

CO rnd

Pick-up rnd

Notes on colors: The background colors are sequenced as follows: the first round of the chart uses dull red-violet heather, #19; rounds 2, 3 and 4 use the slightly lighter purple-gray heather, #FC9; on round 5 is the much lighter pale purple heather, #FC21. Round 6, the center round of the diamonds, uses a relatively vivid—especially in this context of dull, warm colors—blue-violet heather, #131. Round 7 duplicates round 5, and rounds 8, 9 and 10 duplicate rounds 4, 3 and 2. Rounds 11 and 12 use #19 again. On Rounds 13 and 14 the background is orange-brown heather, #122, the color of the ribbing's knit stitches. The background shifts to the lighter red-brown heather, #FC63, on round 15 and 17.

	14 Pale Blue
	19 Muted Red-Violet Heather
	121 Mustard
	122 Orange-Brown Heather
	203 Light Gray Used in ribbing only
	FC7 Light Orange Heather
	FC9 Medium Purple-Gray Heather
	FC21 Pale Purple Heather
	FC22 Deep Pink Heather
	FC37 Blue-Violet Heather
	FC43 Pale Yellow-White Heather
	FC63 Red-Brown Heather
—	Purl on RS
	Begin S
	Begin M, L

Westerwick Cardigan

WESTERWICK CARDIGAN

This sweater is composed of prismatic pastels, and seems to shimmer. An impression of oscillating light is created in the wide bands, where the pattern travels from dark to light (from deep pink to pale yellow) while the background goes from light to dark (from pale turquoise to deep turquoise). In the narrower bands, pattern and background colors are reversed and the sequences are turned inside out; the pattern shades from dark to light blue, and the background shades from light to dark pink. These shifts of background and pattern alter every color's identity, so the pinks seem nebulous here, brittle there; the blues either oceanic or metallic. The yellows flicker where dispersed in the body of the sweater, yet have the effect of a strong emanating light where they are concentrated at the center of the ribbing.

Finished Size: Extra Small (Small, Medium, Large, Extra Large). Shown in size Medium.

Bust/chest circumference, buttoned: 41¼ (44, 46¾, 49¾, 52½)" (105 (112, 118.5, 126.5, 133.5) cm).

Body length: 22¾ (23, 24½, 25¼, 26¼)" (58 (58.5, 62, 64, 66.5) cm).

Sleeve length: 15¼ (16, 16¾, 17¼, 17¾)" (38.5 (40.5, 42.5, 44, 45) cm).

Materials

Yarn: Jamieson & Smith 2-ply jumper weight Shetland yarn (100% wool; 150 yd/oz (137 m/28 g)): #75 pale turquoise, #FC22 deep pink heather, #FC34 medium turquoise heather, #48 light bright turquoise, 3 (3, 4, 4, 5) oz (85 (85, 113, 113, 142) g) each; #95 light pink, #FC43 pale yellow-white heather, #FC6 light pink heather, 1 (1, 2, 2, 3) oz (28 (28, 57, 57, 85) g) each; #70 bright medium pink, 1 (1, 1, 2, 2) oz (28 (28, 28, 57, 57) g) each; #132 very bright turquoise, #FC15 light blue, #FC37 blue-violet heather, 1 oz (28 g) each.

Needles: Body and Sleeves—Size 4 (3.5 mm): 16"/40 cm and 29"/80 cm circular and double-pointed (dpn); Ribbings—Size 2 (2.5 mm): 16"/40 cm and 29"/80 cm circular and dpn. Adjust needle sizes if necessary to obtain the correct gauge.

Crochet hook: Size C (2.5 mm).

Notions: Marker; three stitch holders; tapestry needle; six 3/4" (2 cm) buttons.

Gauge: 28 sts and 28 rnds = 4" (10 cm) with larger needle over St st in color pattern.

Note: Each size begins at a different round and at times at a different stitch in the pattern repeat.

Body: With deep pink heather and longer ribbing needle, CO 278 (294, 310, 326, 346) sts—266 (282, 298, 314, 334) body sts (and 12 extra sts to be cut later for the center front opening). Place marker at beg of rnd (center front). Join, being careful not to twist sts. **Ribbing:** Work 6 extra sts alternating colors [k1 deep pink heather, k1 medium turquoise heather] 3 times, *k2 medium turquoise heather, p2 deep pink heather; rep from * to last 8 sts, end k2 medium turquoise heather and work rem 6 extra sts [k1 medium turquoise heather, k1 deep pink heather] 3 times. Work to end of Body Ribbing chart, always working the extra sts next to the body of the sweater in the knit color, the two center extra sts in the purl color, and the rem extra sts in the established striped pattern. Change to longer body needle and light pink (light pink, light pink, pale turquoise, pale turquoise). **Increase rnd:** Work 6 extra sts, k14 (6, 6, 1, 11), M1, *k17 (15, 13, 12, 12), M1; rep from * 14 (18, 22, 26, 26) times, end k14 (6, 6, 1, 11), then work rem 6 extra sts—281 (301, 321, 341, 361) body sts (and 12 extra sts). Except when only one color is used in the rnd, always work the extra sts next to the

body of the sweater in the background color, the 2 center extra sts in the pattern color, and the rem extra sts in the established striped pattern. Beg on rnd 13 (1, 1, 20, 20) of Main Chart, work through rnd 42, then rnds 1 through 42 (39, 39, 42, 42), and then rnds 1 through 7 (0, 0, 22, 28), for a total of 79 (81, 81, 87, 93) rnds.

Shape Armholes and V-Neck: Rnd 8 (40, 40, 23, 29) of chart: Work 6 extra sts, k2tog (the dec slants towards the extra sts), work 68 (73, 78, 83, 88) right front sts in color pattern, place 1 st on holder for right underarm, CO 12 extra sts with backward loops alternating colors [(background, pattern) 3 times, (pattern, background) 3 times], work 139 (149, 159, 169, 179) back sts in color pattern, place 1 st on holder for left underarm, CO 12 extra sts as for right underarm, work 68 (73, 78, 83, 88) left front sts in color pattern, ssk (the dec slants towards the extra sts), then work rem 6 extra sts—277 (297, 317, 337, 357) body sts (and 36 extra sts). Work extra sts as for the center front. Being careful to keep the pattern motifs in established vertical alignment, dec 1 st each side of center front extra sts in this manner every other rnd 3 (6, 2, 2, 10) times and then every 3rd rnd 19 (17, 23, 23, 18) times total, and *at the same time,* after working a total of 133 (137, 145, 153, 160) rnds, ending on rnd 19 (11, 19, 4, 11) of the chart,

Shape Back Neck: Work across right front sts and 55 (57, 62, 65, 67) sts of right back shoulder in color pattern, ssk, place 25 (31, 31, 35, 41) sts on holder for back neck, CO 12 extra sts as for right underarm, k2tog, work to end of rnd in color pattern. Work extra sts as before. Dec 1 st each side of back neck edge in this manner every rnd 9 (7, 9, 7, 7) times total, ending with rnd 28 (18, 28, 11, 18) of chart—48 (52, 55, 60, 62) sts rem on each shoulder. Work rnd 29 (19, 29, 12, 19) of chart across front sts only (slip sts of left front and 6 left armhole extra sts back to the left end of the circular needle and beg knitting there)—142 (144, 154, 160, 167) rnds total.

Shoulder Seam: Turn work inside out. With medium turquoise heather (pale turquoise, medium turquoise heather, light pink, pale turquoise) and beg at center of armhole extra sts, BO all sts together, matching extra sts to each other.

Sleeves: Cut armhole extra sts up the center. With pale turquoise (light pink, light pink, pale turquoise, light pink), RS facing, and shorter sleeve needle, k1 underarm st from holder, pick up and knit 62 (62, 72, 72, 73) sts along one armhole edge, 1 st at shoulder seam, and 63 (63, 73, 73, 74) sts along other armhole edge—127 (127, 147, 147, 149) sts. Place marker. Join. Be careful to center patterns at top of sleeve as they are at the center back of body. Beg on rnd 18 (11, 15, 38, 3), follow Main Chart in reverse direction, dec 1 st each side of underarm marker every 3rd rnd 2 (0, 17, 9, 2) times, every 4th rnd 21 (10, 12, 19,

26) times, and then every 5th rnd 0 (11, 0, 0, 0) times, working 90 (95, 99, 103, 110) rnds total, ending on rnd 13 (1, 1, 20, 20), and changing to sleeve dpn when necessary. End of sleeve pattern matches beg of body pattern—81 (85, 89, 91, 93) sts rem. **Decrease rnd:** With light pink (light pink, light pink, pale turquoise, pale turquoise) and ribbing dpn, dec 17 (21, 21, 23, 21) sts evenly spaced—64 (64, 68, 68, 72) sts rem. **Cuff:** Rnd 1: *k2 medium turquoise heather, k2 deep pink heather; rep from *. Rnd 2: *k2 medium turquoise heather, p2 deep pink heather; rep from *. Work to end of Sleeve Ribbing chart. With deep pink heather, BO in knit.

Front Band: Cut center front extra sts up the center. With RS facing, longer ribbing needle, and beg at right front bottom edge alternating k2 pale yellow-white heather, k2 pale turquoise, pick up and knit about 1 st for every rnd, ending k2 pale yellow-white heather—about 142 (145, 155, 161, 168) sts along right front edge, 9 (7, 9, 7, 7) sts along right back

neck edge, 25 (31, 31, 35, 41) sts from back neck holder, 8 (6, 8, 6, 6) sts along left back neck edge, and 142 (145, 155, 161, 168) sts along left front edge—about 326 (334, 358, 370, 390) sts total. (Somewhat fewer is acceptable, as long as the number of sts is a multiple of 4 plus 2, but more is not.) Work Front Band Ribbing chart back and forth for 3 rows, keeping floats to the wrong side. **Buttonhole row:** RS facing, rib 3 sts, *work 3-stitch buttonhole (see page 70), rib 15 (15, 15, 16, 18) sts; rep from * 4 more times, work 3-stitch buttonhole—6 buttonholes. Work to end of chart. With deep pink heather, BO in knit. With deep pink heather, crochet about 10 slip sts on the top and bottom edges of the front bands to make them appear continuous with the adjacent cast-on and bind-off edges of the body and neck.

Finishing: Trim the 6 extra sts at neck and armhole edges to 3 or 4 and hem them with a tapestry needle threaded with yarn, turning under 1 st as you go. Overlap the front edges. Using regular

---

Notes on colors: In the large flower-star pattern on rounds 18 to 40, there are three pinks: three rounds of deep pink heather, #FC22, at the outer edges; followed by three rounds of an almost strident, bright medium pink, #70; then three rounds of light pink heather, #FC6; and one round of pale yellow-white heather at the center. The smaller pattern on rounds 41, 42, and 1 to 17 is bordered by seven rounds of a fourth, different, light pink, #95, which is softer, calmer and clearer than the other pinks (it is not heathered). In the background of this smaller pattern, rounds 6 and 10 shade to the brighter, slightly darker pink, #70, and rounds 7, 8 and 9 shade to

the still darker deep pink heather, #FC22. The pattern on these bands begins with one outer round of blue-violet heather (used nowhere else), followed by one round of light blue (also used nowhere else), one round of pale turquoise, with pale yellow-white heather in the center round.

Returning to the larger pattern and rounds 18 to 40, the background sequence of blues contains five rounds, 18 to 22 and 36 to 40, of pale turquoise, #75, then three rounds of the (slightly darker) light bright turquoise, #48, three rounds of the (darker still) medium turquoise heather, #FC34, with the center round in the deep, very bright turquoise.

The little chain pattern on rounds 1 to 3 and 13 to 15 is composed of outer rounds of light bright turquoise, #48, and an inner round of light turquoise heather, #FC34.

The ribbing's purl column is composed of four rounds of deep pink heather, four rounds of medium bright pink (the strident one), and six center rounds of pale yellow-white heather. The knit column consists of six rounds of light turquoise heather, #FC34, two rounds of light bright turquoise, #48, which is lighter than the preceding turquoise, and six center rounds of pale turquoise, #75, the lightest turquoise of all.

Westerwick Cardigan

sewing thread, a tapestry needle, and long sts, baste the overlapped front edges together so that they will remain flat during blocking. Wash in wool-safe detergent. Remove excess water with the spin cycle of a washing machine. Place on a jumper board. Baste the V of the neck to draw it in and shape it. When dry, remove the sweater from the board and pull out basting. Reshape the body and sleeve ribbings by wetting and patting them into place, or by steaming them. Sew on buttons.

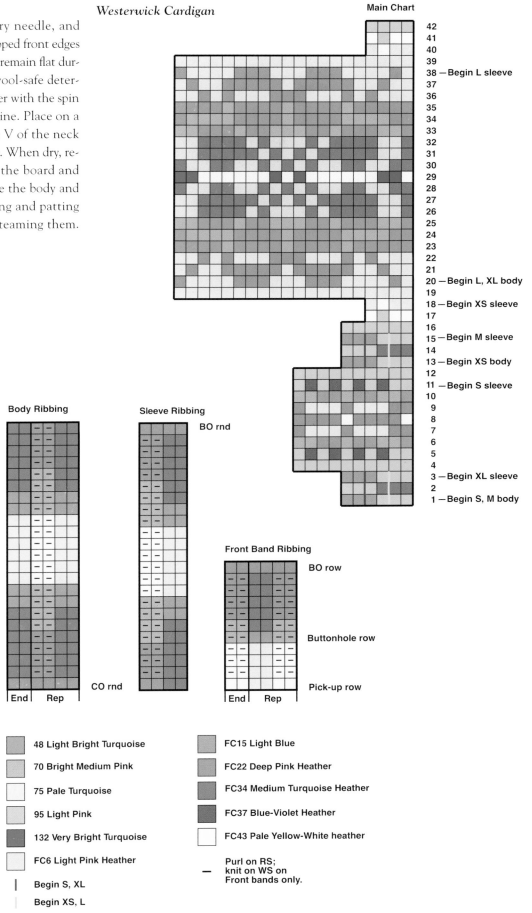

Main Chart

42
41
40
39
38 —Begin L sleeve
37
36
35
34
33
32
31
30
29
28
27
26
25
24
23
22
21
20 —Begin L, XL body
19
18 —Begin XS sleeve
17
16
15 —Begin M sleeve
14
13 —Begin XS body
12
11 —Begin S sleeve
10
9
8
7
6
5
4
3 —Begin XL sleeve
2
1 —Begin S, M body

Body Ribbing

End | Rep

CO rnd

Sleeve Ribbing

BO rnd

Front Band Ribbing

BO row

Buttonhole row

Pick-up row

End | Rep

	48 Light Bright Turquoise
	70 Bright Medium Pink
	75 Pale Turquoise
	95 Light Pink
	132 Very Bright Turquoise
	FC6 Light Pink Heather

	FC15 Light Blue
	FC22 Deep Pink Heather
	FC34 Medium Turquoise Heather
	FC37 Blue-Violet Heather
	FC43 Pale Yellow-White heather

— Purl on RS; knit on WS on Front bands only.

| Begin S, XL
| Begin XS, L

Whalsay Jumper

WHALSAY JUMPER

The large central patterns of this sweater are borrowed from a child's jumper, shown below, which I bought in a Lerwick charity shop. The patterns are engagingly complex and seem to be unique—I've never seen them in any other sweater, nor in any Shetland or Scandinavian pattern book. The child's sweater is made with the traditional Shetland natural colors, undyed, with dark patterns on a light background. I kept the earthy feel of natural colors, but reversed the values, using a dark background and light patterns. I used dyed colors: warm browns, burgundy red, and purple for the background, and a sequence of red, red-orange, orange, yellow-orange and beige for the pattern. The red at the outer edges of the large stars and quatrefoils also appears in the background (in the center row). Using the same color in both background and pattern eliminates the division of background and pattern, unifying them. The child's sweater, my model, does the same thing: the gray at the outer edges of the stars reappears in the center row.

Child's sweater.

Gauge	Finished Bust/Chest Circumference	Body Length	Sleeve Length
28 sts = 4" (10 cm)	48" (122 cm)	28" (71 cm)	20" (51 cm)
29 sts = 4" (10 cm)	46¼" (117.5 cm)	27" (68.5 cm)	19¼" (49 cm)
31 sts = 4" (10 cm)	43¼" (110 cm)	25¼" (64 cm)	18" (45.5 cm)
32 sts = 4" (10 cm)	42" (106.5 cm)	24¾" (63 cm)	17½" (44.5 cm)

Finished Size: Medium.

Bust/chest circumference: 44¾" (113.5 cm).

Body length: 26" (66 cm).

Sleeve length: 18¾" (47.5 cm).

Note: Because of the large pattern repeats, this sweater is given in only one size. However, it can be made slightly larger or smaller by adjusting the needle size to change the gauge, as shown in chart above.

Materials

Yarn: Jamieson & Smith 2-ply jumper weight Shetland yarn (100% wool; 150 yd/oz (137 m/28 g)): #143 chestnut brown, 5 oz (142 g); #80 dark brown, 3 oz (85 g); #72 light red heather, #134 maroon, #1281 yellow-orange heather, #1288 red-orange heather, #1289 orange heather, #FC45 medium dull gold, 2 oz (57 g) each; #133 medium red-violet heather, 1 oz (28 g).

Needles: Body and Sleeves—Size 3 (3.25 mm): 16"/40 cm and 29"/80 cm circular and double-pointed (dpn); Ribbings—Size 1 (2.25 mm): 16"/40 cm and 29"/80 cm circular and dpn. Adjust needle sizes if necessary to obtain the correct gauge.

Notions: Sixteen markers; four stitch holders; tapestry needle.

Gauge: 30 sts and 30 rnds = 4" (10 cm) with larger needle over St st in color pattern.

Notes:

All rounds from cast-on to underarm begin on the back of the sweater below the shoulder blade so that the shift where rounds end and begin is not noticeable. Above the underarms, the beginning of the round is moved to the center of the armhole extra stitches.

Body: With chestnut brown and longer ribbing needle, CO 312 sts. Place marker at beg of rnd. Join, being careful not to twist sts. **Ribbing:** *k2 chestnut brown, p2 medium red-violet heather; rep from *. Work to end of Body Ribbing chart. Change to longer body needle and chestnut brown. **Increase rnd:** *k13, M1; rep from * 24 times—336 sts. Work Pattern 1 (diamonds) over 69 sts, place marker, *work Pattern 2 (left-facing squiggle) over next 3 sts, place marker, work Pattern 3 (large open X) over next 29 sts, place marker, work Pattern 2 (left-facing squiggle) over next 3 sts, place marker, work Pattern 4 (large solid X) over next 29 sts, place marker, work Pattern 5 (right-facing squiggle) over next 3 sts, place marker, work Pattern 3 (large open X) over next 29 sts, place marker, work Pattern 5 (right-facing squiggle) over next 3 sts, place marker, work Pattern 1 (diamonds) over next 69 sts, place marker; rep from * to end of rnd (ending with Pattern 5). Beg on rnd 1 of Main Chart, work through rnd 49, then work the established patterns while maintaining the 23-rnd color repeat for 48 more rnds, for a total of 97 rnds (rnd 5 of charts for Patterns 3 and 4). Break yarns.

Armholes: Rnd 6 of charts for Patterns 3 and 4: Sl 34 sts from left needle to right needle to shift the beg of rnd to the center of the left underarm. Place 1 st on holder (center st of Pattern 1) for

Whalsay Jumper

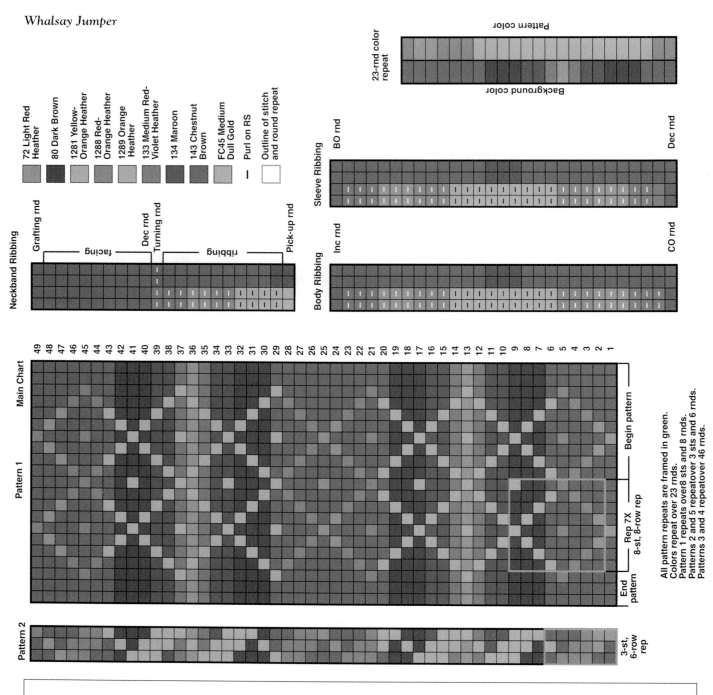

The patterns repeat over 46, 8, and 6 rounds; the colors repeat over 23 rounds. Therefore, the 49-round chart is truly representative of the first 49 rounds only of the smaller patterns. After that, the colors shift in relationship to Pattern 1, Pattern 2, and Pattern 5. Maintain the 23-round color repeat while repeating these patterns as established. Pattern 1 repeats over rounds 2 through 9. Pattern 2 repeats over rounds 1 through 6. Pattern 3 repeats over rounds 4 through 49. Pattern 4 repeats over rounds 4 through 49. Pattern 5 repeats over rounds 1 through 6.

The first three rounds of Pattern 3 and 4 (large X and quatrefoil patterns) are not repeated until just before the neck. On these three rounds, a diamond fills in the space that the overlap of the large patterns otherwise takes up. The sleeve also begins and ends with these three-row diamonds.

Pattern 1 in the sleeve is continuous with Pattern 1 in the body. Patterns 2, 4, and 5 are centered over the center 35 armhole stitches.

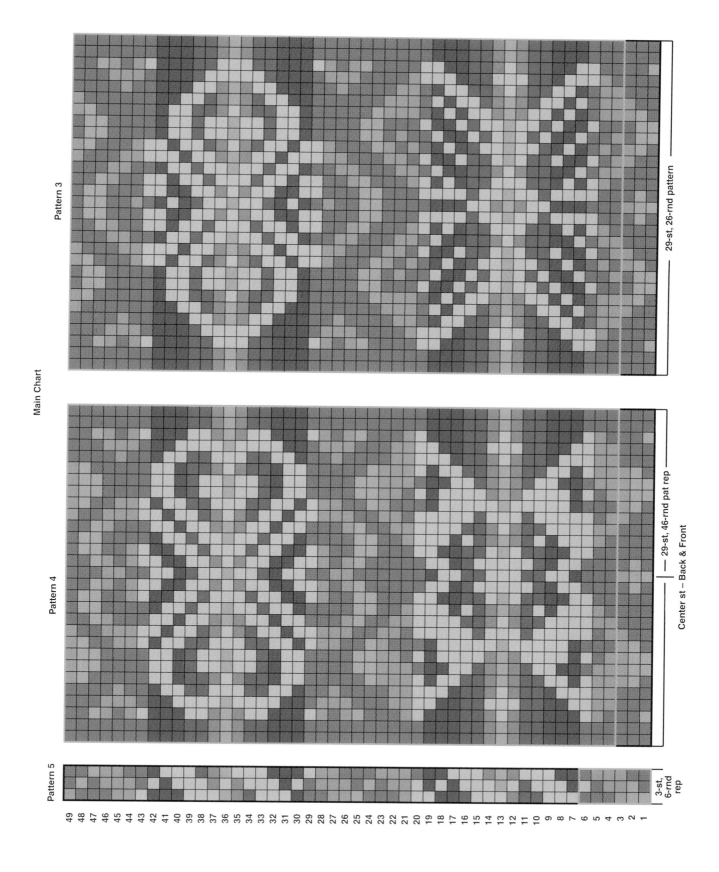

Main Chart

Pattern 3

Pattern 4

Pattern 5

29-st, 26-rnd pattern

29-st, 46-rnd pat rep

Center st – Back & Front

3-st, 6-rnd rep

49 48 47 46 45 44 43 42 41 40 39 38 37 36 35 34 33 32 31 30 29 28 27 26 25 24 23 22 21 20 19 18 17 16 15 14 13 12 11 10 9 8 7 6 5 4 3 2 1

left underarm, CO 6 extra sts, the first 2 with slip knots and the following 4 with backward loops alternating colors [(pattern, background) 3 times], work 167 front sts in color pattern, place 1 st on holder (center st of Pattern 1) for right underarm, CO 12 extra sts with backward loops [(background, pattern) 3 times, (pattern, background) 3 times], work 167 back sts in color pattern (including the slipped sts), and CO 6 extra sts with backward loops [(background, pattern) 3 times]—310 body sts (and 24 extra sts). Rejoin. Always work the extra sts next to the body of the sweater in the background color, the 2 center extra sts in the pattern color, and the rem extra sts in the established striped pattern. Work for a total of 160 rnds. (You will have completed rnd 22 of the chart for Patterns 3 and 4.) For the next 3 rnds, rep rnds 3, 2, and 1 on Patterns 3 and 4 while maintaining the other patterns as established—163 rnds total.

Shape Front and Back Neck: Rnd 26 of charts for Patterns 3 and 4: Work 57 left front shoulder sts in color pattern, place 53 sts on holder for front neck, CO 12 extra sts as for right underarm, work 57 right front and 57 right back shoulder sts in color pattern, place 53 sts on holder for back neck, CO 12 extra sts for right underarm, work 57 left back shoulder sts in color pattern. Work extra sts as before. Work decs at neck edges as follows: work left front sts to 2 sts before front neck extra sts, ssk, (the dec slants towards the extra sts), work extra sts, k2tog (the dec slants towards the extra sts), work to 2 sts before back neck extra sts, ssk, work extra sts, k2 tog. Dec 1 st at each side of front and back neck edges in this manner every rnd 4 times—53 sts

on each shoulder. Work through rnd 35 of the chart for Pattern 3 (173 rnds total). Work rnd 36 of chart for Pattern 3 across front sts only.

Shoulder Seam: Turn work inside out. With chestnut brown and beg at center of armhole extra sts, BO all sts together, matching extra sts to each other.

Sleeves: Cut armhole extra sts up the center. With chestnut brown, RS facing, shorter sleeve needle, and beg at center of underarm, k1 underarm st from holder, pick up and knit 76 sts along one armhole edge, 1 st at shoulder seam, and 77 sts along other armhole edge—155 sts. Place marker. Join. Beg with rnd 1 of the *color chart* for all patterns. Beg with rnd 9 of Pattern 1 (diamonds), match sleeve diamond pattern to body diamond pattern over 60 sts; rnd 3 of Pattern 5 (right-facing squiggle) over 3 sts; rnd 1 of Pattern 4 (large solid X) over 29 sts; rnd 3 of Pattern 2 (left-facing squiggle) over 3 sts; rnd 9 of Pattern 1 over next 60 sts, again matching sleeve diamond pattern to body diamond pattern. Follow Main Chart in reverse direction, dec 1 st at each side of underarm marker every 3rd rnd 15 times, then every 4th rnd 18 times, working 118 rnds total, and changing to sleeve dpn when necessary. End of Pattern 4 on sleeve matches beg of Pattern 4 on body—89 sts rem. **Decrease rnd:** With chestnut brown and ribbing dpn, dec 21 sts evenly spaced—68 sts rem. **Cuff:** Rnd 1: *k2 chestnut brown, k2 medium red-violet heather; rep from *. Rnd 2: *k2 chestnut brown, p2 medium red-violet heather; rep from *. Work to end of Sleeve Ribbing chart. With chestnut brown, BO in knit.

Neckband: Cut neck extra sts up the center. With RS facing, shorter ribbing needle, and beg at right side of back neck, *k2 maroon, k2 medium dull gold; rep from * across 53 sts from back neck holder, and continuing to alternate colors, pick up and knit 21 sts along left back and front neck edges, knit 53 sts from front neck holder, and pick up and knit 21 sts along right front and back neck edges—148 sts. Place marker. Join.
Ribbing: Following Neckband Ribbing chart, rib 10 rnds. **Turning Rnd:** *p2 chestnut brown, p2 medium red-violet heather; rep from *. **Decrease rnd:** (Dec about 10% of the sts.) With chestnut brown, *k8, k2tog; rep from *—134 sts rem. **Facing:** K8 rnds. Break yarn, leaving a long end for grafting.

Finishing: Trim the 6 extra sts at neck and armhole edges to 3 or 4 and hem them with a tapestry needle threaded with yarn, turning under 1 st as you go. Using the long end from the neckband and a tapestry needle, graft neckband sts on needle to purl bumps and innermost neck extra sts, spacing sts to allow for 10% fewer sts on inner band. Wash in wool-safe detergent. Remove excess water with the spin cycle of a washing machine. Place on a jumper board. Using regular sewing thread, a tapestry needle, and long sts, baste the neck edge to shape it and draw it in. When dry, remove the sweater from the board and pull out basting. Reshape the body and sleeve ribbings by wetting and patting them into place, or by steaming them.

GLOSSARY OF SHETLAND KNITTING TERMS

Basque: The bottom border of a sweater (ribbing).

Beret: (Pronouced to rhyme with 'ferret.') A hat with a star pattern on the crown, stretched to shape on a plate. The term 'Tam o' Shanter' for this type of hat appears in knitwear catalogs at the turn of the century, but is not used today.

Cardigan: V-neck sweater that buttons down the front.

Cravat: Narrow scarf.

Clew: Small ball of yarn, a leftover.

Dag: Fingerless mitten.

Fawn: Undyed wool, light beige in color.

Hank: Two ounces of yarn.

Head: Half a pound of yarn, one-ounce skeins loosely twisted together. Called a head because it is the amount that one sheep, that is, one *head* of sheep, would yield.

Hosiery: Knitting in general, not footwear per se. The Shetland knitwear industry is referred to as 'Shetland Hosiery.'

Jumper: Crew-neck, long sleeved pullover.

Lay up, or lay on: Cast on.

Loop: Stitch.

Lumber or lumbercoat: Round-neck sweater that buttons down the front.

Moorit, or murat: Undyed brown wool.

Makkin': What you are making; your knitting. "Takkin' your makkin' " means bringing your work with you, implying that you should take it wherever you go, and be industrious.

Makkin' off: Binding off.

Marled: Refers to yarns with two or more colors subtly mixed.

One and one (in dialect, 'een and een'): alternating stitches.

Peerie: Small pattern used to separate larger ones or as borders.

Shetland black: The deepest shade of undyed wool, really a dark brown.

Slipover: A sleeveless V-neck pullover, what Americans call a 'vest.'

Sock: Knitting in general. "Tak dy sock," in dialect, or "take your sock," means the same thing as "takkin' your makkin'": be diligent.

Spencer: Long-sleeved knitted undershirt.

Spret: To rip out.

Sweerie geng: The first row. There is a superstitious saying: You shouldn't get up until you've completed the entire sweerie geng—otherwise the garment will never be finished.

Take back: Rip out.

Take in: Decrease.

Take up: Increase.

Twin pins: Double-pointed needles.

Waistcoat: A sleeveless V-neck button-down-the-front garment.

Wire: Needle.

KNITTING ABBREVIATIONS

beg	begin(s); beginning	M1	make one	St st	stockinette stitch
BO	bind off	p	purl	WS	wrong side
CC	contrasting color	psso	pass slipped stitch over	*	repeat starting point (i.e., repeat from *)
cm	centimeter(s)	p2tog	purl two stitches together		
CO	cast on	rem	remaining	**	repeat all instructions between asterisks
dec(s)	decrease(s); decreasing	rep	repeat		
dpn	double-pointed needle(s)	rib	ribbing	( )	alternate measurements and/or instructions
g	grams	rnd(s)	round(s)		
inc	increase; increasing	RS	right side	[ ]	instructions that are to be worked as a group a specified number of times
k	knit	sl	slip		
k2tog	knit two stitches together	ssk	slip, slip, knit 2 slipped stitches together		
MC	main color				
mm	millimeter(s)	st(s)	stitch(es)		

SOURCES OF SUPPLY

To order Jamieson & Smith yarn direct:
Jamieson & Smith
Shetland Wool Brokers Limited
90 North Road
Lerwick, Shetland Islands ZE1 OPQ
44-1595-693579
www.Shetland-wool-brokers.zetnet
.co.uk

American shops that carry Shetland wool:
Blue Hill Yarn Shop
R.R. 172
Blue Hill, ME 04614
(207) 374-5631

Northampton Wools
11 Pleasant Street
Northampton, MA 01060
(413) 586-4331
www.northamptonwools.com

Schoolhouse Press
6899 Cary Bluff
Pittsville, WI 54466
(800) 968-5648
www.schoolhousepress.com

Unicorn Books and Crafts
1338 Ross Street
Petaluma, CA 94954
(800) 289-9276
www.unicornbooks.com

The Weaving Works
4717 Brooklyn Avenue NE
Seattle, WA 98105
(206) 524-1221
www.weavingworks.com

The Wooly West
PO Box 58306
Salt Lake City, UT 84158
(801) 581-9812
www.woolywest.com

BIBLIOGRAPHY

Allen, John. *Fabulous Fairisle: A Complete Guide to Traditional Patterns and Classic Styles.* New York: St. Martin's Press, 1991.

Bennett, Helen. *Scottish Knitting.* Shire Album 164. Aylesbury: Shire Publications, Ltd., 1986.

————. "The Shetland Handknitting Industry," in Butt and Ponting (eds.), *Scottish Textile History.* Aberdeen, 1987.

Best, Betty and Cathy Stout. *Fair Isle.* Edinburgh: Marketing Services Division of the National Trust for Scotland, 1988.

Beukers, Henriette, "Voorbeelden: Patronen en Ideeen," *Handwerken Zonder Grenzen* 4/85, September, 1985, p.10-14.

Bing, Valentijn and Braet von Ueberfeldt, *Nederlandsche Kleederdragten* [Dutch Costume]. Amsterdam: Frans Buffa En Zonen, 1857. Facsimile edition, Canaletto Alphen Aan Den Rijn: Uitgeverij Westers Utrecht, 1976.

Bliss, Debbie, ed. *Traditional Knitting from the Scottish and Irish Isles.* New York: Crown Publishers, Inc., 1991.

Compton, Rae. *The Complete Book of Traditional Knitting.* London: B. T. Batsford, Ltd., 1983.

Don, Sarah. *Fair Isle Knitting: A Practical Handbook of Traditional Designs.* New York: St. Martin's Press, 1979.

Flinn, Derek. *Travellers In a Bygone Shetland: An Anthology.* Edinburgh: Scottish Academic Press, 1989.

Fryer, Linda. *Knitting by the Fireside and on the Hillside: A History of the Shetland Hand Knitting Industry c. 1600-1950.* Lerwick: The Shetland Times, Ltd., 1995.

————. "The Shetland Hand Knitting Industry, 1790-1950, With Special Reference to Shetland Lace." Unpublished thesis submitted for degree of Master of Literature to Department of Scottish History of the University of Glasgow, September 1992.

Ginsburg, Madeline, ed. *The Illustrated History of Textiles.* New York: Portland House, 1991.

Hinchcliffe, Frances. *Knit One, Purl One: Historic and Contemporary Knitting from the V & A's Collection.* London: Victoria and Albert Museum, Department of Textiles and Dress, 1985.

Jakobsen, Jakob. *An Etymological Dictionary of the Norn Language in Shetland.* London: David Nutt, 1928.

McGregor, Sheila. *The Complete Book of Traditional Fair Isle Knitting.* London: B. T. Batsford, Ltd., 1981.

————. *Traditional Knitting.* London: B. T. Batsford Ltd., 1983.

McKee, Alexander. *Merciless Invaders: The Defeat of the Spanish Armada.* Kent: Mackays of Chatham, Ltd., 1987.

Mitchell, I., A, Johnson, and I. Coghill, eds., *Living Memory.* Shetland, 1986.

Mitchell, I., ed., *A Hint Da Daeks.* Shetland, 1987.

Nicolson, James R. *Traditional Life in Shetland.* London: Robert Hale, 1978.

————. *Shetland.* London: David and Charles, 1972.

Norbury, James. *Traditional Knitting Patters from Scandinavia, the British Isles, France, Italy and other European Countries.* New York: Dover Publications, Inc., 1973.

Pearson, Michael. *Traditional Knitting: Aran, Fair Isle and Fisher Ganseys.* London: Collins, 1984.

Rutt, Richard. *A History of Hand Knitting.* London: B. T. Batsford, Ltd., 1987.

Smith, Hance. *Shetland Life and Trade, 1550-1914.* Edinburgh: John Donald, 1984.

Smith, Mary and Chris Bunyan. *A Shetland Knitter's Notebook.* Lerwick: The Shetland Times, Ltd., 1991.

Smith, Mary and Maggie Twatt. *A Shetland Pattern Book.* Lerwick: The Shetland Times, Ltd., 1979.

Starmore, Alice. *Alice Starmore's Book of Fair Isle Knitting.* Newtown, Connecticut: Taunton Press, 1988.

Thom, Valerie. *Fair Isle: An Island Saga.* Edinburgh: John Donald Publishers, Ltd., 1989.

Waller, Jane. *The Man's Knitting Book: Classic Patterns from the '20s to the '50s.* London: Thames and Hudson, 1984.

Weston, Madeline. *Classic British Knits: 40 Traditional Patterns from England, Scotland and Ireland.* New York: Crown Publishers, Inc., 1986.

Withrington, Donald J. ed., *Shetland and the Outside World, 1469-1969.* London: Oxford University Press, 1983.

Newspapers:
The Shetland News
The Shetland Times
Shetland Journal
Shetland Advertiser

INDEX